# CYCLING TO THE SUN

# Cycling to the Sun

---

## *One Woman's Journey from Norway to Malta*

### TERRI JOCKERST

Terri Jockerst

Cover design and internal illustrations by Angélica Baldit

First Printing, 2020

For Jacquie and Mark, who helped me to get started

AND

For Anne-Rose, who helped me get to the end

# CONTENTS

## PART 3

**PART 4:**

## PART 5:

# PART 1

## First We Headed North

*To the North Cape*

# | 1 |

## The Dream

"AIM FOR THE DRUMS," my brother said. I was four years old and perched on top of an old, rackety bicycle. He pushed, the bike rolled, he ran next to me, faster and faster, wind rushing through blonde curls, squealing with delight as we rattled and bounced down the hill. The row of large oil drums lined across the driveway at the bottom were there to stop me landing in the pond at the side. We never made it. My legs, short and stubby, weren't long enough to reach the pedals; they waved around in the air until one foot caught in the wheel and then the chain. Bike, child, feet and brother all came crashing down in a tangle of limbs, pain, and technology.

Fast forward to the present. I'm just over sixty years old and time races faster than the speediest bicycle. My blonde locks have become a non-descript non-colour laced with silver. The curls, shorn to a dignified length, are only a tad longer than a marine's crew-cut. I still regularly fall off my bike, but I've learnt not to squeal.

For me, the 1960s were spent growing up, getting a standard education, and waiting for my legs to grow long enough so I could get my own bicycle. We lived on a dairy farm in a rural area of Victoria, Australia, where life was frugal and living with a light environmental footprint was so common that it didn't need a movement or a name; it was just lived. Every family grew all their own fruit and vegetables. The women made their own jam, swapped cake recipes, knitted pullovers, and sewed all the family's clothing needs. Everything which couldn't be produced at home was recycled and rotated amongst the local families until it finally fell apart to a point of no repair.

Bicycles were handed around according to the size of the needy child compared to the sizes of the bikes available. When I was tall enough, my parents exchanged a dark blue and very scratched child's bike for a light green adult version which had previously been ridden by an elderly neighbour. There were no lights or gears, the tyres were bald, and the brakes only worked spasmodically but it did have a reflector on the back and a basket on the front, so it was deemed a suitable bike for me to ride.

During my six years of secondary school, I had to ride my bicycle three kilometres to the school bus at the nearest bus stop, and back every day. There was a steep hill on the way. My plan of attack in the mornings was to walk the bike half-way down the hill, then clamber aboard and hurtle to the bottom with my feet just touching the ground. If I felt I was gaining too much speed, I dug my heels into the dirt and prayed that I could turn the bike around the corner at the bottom before I got collected by any oncoming vehicles. Having arrived at the bus stop, my bike was left, unlocked, leaning against a tree in a farmer's paddock, in full view of passing traffic, all day, every day and was never stolen. How times have changed! But then again, the tyres were quite bald, and it had no lights.

I developed a love for the outdoors too. Every year, our family went for two weeks to the beach, camping in a big canvas tent, the sort which leaks whenever it rains. My teachers introduced me to the joys of hiking through the rugged Australian bush where the reward for the day's hard work was a swim in the sea at an isolated cove. Mornings were a symphony of bird song and the laughter of my classmates preparing their breakfast before breaking up camp and setting off on the trail again. It was an idyllic way to grow up; quiet, calm, settled, and grounded in the love of family and the natural environment.

Eventually though, it was time to leave home and tackle the wider world. I moved to the city and in the ensuing years gained a university degree, learnt to drive everywhere in a rattly old Datsun, and fell for Matt, a handsome young Dutchman who had migrated from the Netherlands to Australia. It should have been enough, but it wasn't. I was restless. There had to be something more in my future than city, work, and family.

Like many young, adventurous Australians in those days, we took time out from the serious business of life to backpack overland through Asia to Europe, ending up in the Netherlands with Matt's family. I was astonished to see how many people rode bicycles to school, to work, for shopping, or just for fun. There were safe bicycle routes in every direction, often running next to the roads, but also through fields and forests. I could see that it was possible to ride from one end of the Netherlands to the other and an idea started to germinate in my mind: a bike trip!

We bought some bicycles; my first ever brand-new set of wheels. Not knowing anything of importance about bikes, we went to the closest bike shop and bought the first ones the salesman showed us. Admittedly, the selection was much smaller in 1983 than it is these days, many of the modern requirements for touring bikes hadn't been invented or were certainly not available in the average bicycle shop. This was in an era long before computers and surfing the net for information. Our only means of research were to ask family and friends or to ask at the bike shop.

My bike was a Raleigh. It had three gears and was maroon in colour. It was a lady's bike, which quite annoyed me, but, most importantly, it had proper tyres and functioning brakes. We each had two rear panniers and a front basket for all our sleeping bags, cooking utensils, and clothing. Matt tied our tent on top of his rear panniers and, loaded with all we needed in life, we set off on a tour of one of the world's flattest countries.

The first day nearly wrote me off! We cycled thirty-five kilometres from Kerkrade to Maastricht which included hills. I wasn't expecting hills but there they were, in all their green exhausting glory. I had never ridden a bicycle with gears or panniers or even properly functioning brakes. My bike was heavy, my panniers were unbalanced, and I didn't know how or when to change gears. Going downhill was a nightmare! "I didn't sign up for this!" I wailed as I struggled up yet another hill. "I want to go home!"

Somehow, we made it to Maastricht. We cycled past a watermill with a big wooden wheel and into a campground; a soft meadow sprinkled with an assortment of colourful flowers and shaded with old trees. I collapsed in a heap; looked around at the flowers, at the buzzing bees, and at all the bicycles parked next to tiny tents. I felt revived in an instant and all was forgiven.

In the following days, we headed north, cycled along a canal, and traversed a wet and watery landscape of fens, marsh, and biting insects. We cycled past herds of deer in the Hoge Veluwe National Park, through the busy streets of Rotterdam, over the flat lands of northern Holland, and along the Zuiderzee, before turning around and heading for home again. Usually our cycle paths were of bitumen, sometimes of compacted sand, and even occasionally of crushed shells. The paths were generally well signposted, the campgrounds were beautifully tended, and it was all terribly easy and civilized.

We saw some astonishing sights such as a Friesian cow with such a large udder that she was wearing a supporting net, a bra. We cycled past a man washing a route sign in the middle of a small forest with a bucket of hot, soapy water. Where did he get his bucket of hot water? We saw boats sailing across the fields, actually on canals. The visual effects of long distance on such flat land made field-sailing seem quite normal. We went shopping in a market and bought so much food that we couldn't carry it all on our bikes. We then had to find a quiet corner in a park and have an immediate picnic, even though we weren't hungry, so the rest of the food could fit into our panniers.

I learnt to ride through traffic in Rotterdam. Being on bike paths which were separated from the trucks and traffic cut my hysteria down to manageable levels. I learnt to pedal as fast as I could when coming up to a dyke so that my momentum helped me get to the top before swooping down the other side. One thing I never learnt, though, was to enjoy the wind. The wind in Holland is amazing. It is always there, either steady and strong, or just a breeze hinting at the possibilities. It didn't matter in what direction we were riding we always had a head-wind! And I hated it. I still do.

By the time we had been cycling for four weeks, we were able to cover fifty kilometres by lunchtime and I felt fitter, trimmer, and healthier than ever before. The initial idea of cycling around Holland grew into a vague dream of long-distance cycling. Where else could we go? What else could we see? I was hooked!

"Life" got rather in the way of my vague cycling dream over the next thirty years. I qualified to become a secondary school teacher, we raised a family, ran the family farm, got divorced, and did all the things which are expected of adults in our frenetic western culture. Occasionally, I thought back to "the dream" but then resolutely pushed it to the back of my mind so that I could focus on those all-important responsibilities which had somehow become a part of my life.

By the time I was fifty, I had been working full-time as a teacher for many years. I was a loving daughter of an increasingly frail parent as well as being a single parent of three vibrant teenagers and a sloppy Labrador. I was so busy being everything for everyone that I had no time at all for myself, no time to ride a bike or even to dream of the freedom which that entails. I didn't even own a bike. In short, I was an ordinary woman living a fairly uneventful life in rural Australia.

Eventually the teenagers morphed into young adults and moved away in pursuit of careers and life off the farm. Cooking for four or five became cooking for one and the eternal question: "What can I make with the leftovers?" I looked at life after retirement and was daz-zled with the possibilities. I looked at my garden, my house, and at the burgeoning pile of retirement projects. My crafts/hobby cupboard overflowed with photos which needed to be sorted out and stuck into albums, embroidery patterns cried out to be completed, and boxes of "stuff" demanded to be tidied. None of it really inspired me and in the back of my mind was that ever-present niggle of restlessness.

In 2014, fifty-six years old but not yet retired, I walked from Sevilla to Santiago de Compostela in Spain; a trek of about one thousand kilometres based on the medieval pilgrimage, the Camino. My reasons for doing so were very similar to many people who had walked this route before me; to get away from life's every day cares, to develop Olympic sized blisters on each foot, to get out of the single parent/dutiful daughter/overworked teacher rut, and to spend some time just being "me" while experiencing something else for a change. In amongst all those reasons was also the need to have a short look at what life as a retiree could look like and to spend time mulling over the "when" and the "how" of retirement.

At the end of the pilgrimage I thought to myself: "Wow, that was fantastic! What's next? Maybe I should do a long bike trip. Where from? Where to? Norway sounds nice and I've always wanted to go to Malta." All those pressing issues on the theme of "retirement" had magically dissolved into unimportant background chatter while the dream of my next adventure became the focal point of my consciousness.

The idea of cycling from north to south in Europe was born.

# | 2 |

# The Long Lead-up to Take-off

I casually mentioned my dream to family and friends. Other people heard about it and before I could say "Cycling trip" my friends Jacquie and Mark offered to ride part of the way with me.

Jacquie and Mark are both a little younger than me, but not much. I have known Jacquie since early primary school. She is petite and slender but with an inner core of steely determination which comes in quite handy when riding up steep hills. She is one of those blessed people who never fails to see the positive and good side in others. Mark is quiet and calm, one of those handy people to have around in a crisis. He is great at researching the best pedals, the best tyres, the best way to get from A to B but he loves nothing better than racing down steep hills like greased lightning. I was very glad to have them join me for the beginning of my long ride.

We studied the Eurovelo map of Europe. The Eurovelo is a network of about fifteen cycling routes criss-crossing Europe in all directions. Some parts of some of these routes have been completely set up with good quality cycling paths, signage, and accessible information. These sections are marked in green on the Eurovelo map. Other parts are still "works in progress" which are marked in orange. A third category of the routes are those which are still only mere suggestions. There might be a cycle route along these stretches, but there is every chance that there is no cycling infrastructure there at all. These sections are marked in red.

We decided to follow the Eurovelo Sun Route beginning at the North Cape of Norway and cycling south. Unfortunately, there were still a great many red lines on the map, so we solved that issue by deciding to make our own route and just generally aiming towards the sun. At this stage, we didn't know whether we would cycle down the coast of Sweden or the coast of Finland, but we did know that we wanted to have a few days on the Lofoten Islands prior to setting off from the North Cape. Jacquie and Mark wanted to finish at their friends' house in Switzerland while Malta seemed a reasonable target for me. None of us had any idea what we were signing up for, but we couldn't pull out, even if we wanted to, because word of our adventure quickly spread through the community and we were "famous" before we even started.

It took us the best part of two years to prepare. Two years of researching and buying bicycles, panniers, sleeping bags, tents, and maps. Two years of working out holiday dates, visas, bicycle transport, and the cheapest air tickets. Living in Australia meant that the logistics of organising a long trip like this were infinitely more complex than if we lived in Europe. Holiday and visa restrictions meant that our time was limited; we would have to start cycling immediately we arrived in Norway. There would be very little opportunity to purchase forgotten items and no time at all to try out different items of cycling equipment. We had to get it all properly sorted out before we left.

The most important items of equipment were, of course, the bikes. I went into all three of our local bike shops and discovered that while there was a great deal of information available about racing bikes, road bikes, and mountain bikes, there was next to nothing about touring bikes. One young man suggested I look on the internet which I did, to no avail. Every page which I found was so full of techno-babble that I found it virtually impossible to understand anything, let alone use the information to make a purchasing decision. Luckily, Mark came to the rescue. He was happy to do the research and I was happy to buy whatever he recommended.

We ended up going to a large bicycle store in Melbourne and purchasing Australian made Viventes for each of us. The bikes had steel frames, hydraulic disc brakes, Shimano derailleur gears, trekking handlebars and Schwalbe Marathon tyres. I learnt those specs by heart so that I could answer a few very basic questions from friends. Other than that, I knew that my bike was black, had good lights and, most importantly, it had a USB port for charging my phone while riding.

I already had most of the camping gear which I needed as I had recently completed a six-day walk in Tasmania's wilderness for which I needed a good quality tent, a three-season sleeping bag, and a very good air mattress as well as warm and waterproof clothing. However, I had no cycling clothing of any kind. I dived into the world of lycra but quickly decided that I didn't want most of the cycling "essentials." Padded cycling shorts and long pants made sense, as did cycling gloves, a helmet, and a fluoro vest. The rest of my clothing came out of my cupboard. The advantage of this is that I didn't have to take much extra for rest days, just a pair of shorts and a pair of jeans. At the end of a cycling day, I often changed into my casual shorts and immediately looked like any other hot and sweaty tourist.

Training for the long ride was the least of our worries. We weren't very fit but the thought of riding from the North Cape to Malta sounded OK. After all, according to the world globe, it was downhill all the way, wasn't it?

We did manage to do some bike rides, more as an opportunity to test out our new equipment, to discuss arrangements, and to keep our enthusiasm for all the preparations at a high level. A favourite ride was along a thirteen-kilometre rail-trail from our local village through bush and farmland to a nearby town. This trail slowly ascends a hundred metres over the thirteen kilometres and finishes in a patch of very fine cafés and coffee shops. An hour or so of riding was followed by a long, leisurely coffee or lunch but the highlight of each of these rides was the return cruise, downhill all the way.

Another popular ride was in the other direction towards a small national park. On one edge, there is a small picnic area of the type which is quite common and beloved in Australia. It's just a grassy clearing with views over the surrounding farmland. A large ancient eucalyptus tree cast its shade over a simple picnic table, a fireplace, and a very basic toilet block. We would ride there, Mark would extract water, gas cooker, pot, coffee, and plunger from his pannier. Jacquie would bring out the cups, milk, and sugar while I supplied a packet of biscuits. Once it all was set up, we would each find a spot to sit between the trails of ants and discuss our plans, our supplies, and other possible purchases.

Our only realistic practice run before flying to Europe was a two-day cycle along another rail-trail to Stratford in eastern Victoria. Even though we knew we didn't need all our equipment for the two days, we still packed and carried everything with us as though we were setting off on a year-long journey.

We hadn't ridden for more than twenty metres before I realised that my knees were exceptionally unhappy. I had ridden a Great Victorian Bike Ride two months previously. This is an annual cycling tour covering about 650 kilometres over ten days every November. The organisers always include one, or even two days, of over a hundred kilometres per day, and a few steep hills to climb; distances which I find quite challenging, even without luggage. I completed the bike ride with my knees yelling abuse at me with every turn of the pedals. My knees calmed down afterwards, with a few weeks rest, and I had hoped that that was the end of the matter. Our two-day jaunt proved otherwise, so, the minute I got home, I organised an appointment with a physiotherapist.

A week later, I discovered what every old cyclist (except me) knows; one must stretch certain leg muscles to warm them up before every ride. Smart cyclists stretch during and after their rides too. I threw myself into a tough regime of rehabilitation stretches three times a day. Tough, because any routine of planned exercises is as boring as it gets for me. I have a long and sad history of starting out on a good exercise plan which then falls in a heap within forty-eight hours. This time, I persevered. I had a long bike trip to look forward to.

As well as planning our trip, purchasing our gear, and going on a few coffee-fuelled training rides, Jacquie and I wanted to learn a bit about bicycle maintenance. Mark was our recognised expert. He taught us the names and uses of the various tools and spare parts which we needed to take with. We learnt to pump the tyres to the recommended level, to clean and oil the chain, and most impressively, how to dismantle and re-assemble our bikes for the flight to Europe. Taking my bike apart and re-assembling it were, for me, fairly long and complex procedures. Typically, for a female of my generation and education, I had next to no understanding of anything slightly mechanical or technical. I took notes, copious notes and transformed them into a forty-three-point instruction manual, complete with five pictures on how to dismantle and pack my bike. Assembling it was not quite so complex; only thirty-five points and two pictures.

A week before I was scheduled to fly out to Thailand for a four-week stop-over on my way to Europe, Mark delivered a Qantas bicycle box for me. I took my bike apart, packed it all into the box, added the panniers, sleeping bag, tent, camping stool, miscellaneous camping gear, and thought: "Too much! I have to take something out!" I took out the camping stool and swapped my nice, warm sleeping bag for a much lighter version; a decision I was to regret in the coming months. We drove my packed bike to the courier company in Melbourne, sent it off, and breathed a huge sigh of relief. All the preparation and planning were over. It was time to move on to the next stage of our great bicycle journey.

# | 3 |

# Some Tricky Questions

On arriving in Germany, I stayed a few days with a cousin in Frankfurt. My first task was to collect my bike from the shipping company which had transported it for me and to reassemble it. Despite our practice sessions at home, I was still rather daunted when faced with a big cardboard box full of bicycle bits in my cousin's garage. I read and reread my notes, carefully sorted out the various pieces and set to work. I was mightily relieved when I was able to put it all together again with no pieces left over. I hopped on, turned the pedal forwards, and was so happy when the bike moved in the right direction. The first of many challenges met and overcome!

I eventually made it to the island of Föhr to visit my friend, Renate. I had first met her while walking the Camino and our friendship had developed from there. She had celebrated her seventieth birthday while visiting me in Australia for three months, two years previously and I was really looking forward to seeing her again. Renate chose to move to Föhr after retirement, partly because it is such a positive cycling community with bicycles significantly outnumbering cars and with protected cycling lanes everywhere.

Föhr, lying just off the coast of north-west Germany, was once a thriving fishing community, but it has since changed identity and become a popular holiday island. It is flat, windy and ringed by dykes to keep the mudflats, the marshes, and the extreme tidal flows at bay. Renate lives in one of eight tiny apartments in a converted barn, surrounded by farmland to the north, marshlands running to the sea in the south, and an Italian restaurant next door.

During my two days there we cycled across the island. The terrain, being flat, was easy but the wind against us was merciless. It belted me around the ears, pushed me across the road, and demanded to know what I was thinking of, trying to cycle in the Arctic Circle. Coming up with a sensible rationale for a venture like ours was a bit tricky. I wasn't planning any research, I wasn't going to make an income, write a book or do anything remotely useful on the journey. It was all a huge self-indulgence. But then again, isn't that what retirement is all about; the chance to live "the dream" in whatever form it may take, before the body falls apart and its owner gradually sinks into the fog of old age?

The wind dropped in the evenings and we relaxed on Renate's balcony overlooking the fields, watching the swallows as they dipped and darted, chasing insects in the warmth of the evening sun. Our conversation on that first night unsurprisingly started with: "Wasn't it great on the Camino when …" but quickly moved on.

"Where are you cycling from here?" Renate asked, curiously.

"Into Denmark."

"Where will you meet Jacquie and Mark?" Renate had met them in Australia; they had even helped us to celebrate her birthday with a true Aussie meal at our local pub.

"I'm meeting them in Oslo."

"Oslo! That's in Norway. Does that mean that you'll be cycling alone in Denmark?"

"Err, yes."

"What will you do if you get a flat tyre?"

"Um, panic???"

And then came the big question: "You'll be all by yourself. Aren't you afraid?"

In the quiet of the night, I pondered the big question. Was I afraid? Yes, most definitely! But what was there to be afraid of? I wasn't afraid of being alone in a strange land. Most of my travels in the last few years had been by myself. I had previously travelled alone through Sulawesi in Indonesia, through western China (very few people speak English there and I don't speak any of the Chinese languages) and most recently in northern Thailand. No, I wasn't afraid of being alone. Besides, I was going to meet Jacquie and Mark in two weeks' time in Oslo.

However, I was absolutely terrified of my bike getting a puncture, a broken chain, or of it developing a mysterious clunking sound. I was nervous about getting lost or not being able to find a campground at night. I was worried that my knees would seize up and refuse to co-operate or that my backside would hurt from all the hours in the bike saddle. There was plenty to be afraid of, but I couldn't let that stop me. Cycling through Europe had been a dream for so long. What was I going to do? Go home because I had no-one to hold my hand in Denmark, one of the most civilised countries in the world? I didn't think so!

# | 4 |

# Just Me, My Bike, and Some Friendly Vikings

I left the relative luxury of Renate's house in late May and headed stoically off into the distance. I planned to make my way north through Denmark, in an effort to get bike fit, before meeting Jacquie and Mark in Oslo. Being keen on Viking history, I wanted to see Ribe which has a working outdoor Viking museum in addition to Denmark's oldest cathedral.

The first day of cycling was quite uneventful. I covered forty-six kilometres. The route was easily marked so there was little chance of getting lost. The land was pancake flat, I found the campground easily, my bike didn't get a puncture, and the chain didn't break. The lack of Danish money, however, looked to be more of an issue. There hadn't been anywhere to change money at the border. In fact, I hadn't even seen a border. I only realised that I was in Denmark when the road signs changed style and included funny letters which are not used in German. The manager of the campground was very friendly; she let me pay for the site in euros and gave me milk for my breakfast cereal, so I didn't worry too much about my lack of Danish kroner.

I woke up in my sleeping-bag cocoon the next morning and gingerly tested knees and backside. My knees were not happy, nor was my lower back. I rolled out of bed and somehow crawled out of my tiny tent. That wasn't so easy, but a few stretches and a gentle stroll to the amenities started to get the body working again. My knees kept protesting so I determined to do stretching exercises at least three times a day until they settled down. Creaking knees and a sore back were never part of the dream.

My route started with a seven-kilometre ride due west. It was a disaster! There was a howling wind coming off the North Sea towards me. It was so strong that I had to push really hard on the pedals to make any progress and every time I slowed to catch my breath the wind pushed me back again. It took me over an hour to ride the seven kilometres. Tears of frustration pooled in my eyes and I wondered how I would manage to cycle the sixty kilometres planned for the day.

Relief came when I was able to turn north and cycle in the shelter of the dyke which was a long mound covered in grass and stretching into the distance. Sheep grazed all over the dyke to keep the grass short. I pedalled along slowly, dodging sheep pellets, gambolling lambs and doting ewes. Sheep odour and constant bleating wafted over me to be carried off by the wind. Eventually, I had to turn east again towards a town with an ATM, and hopefully some Danish kroner for me. With the wind at my back, I covered the fifteen kilometres in under half an hour and learnt a strong lesson; that while small differences in terrain and weather take on tremendous importance when cycling, these conditions change continuously during the day. Good becomes bad and then gets better again. I just had to keep going through the tough sections to get to the good bits. Unfortunately, I'm a slow learner and have had to relearn this lesson any number of times.

By late afternoon, I arrived at Ribe having successfully cycled the planned sixty kilometres and felt quite proud of myself.

I spent some time at the Viking village, and checked out the church but the high point of Ribe was the Watchman's Night Tour. We walked around the town looking for burglars and checking that all was well, all the while listening to stories of the glorious days gone by. Our Watchman was a lovely old gentleman who carried a long stick with a wicked looking spiked mace on the end of it. He had a great sense of humour in Danish (the Danes laughed a lot) and made a valiant effort to entertain us with his stories in English too. The Watchman told the story of the meadow called "Hovedeng."

*Many years ago, there was a ship carrying goods from Belgium to Poland. It was crewed by a captain and three sailors. They were attacked and the ship was captured by nine pirates who, upon realising that part of the cargo was alcohol, proceeded to raid the hold and got quite drunk. The captain and crew managed to free themselves. They threw three of the pirates overboard, locked the remaining six in the hold and sailed in to Ribe harbour. The six pirates were executed, and their heads were stuck on spikes in the meadow.* Hovedeng (Head Meadow).

I knew that I wouldn't have the time to cycle all the way from Ribe to Frederikshavn from where I would catch the ferry to Oslo, so I decided to take the train part of the way, to Jelling, which is of terrific importance in Danish Viking history. Taking a fully loaded bicycle on the Danish rail network was an experience in itself. Denmark may be a world leader in the use of bicycles for transport, but this culture did not seem to extend to the rail system on that particular day. Steps into the carriages were high and steep, information was lacking, and train attendants were nowhere to be seen. Luckily, the people themselves were incredibly considerate and helpful. One young man helped me to buy a ticket from a machine, and a lady helped me manoeuvre my bike in and out of the elevators to get to the correct platform.

Best of all was getting onto the last train at the end of a long and tiring day. Hundreds of young people were milling around on the platform. The train pulled in but the steps into the carriage were too numerous and too high for me to lift my bicycle in. What should I do? I had no idea, but then a young man approached me. "Would you like to get on the train?" he asked. My young friend picked up my bike with all my gear and heaved them into the carriage as though he did it every day before breakfast. At Jelling, three others co-operated to hand the bike down onto the platform for me. It was brilliant!

On arrival in Jelling, I discovered that there was a very loud and well attended music festival happening over the weekend – right next to the campground! "Never mind," I told myself, "Survival is only a matter of attitude."

The campground manager suggested I stay close to my tent and bike to ensure I still possessed them the following morning. Somebody had already taken her car for an unauthorised joyride. I stuck close to my tent with the thumping and raging of heavy metal and hard rock vibrating through the airwaves and scaring the local birds witless. I fell asleep at last, half-way through a serious musing of the link between Viking ferocity and modern pounding music. There are an awful lot of very loud heavy metal festivals every summer in Scandinavia.

Waking to the soft trilling of the local stunned bird life, I packed up and left the campground early. All was quiet, the festival goers were either sound asleep or nursing huge hangovers.

Jelling is not only a centre of heavy metal music, but it's also the centre of Viking Denmark's soul. Way back in the tenth century, the Vikings were ruled by King Gorm the Old and Queen Thyra. They were both dedicated pagans and after they died, they were interred in burial mounds in the traditional way. Their son, Harald, became king, and in the way of newly minted kings wanted to display his importance for all the world to see. He built a huge wooden palisade in a tilted square shape and within it placed important symbols of his rule and Viking culture. A row of beautiful white pillars now marks out the boundaries of this square. Taking up most of the inside of the square are two curved rows of stones symbolising a stone burial ship. In the centre of the square is King Gorm's burial mound and on the other side of the square is another mound. Midway between the two mounds stands a simple white church.

I have always thought of the Vikings as ferocious wild men who loved nothing better than brawling amongst themselves and murdering, raping, and pillaging their quieter neighbours. Long-haired and wild-bearded they sailed the seas in their long-boats and terrorised all in the known world as far away as modern-day Istanbul. That's what I learnt many years ago in school. The museum and the church next door told me a different story.

The museum focused on the story of Gorm the Old, King Harald, rune stones and Viking life in general. It used the best of modern technology, sound, light, and interactive experiences to bring the information to life. I loved the display of farm life; buildings and trees drawn in grey on a black wall. At the touch of a button, a series of animals lit up; chickens, geese, a dog, a cat, sheep, pigs and a horse. The horse was led to a frame, hoisted up by its back legs, and its throat cut. The blood pouring out was bright red!

I discovered that the Vikings were farmers, fishermen and traders. They loved bright colours and jewellery, they loved their sagas, their gods and family life. King Harald converted to Christianity and then commanded his people to follow the new loving, sharing and caring God too. He built a church in the centre of the Jelling site and moved Gorm's body into the church.

I entered the church, the fourth one on this site. The floor had a series of zig-zigs of bright metal set into it, symbolic for the confused path that a pagan treads through life. On the outer edges, straight lines symbolised the straight and narrow path of a good Christian. Years ago, the body of a man was excavated from under the church. This is believed to be the body of Gorm the Old, the precise point being marked by a silver stripe on the floor. Why did Harald move his father's body into the church? Did he think Gorm needed very close contact with the new God for a very long time to counteract all his wild deeds as a Viking chieftain? Or was Gorm really a closet Christian, unable to convert officially for fear of his even wilder followers?

Seemingly oblivious to these all-important questions and the weight of Viking history, the sun shone through the stained-glass windows, a man practised the organ, and a pastor quietly organised the next service. It seemed appropriate to spend a moment in silent prayer before I wandered out into the wider world again.

Of course, King Harald had to advertise his good deeds. He erected a rune stone which now stands outside the church. It proudly states that as he was the son of Gorm and Thyra, he was by right the king of Denmark and Norway, and also that he brought Christianity to Denmark on behalf of all Danes.

Next to this is another rune-stone put there by Gorm the Old to honour his wife, Thyra. It is the oldest known mention of Denmark as an entity, so the stone is viewed as Denmark's birth certificate.

As a footnote to all this history, Harald was usually called Harald Bluetooth. Did he also invent a method of sending written documents and photos wirelessly from device to device? He probably wasn't even literate, so maybe not. The modern symbol for Bluetooth is made of the Viking runes for H and B superimposed one on the other. But why was he called "Bluetooth"? Surely a dead tooth would not have been that unusual in those days so was there another reason? Too much liquorice, maybe?

# | 5 |

# On the Hærvejen Road with a Puncture

With this momentous question to ponder over, I hopped on my bicycle and started riding the thirty-eight kilometres up the ancient Hærvejen Road towards Bryrup. This road is an ancient path, over a thousand years old. It winds for five hundred kilometres from Padborg on the border with Germany, along the Jutland Ridge to Hirtshals on the northern tip of Jutland. The route was used by pilgrims, traders, cattle drovers, and kings with their armies. They preferred to travel along the Hærvejen Road because there were less rivers to cross. They usually chose the easiest path rather than the most direct, resulting in a route which often meanders around the countryside in a manner which is very romantic but not terribly efficient. Nowadays the route is used by walkers and cyclists wanting to connect with Danish history and travel a quieter, slower, and more thoughtful way.

I deliberately chose to cycle through this area because, being the hilliest part of Denmark, I thought it would be good preparation for cycling in Norway. The strain of cycling uphill was rewarded with the cooling wind on my face as I coasted down the other side. I rode past skittish horses racing each other in the spring air, and placid cows meditatively chewing their cud. I rounded gentle corners to be surprised with a view of a village or a farmhouse. Everywhere I looked were patches of forest - Hansel and Gretel country. A church spire in the distance was partially hidden by trees. It was bucolic in the extreme.

It took me four days to cycle from Jelling to Aalborg and I hadn't had any issues. I was feeling quite confident in my cycling, camping and navigational abilities. I hadn't starved, got freezing cold, or fallen to the ground in a snivelling heap – yet.

From Aalborg, I had to cycle a short way along the Hærvejen Road and then head east to the coast. I packed up my gear in Aalborg with a slight sense of impending doom. A howling wind from the north-west did not bode well, particularly as I was going to be cycling north-west.

I managed to navigate my way through the industrial area of town and on to the Hærvejen trail. All was going well until a sudden left turn took me on to a narrow muddy trail through more forest and land scattered with rubbish; a trail fit for mountain bikes but not for tourers carrying eighteen kilograms of luggage. The trail disgorged me onto a wider track of deep sand with pebbles, stones, and sharp-edged rocks. I could feel something was wrong with my back tyre, but when I checked I couldn't feel anything. I came to a three-way intersection with sand roads in all directions. A right turn led to a different bike route, the sign for Route 3 indicated left but which left? There were two different trails leading to the left but there was no other sign. I took the better trail. Coming on to a small bitumen road, I could feel there was definitely something wrong with my back wheel. A flat tyre! Oh no! Our bicycle maintenance lessons hadn't covered changing tyres or mending punctures and I was at a complete loss as to what to do.

Luckily there were some houses and a bus stop a short distance ahead. There was a bus to Aalborg every thirty minutes. Maybe I could dump my gear in some-one's garden for a few hours so that I could take my bike on the bus to a repair shop in Aalborg. Walking up to a nearby house, I met a gentleman in the driveway. He spoke perfect English and explained that I wouldn't be able to get my bike on the bus, that bicycles were not allowed on city buses. My next idea was to take the back wheel off somehow and to take it to Aalborg. When I asked about that the man looked puzzled and asked why I wanted to take just the back wheel.

"To get the puncture repaired."

"Is that all you want? Then you're in luck. You relax, come inside, sit down and have a coffee with my wife, Eva, while I repair your bike."

"He's a mechanic, he can fix anything," Eva explained, much to my bemusement.

So, I sat and had a coffee while the gentleman not only replaced my tube but also oiled the chain for me. While chatting with Eva she realised my glasses were broken; one of the screws had come out. She rummaged around in a drawer and came up with a new pair of the right strength which fitted perfectly. Then she looked online to find the best way for me to cycle to Asaa.

"Forget the Hærvejen," she said. "It's very romantic but too fiddly. It takes you into the hills and all over the place instead of where you need to go. The path is also not very good." She suggested I follow the 180 road which had a proper bike path all the way along it rather than going back on to the Hærvejen trail.

Cycling from there to Asaa I had a good straight path, a gentle descent, and a strong wind from behind. My newly oiled bike travelled beautifully with scarce a whisper, every cyclists' dream. As I turned the pedals so effortlessly and smoothly, I thanked the Viking gods for the wonderful people I had just met and prayed that they would also receive such kindness in their lives.

The further north in Denmark I cycled, the more I realised how cold it was getting at night. Back in Australia, I had packed my warm sleeping bag along with a mountain of other gear. Looking at the huge pile, I had panicked. How was I supposed to cart all that stuff around? What could I get rid of? The sleeping bag was rated to minus eight degrees, so I thought I wouldn't need something that warm. After all, it was going to be summer at the North Cape.

I had taken out the sleeping bag and replaced it with a lighter version rated to zero degrees. Bad idea. Some warm-blooded souls might be able to sleep well in such a thin sleeping bag. but I certainly couldn't.

Just before Frederikshavn I found a camping shop which had just begun trading that very day. They stocked merino thermal long-sleeved vests and pants made in Australia, of all places! I bought one of each, they threw in a torch for good measure and we were all happy. Fancy a brand-new shop in the north of Denmark selling Australian made thermals to an Australian cyclist on their first day of trading!

# | 6 |

# Across the Arctic Circle

In early June, I took the ferry from Frederikshavn to Oslo, capital city of Norway. I met Jacquie and Mark there. They had just flown in from Australia and had booked further flights to Bodø where we would meet again for the start of our combined bicycle tour. While they spent the next two days seeing the sights of Oslo and getting acclimatised, I took two trains, first north to Trondheim and then, the following day, even further north, across the Arctic Circle and into Bodø. My feelings of awe at the beauty of the Norwegian lakes and mountains turned to dismay as I saw how much snow was still lying on the ground. "I'm supposed to ride through *that*? And sleep in it at night? Oh dear!"

I was relieved to see there was no snow at Bodø although the wind was strong and cold enough to turn my every thought into a tinkling icicle. The train pulled in, and there were Jacquie and Mark, beaming with pleasure at the thought of all that cycling ahead of us. After dinner, we realised that it was still broad daylight outside, at 9 p.m. On checking our tourist brochures, I discovered that there are twenty-five days of constant daylight in summer at the Arctic Circle. This increases the further north one travels, to thirty-five days at Bodø, sixty-seven days at Alta and seventy-nine days(!) at the North Cape. Seventy-nine days of 24-hour sunlight! We weren't going to see any darkness again until we returned much further south on our big bike ride.

I had still been stressing about my stupidity in not bringing my very warm sleeping bag to use on this trip, so the following day, with a few hours to spare in Bodø I set off to see what the town had to offer in the way of camping gear. I bought an extra liner for my sleeping bag which the makers claimed would give me an additional fifteen degrees of warmth. I also invested in two pairs of extra warm socks, a waterproof cover like a shower cap for my bike helmet, and a few more packets of dried food in case we had to camp somewhere far away from a food source. I hoped all these additions would keep me dry, warm, chirpy, and energetic.

With our minds grappling the mysteries of 24-hour daylight, and fields of snow in summer, we boarded the ferry for the 3 ½ hour trip to the Lofoten Islands and the beginning of the next phase of our big adventure.

# | 7 |

# Loving the Lofoten Islands

The first time I ever came across the Lofoten Islands was when I was rifling through some old postcards which my mother had stored in a shoebox at the back of her wardrobe. There was a black and white postcard showing a mountain spilling down into the sea. Some tiny wooden buildings were perched precariously on the edge of land. It all looked so dramatic, but I had never even heard of this place. A quick search on the internet showed a chain of islands off the west coast of Norway, quite close to Narvik where my grandfather had been in business and where my mother was born in 1921. It seemed that this place was part of my family history. The name stuck in my brain and in the way of things mysterious, I kept coming across references to these islands. They were pictured in a calendar, they were listed as one of the "new" places tourists should visit, and they were a centre of the stockfish industry. Even as I edited this chapter, it was listed by my favourite travel site as one of the ten most beautiful archipelagos in the world.

The Bodø ferry docked at Moskenes on Moskenes Island, in the Lofotens. We wheeled our bikes off and turned south to Å. This was a slight detour as we were supposed to be heading north but a town with only one letter in its name needed to be investigated. I wasn't sure how to pronounce a letter with a circle above it. I learnt that the circle transforms the A sound to an "aaw" sound as in "dawn." Å turned out to be a quaint and incredibly scenic fishing village scattered over the rocks at the edge of a bay.

Dried stockfish has traditionally been the major export of the area. There were fish drying racks and red-painted fishing sheds scattered all along the shore. I could tell that we would be eating quite a lot of fish over the coming days. The town's restaurant jutted out over the water in the style of the old fishing sheds. I tried battered cod cheeks for dinner. It was beautifully presented with steamed potatoes and locally sourced berries which more than compensated for the bland taste of the fish.

No tents were allowed in the campground but we were able to spend the night in a two-bedroom wooden cabin which was tied down with wire cables attached to the rocks in the ground. Winters in the Lofotens must get rather wild.

On our first full day of cycling, we followed our noses to a bakery which was still using an oven from the 1800s to produce sensational cinnamon buns and a dozen different types of bread. Having filled our stomachs, we cycled through a short tunnel to the southernmost point of the island, peered over the water and admired the view, then turned our bikes and headed north towards the midnight sun.

The weather was glorious, the sun shone, the wind was just a mild breeze, and our spirits were high. We cycled along the coast, the scenery was stunning; small rocky bays and blue water sparkled to our right, a narrow road twisted, turned, rose and fell in front of us while steep mountains reared high on our left. Reine hosted our picnic lunch. It was another stunning village which I am sure has graced many a calendar over the years. It was also a proper working village. There were more racks of fish drying in the sun and men driving crates of fish around, readying them for export. We ate our picnic at some tables in the centre of town. A sign on a doorway of an outdoor adventure shop nearby proclaimed that there was "No ass sitting in the Lofotens." I assumed it wasn't aimed at us; we had just cycled a whole 9.3 kilometres!

Some three or four kilometres past Reine we came to a small hump-backed bridge, steep ride up one side and steep ride down the other.

These bridges were designed to allow tall boats to easily motor under them. This particular bridge had only one lane but had traffic lights at each end to control the traffic. Our light was red, so we lined up behind a waiting car. The light turned green, the car took off, and we pedalled behind. The incline was so steep that I had to get off and push to the top. On the other side, there were three cars waiting for the opposite green light at the bottom. I began to cycle down the slope and started to move to the side of the road to make way for the cars as they came towards me. Their light turned green, but the oncoming cars didn't move, the drivers waited patiently until I was safely out of their lane and completely off the bridge then with a smile and a wave, they pulled out and went on their way. "Wow," I thought, "That's courtesy. If all the drivers are like this, we're going to *love* this trip."

We camped that night at Ramberg, having cycled thirty-four kilometres. Neither Jacquie nor I were terribly fit, and we also felt a definite need to stop very often to take photos of the glorious scenery. Ramberg had the most stunning beach, a long sweeping curve of pristine white sand bordered by clear blue water. All that was missing were some palm trees and a bit of warmth in the sunshine so that I could imagine myself in Paradise. Supper in the restaurant was battered cod's tongue. Like the cod's cheek, it was quite bland but once again beautifully presented with steamed potatoes and berries.

The following morning, we saddled up and set off along the narrow road past fjords and mountains, over bridges and under the deep blue sky until a descent into a tunnel to the next island, 1.7 kilometres long, going deep underground, and under the sea. This was a serious tunnel. From outside we could see that there was a path on the left side for cyclists and pedestrians. It was just wide enough for a bike with panniers. The edge of the path was a ten centimetre drop to the road. Riding too close to the edge could be quite dangerous as the bike and rider could easily fall into the path of oncoming traffic. I wasn't happy.

Channelling the courage of the old Vikings, I entered. The howling of the wind, and the roaring of the traffic soon knocked my confidence to zero. I fully expected a burst of flame to come racing up the tunnel followed by the angry roar and foaming features of a huge dragon! It was really dark. Mark yelled something at me. I stopped and looked back at him. "What?"

"Take off your sunglasses!"

The descent steepened, the roaring increased and I started to get the wobbles but managed to hold firm. A truck roared past inches from my side; the slipstream knocked me sideways; I fell into the wall, scraping knuckles, elbows, and bags as I slowed to a stop. The tunnel bottomed out and I began the tortuous climb uphill, staring hopefully into the distance trying to find a glimmer of daylight. A light! But no, false hope dashed. It was just a car's headlights. I plodded on, heart thumping, sweat trickling, and muscles screaming. Another cyclist came down the path towards us. I moved right to the edge of the path, just a whisker from the road and waited. He slowly inched past, concentration etched on his face, no time for a smile or glimmer of thanks. I moved on until, after an age of pulling and heaving, puffing and panting, ignoring the traffic as it raced past, I saw a tiny circle of light, growing slowly ever larger and then, with a cheer of relief and jubilation I reached lovely, glorious daylight! The other side! I took a few gulps of fresh air, settled my panniers back into the correct position, patted my bicycle on the saddle, hauled myself aboard, and on seeing Jacquie and Mark emerge unscathed, slowly wobbled down the road.

The last ten kilometres of the day we followed the shoreline of yet another deep bay. The road was narrow but with very little traffic. The sun had moved to the other side of the mountains, the light softened and caressed the shallow waters. It was bliss.

We camped that night at Rolvsfjord and discovered the importance of having some emergency food supplies with us. The camp manager had a small café with a choice of hamburgers (out of the freezer) or pizza. (also out of the freezer) She was not planning to open for breakfast. After a supper of hamburgers it was still quite light outside, so we wandered around a little, did some washing, yawned and looked at the time. Crikey! It was eleven o'clock, broad daylight and way past my bedtime. This camping life in the Arctic Circle was going to take some getting used to.

Our third day of cycling in the Lofotens started with a pitiful breakfast of muesli bars; just enough to stop the tummy rumbles but not quite enough to power a day's cycling. I did my daily ten minutes of morning stretches and left camp by nine. Jacquie and Mark planned to follow when they were ready. It was another beautiful day with bright sunshine, a cloudless blue sky, and chirruping birds. Full of energy but just a tad hungry, I pedalled hard up the rises and swooped down the other side. I rounded the headland to see the water sparkling in the distance where the white peaks of a range of mountains on the mainland glimmered in the sunshine.

Jacquie and Mark caught up with me as I was staring hard at some low shrubs by the side of the road. There were some birds in there creating an awesome racket and I wanted to know what they were. Together we rounded a corner and spotted a building and cars in the distance. As we neared, the excitement rose as it became clear this was possibly a shop, a café, or a restaurant. It was an old weatherboard building with a deck with tables and chairs out the front, cabinets of curios inside, and a menu! A simple menu of simple food, but nonetheless a welcome addition to a fruit and nut muesli bar. We each ordered a fish-burger with salad and sat outside in the sun.

A young man rode up on an overloaded bicycle. He also ordered a fish-burger (the choices were limited) and asked if he could sit with us. He was Dutch and had ridden from the North Cape. The weather up there had been foul, with howling winds, rain and sleet. The worst was the fog. It had been so thick that he couldn't see anything at all of the magnificent views from the lookout point. Apparently, it's like that most days.

Our young friend usually rode one hundred and fifty kilometres a day. When asked how far we rode in a day, we didn't answer, just mumbled something about being at the start of our trip, hadn't established a routine yet, blah, blah, blah. I felt better when he explained it took him all day to cycle that distance and he had no time for chatting or sightseeing. He scoffed his fish-burger and raced off in enthusiasm. We sat back and relaxed, mindfully enjoying our coffees as we watched a hiker hoist his backpack and traipse into the hills after which, having had a good rest, we slowly wheeled our bikes back to the road and cruised onwards.

In the afternoon, we cycled along another fjord and had to cross two hump-back bridges in order to cross over to the next island. I was quite happy to push my bike up to the top of each bridge. Anything was better than having to go through another tunnel under the sea. We camped that night in a remote little place, Kabelvåg, having cycled a terrific forty-seven kilometres.

# | 8 |

# Being Spoilt on the Hurtigruten Ferry

Kabelvåg to Svolvær was just a short jaunt of six kilometres, hardly worth saddling up for. We wanted to take a tour of the Trollfjord from Svolvær; it was on all the tourist brochures although we weren't sure why. Jacquie has a soft spot for trolls and had been stopping at every tourist gift shop looking for the perfect troll to adopt. Maybe she could find one in Trollfjord? When we arrived in Svolvær we discovered that the Hurtigruten ferry which would take us on the next stage north also did the Trollfjord tour en route. We found a café and booked our passage; Svolvær to Honnigsvåg, jumping off point for the North Cape.

Also waiting for the ferry were two excitable Frenchmen with their bicycles. They were on their short summer break and were slowly making their way up the Lofotens and around some other islands. They often wild camped and were having a lovely time fishing for their supper every day. "You don't need to know how to fish," they explained. "Just throw the line in the water and the fish will come to you." They were very intrigued by our bicycles and asked many technical questions which Mark was able to answer to everyone's satisfaction.

Shortly before midnight, the passengers were lured out of the lower decks by the promise of delicious warming cups of soup served outside on the top deck. As I sipped on my steaming mug, we entered the Trollfjord. A hundred metres wide at the entrance; it had steep cliffs and a narrow waterfall. We motored to the end, which was even narrower, and very, very slowly turned around to motor back out. How the captain managed not to bump into the cliffs on either side is one of technology's modern miracles. I looked for trolls but didn't spot any. Maybe they didn't like all that midnight sun. The scenery was sublime; dark blue water, ripples shimmering in the light, and sunlight on peaks.

Our journey north on the Hurtigruten ferry was one day and two nights, as they say in travel brochures. The Hurtigruten Line, established in 1893, initially transported freight, mail, and passengers back and forth between Bergen in the south and Kirkenes in the north, near the Russian border. They soon began to take tourists who wanted to see the wild north. By 2017, Hurtigruten had eleven ships plying this route, stopping at thirty-four ports on the way. They were still transporting freight, mail, and passengers, but the major money spinner was most likely the tourists who were keen for a week in another world, the world of the cruise ship. The ships are no longer simple ferries but rather fully decked out cruise ships with all the modern conveniences required by tourists in the 21st century. Our ship was the Midnatsol (the Midnight Sun) and was full of retired folk, mainly from Germany with a scattering of other European nationalities.

# | 9 |

# To the Cape!

By the time we had spent two nights surrounded by such luxury, I was ready to leave. We disembarked just before lunch at Honningsvåg on the island of Magerøya, ready for the thirty-five-kilometre push to the North Cape. What a hard slog! Thirty-five kilometres of mountainous riding through ice and snow took us up never-ending ascents and down long, but all-too-short descents, past small lakes frozen around the edges, some still completely covered in ice. Sometimes a patch of lovely blue colour glowed invitingly, but I knew there was a lake hiding under all that snow, beautiful but deadly to the unwary. We saw our first reindeer, scratching amongst the rocks and ice, looking for some tender green shoots to graze on. At first there was a strong crosswind which kept threatening to knock me off my bicycle but by mid-afternoon it dropped to a gentle whisper of a breeze. Although the air was freezing, the day was clearing to be sunny and warm-ish, just perfect. I was surprised by how many campervans and tourist buses were passing us. The whole world was on its way to the North Cape to view the midnight sun.

At the top of the last hill, just past the "North Cape" sign, I puffed and panted as I slowly cycled my way across the carpark to the young man in the ticket booth. It had been such hard work to get there and I was so hot and sweaty from my efforts that I prepared myself to ask for a discount on the entrance ticket, maybe for my age.

The young man opened his window, smiled a dazzling smile and said, "It's free for you, you don't have to pay."

"Huh?"

"Yes", he said. "Cyclists and walkers do not have to pay"

Wow! I was so happy! Not because I had saved some money, but because some nameless bureaucrat somewhere had recognised the effort which walking or cycling to the North Cape takes and had decided that such effort should be acknowledged in a small way. So good!

Jacquie and Mark arrived an hour later, full of chatter about the steep hills we had to ride or push up and the beautiful weather. We walked outside to the large world globe which was made of metal bands and had been placed at the northernmost point of the island. It sat on a platform above a short flight of steps.

Clustered in front was a large group of German tourists trying to get themselves organised to get their photo taken. I obliged, and in return, their guide waited patiently while the three of us carried our bikes up the steps and posed with them for our official "Beginning of the Bike Trip" photo.

"Smile!" she commanded. We smiled obediently. Click went the camera. We smiled more, noses red from the cold and teeth aching with the chill, but this moment was not allowed to go unrecorded for posterity. The midnight sun shone in front of us, casting long shadows behind as we posed with our bikes and our smiles underneath the huge metal globe. More cameras clicked and suddenly we were done. All that remained was for Jacquie and Mark to cycle to Switzerland, and for me to cycle the 7,000 kilometres to Malta.

# PART 2:

## Then We Turned Around and Headed South Again

*Scandinavia*

*The North Cape to Vordingborg, Denmark*

*2,847 kilometres*

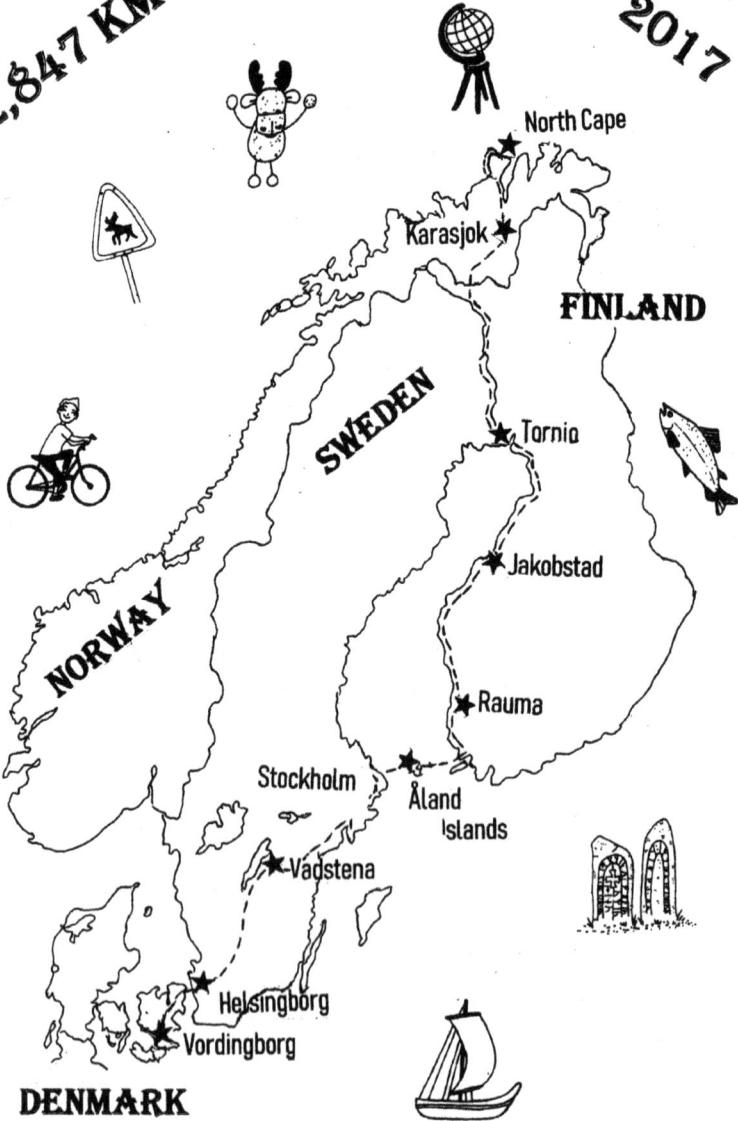

*Scandinavia*

2,847 KM

2017

North Cape

Karasjok

FINLAND

SWEDEN

Tornio

Jakobstad

NORWAY

Rauma

Stockholm

Åland Islands

Vadstena

Helsingborg

Vordingborg

DENMARK

# | 10 |

## Of Ice, Snow, and Reindeer

### The North Cape to the Norway-Finland Border, 409 km

The ride from the North Cape back to Honningsvåg had a surreal quality. All was quiet except for the whoosh of the bike wheels and the occasional call of a passing bird. The air was still and cold, the low, bright sun and the chilled air forced sunglasses on me, fogged by the vapour from my breath. Our shadows raced along with us, one moment swooping ahead as long streaks, then later, short and squat by our sides as we rounded a corner and changed direction. We crossed a plain, the snow glistening in the light, or brooding blue where it hid from the sun. We had a brief rest, shivering as we peeled off gloves and neck warmers to munch on some muesli bars. The crunch of nuts echoed the crunch of the dried grass under our feet. A last quick descent brought us to the edge of a lake where our shadows sat up straight, crisp and clear on the rock wall lining the road. Flushed with exertion and glowing from the exhilaration of the ride, we coasted back to our hostel at 12.30 a.m. It was still daylight.

Having had about four hours rest but even less sleep, we had to get ready to board the Hurtigruten ferry, the Lofoten, at 5.45 a.m. which is a ridiculous hour to be doing anything. With twenty-four-hour daylight, the time didn't really matter but my beauty sleep was still quite important to me. The alternative was to ride through a seven-kilo-metre tunnel under the sea to the mainland, a thought which, quite frankly, terrified all of us. Our proposed route on the ferry took us back one stop to Havøysund which is linked to the mainland by a short bridge, so I thought it was well worth the early start.

Built in 1964, the Lofoten was the smallest and oldest of the Hurtigruten ferries. She only carried about a hundred passengers on each journey up the coast and back again and she was going to be retired from this route in December 2020. With her ingrained smell of sea and salt, the coiled ropes and the slow creaking of the boards as we rocked gently in the waves, the old girl had an ambience that was missing on our previous modern cruise ship. I'm rather embarrassed to confess that rather than walking about and sampling all her delights, I stretched out on a bench in the lounge and immediately fell asleep.

I was woken in time to hastily untie my bicycle and disembark at Havøysund. It was raining and chilly, so time to rug up well. I pulled on almost every item I possessed and completed my outfit with my yellow high visibility clothing and a bright blue neck warmer. The result – large, bright lemon masquerading as a cyclist. We headed for the first warm café we could find and stayed there for at least two hours. It took so long to take off and hang up my two outer layers of clothing that any stay of less than two hours simply wasn't worth the effort. How do people in these latitudes ever get any work done? They must spend hours every day getting themselves weatherproofed. On the other hand, maybe they are a lot tougher than us weak southerners.

The day just refused to warm up. Rain, cold wind and a steep climb to a high plain with all the snow and ice helped us to understand some of the difficulty of living in such an inhospitable environment. And it was summer! We spotted some snow sleds just left sitting in situ until the following winter's snow allowed them to be used again. The trek across the high plain was followed by a long descent back down to sea level. We circled a fjord, picnicked on hot chocolate and muesli bars at a waterfall, then realised we had another steep climb ahead of us. At least the weather was clearing. Half-way up the next climb, a flash of colour flew past us, followed later by two more sedate cyclists. They were an older German couple, on a cycling tour of Norway with their adult daughter who was studying for her doctorate somewhere in the north. The daughter must live life in a hurry, she was long gone!

We camped that "night" high above a fjord. Jacquie and Mark pitched their tent in a hollow, out of sight of the road. I pitched mine behind a pile of rocks, also out of sight of the road. My view of the fjord was sublime. A few birds cried out as they flew across the heather. The water was still, only a few ripples disturbed its surface. Otherwise all was calm. I supped on dried Spaghetti Bolognese reconstituted with boiling water followed by some biscuits. Getting ready for bed was easy. I simply brushed my teeth, divested myself of my outer layer of clothing and crawled almost fully dressed into my very thin sleeping bag with its fifteen-degree liner. I was very snug, a bit like a baby swaddled in a tight blanket so it can't move around much, but I was quite warm and toasty. Getting out of my cocoon to go for a toilet break in the middle of the "night" was a tad more difficult but at least I didn't have to scratch around for my torch. At three o'clock in the morning, it was still broad daylight.

The ride down to Olderfjord wasn't nearly as tough as the previous day. It was still quite cold with some patches of snow and ice but nothing like what we had just experienced. We started to see trees, albeit only just starting to develop buds so the scenery was still mainly browns and greys with a slight tinge of green to break the monotony. A short, gentle climb uphill led to a very long, straight, calm descent down to Olderfjord. Road signs warning of reindeer kept me entertained. Some of them were peppered with small, round holes and had obviously been used for rifle shooting practice. I've seen similar road-signs in Australia but with pictures of kangaroos or wombats instead.

In Olderfjord, we had our first big dilemma. I wanted to head west to Alta with its pre-historic rock carvings in a canyon. They had long piqued my interest. Unfortunately, Alta was over a hundred kilometres away with a large high-plain to cross and no campsites or accommodation on the way. The weather was predicted to get worse again, dumping more snow and we were simply not prepared to wild camp in those conditions. It would have been too dangerous. We could have taken the daily bus but doubted that it could take all our bikes and gear as well. The decision was taken to keep heading south. While I agreed that this was the most sensible solution, I was still rather disappointed.

We headed south along the Porsangerfjorden, a long fjord with the town of Lakselv at its furthest point. Navigation was easy, we simply followed the fjord for the whole day until we reached the town. The scenery was sublime, as usual. The fjord, to our left, rippled grey in the breeze. Its shores were sprinkled with red houses and barns. A small white church was a welcome change of colour. To our right were woods, green with new growth and thick underbrush. The trees quickly gave way to steep hills, still quite brown and barren. Every now and then, some reindeer would emerge from the trees, give us a startled look and bolt for cover as quickly as possible. I stopped to take some photos, walked up a knoll and was surprised to see a whole herd of reindeer sheltering between the knoll and the fjord. They looked equally astonished and started milling around in confusion, so I quietly backed off and left them in peace.

Shortly before Lakselv, Mark rode ahead to try to see if he could find a bicycle shop before closing time. Jacquie and I continued at a more sedate pace. We came to the top of a hill, Jacquie sped down it with glee. I waited for her to get a head start, then started to follow. I saw a black blob moving towards me out of the corner of my eye. The blob quickly morphed into a huge, slavering dog furiously barking and racing to get me. I put on a spurt of speed and shot down the hill as fast as I could. The dog was catching up, still baying for my blood. The road dipped into a hollow and rounded a corner until I was out of sight. The barking faded away into the distance and I was safe again, until next time.

I was becoming intrigued with the directional road signs in the area which often had the same place name twice. Kárášjohka and Karasjok were obviously the same place but written quite differently on the same sign. We pulled in at the ticket office for the local national park. There was a young lass at the desk who looked like she didn't have much to do so I asked the question.

"Why are the town names written twice?"

The lass explained in perfect English that wherever there is a Sami community, the road signs are always in Norwegian and Sami. The group with the largest population in a given area has their language in first place followed by the other language. Sometimes, another indigenous language, Kven, is also added.

By the end of the day's ride we had covered sixty-four kilometres, a vast improvement over our earlier efforts, although we were assisted by the reasonable flat route and the fairly kind weather. It had been cold but without wind or rain. It was quite affirming to cover a distance greater than fifty kilometres without having to struggle and sweat the whole way.

By this stage, we seemed to have established a pattern of riding which saw me leaving when I was ready and the others following when they were ready. I was usually ready to leave at least thirty minutes before they were. I preferred leaving earlier because then I could ride at my own pace and be independent. I was still stopping very often for a short breather and tended not to stop for snack breaks. Jacquie and Mark were having less breaks but stopping for much longer so they could eat some snacks. Different people – different styles.

From Lakselv, we followed a large river upstream to its headwaters then zoomed downhill to finish in Karasjok which is the site of the Sami Parliament in Norway. We spent two days catching up on the important things in life - washing, sleeping, and shopping. We also spent some time investigating Sami culture.

A Sami Parliament was established in 1989. I toured the Parliament House, a beautiful building, very light and airy with massive windows and lovely lighting in the entrance hall. One of the parliament's main roles is to ensure the survival of the Sami languages and culture. There are nine or ten Sami languages in total and the Sami in Norway speak three of those languages – Northern Sami, Southern Sami and Lule Sami. The languages are not interchangeable so that Northern Sami speakers cannot understand Lule Sami speakers unless they have learnt Lule as well. Everything said in the parliamentary sittings is reported on-line and everything is translated into the three Sami languages of Norway.

The entrance hall of the parliament building is also the major Sami library, housing over ten thousand works in and on Sami language and literature. I looked at some of the children's books and was amazed at the words to be found in them. Some were so long and so complicated that I wondered how the children learn to spell. One book was called "Bluppe ja gaskaijabeaivváš" and showed a child sitting on a reindeer on its front cover. I was pleased to see that Sami children's books focus on what is important in their lives, reindeer!

The parliamentary sittings are held in a semi-circular room which is modelled on the traditional Sami Laavuu, a tent or circular hut where families traditionally lived and held important meetings. A stunning blue painting on one wall represented various aspects of their culture and history. The furniture and fittings were of soft coloured birch and other local woods, they glowed in the afternoon light.

I also went to the Sami Cultural Centre and listened to a young lady perform Joik songs. She had us transfixed with her deep, rich voice, which she used with great confidence. Joiks are short songs or chants which can be happy, sad, lively or mournful. They can be about any topic, tell a story or simply recreate an emotion. Anyone can create a joik but they are not allowed to create one about themselves, that would be like bragging. One joik was for a nine-year old boy who was very sad because his parents had died in the mountains. Another joik was happy. It was about a reindeer who loved to take tourists for a ride and tip them off the sleigh.

One evening, the three of us went to a traditional restaurant to sample some local fare. The restaurant was built of logs and lined with more wood. The whole building was covered in a mound of earth and grass, a traditional way of keeping buildings insulated in this bitterly cold climate. Inside, it was shaped like a cross with a large round open area in the centre. Each arm of the cross was lined with benches covered in soft cushions and had a small crackling fire in a fire pot for each group of diners. It was very cosy. I ate reindeer stew with forest berries.

While in the Arctic Circle, I had an important question to research. My great-great-great-great grandmother's brother travelled in this area as a young man in the mid 1800's. He grew up in a family of wine merchants based in Lübeck in north Germany. In those days, it was common for well-educated young men destined for a life in business to undertake a type of Grand Tour around Europe before settling down to desk and quill. His first tour was into the Arctic Circle and was undertaken in the dead of winter with the expected ice and snow. He sometimes travelled in a pulk drawn by a reindeer and commented on the difficulty in getting the reindeer started in the correct direction, a process which involved running along the proposed route while tugging the reindeer along with him. As the reindeer picked up speed, he had to jump in the pulk as it shot past him. If he miscalculated, he ended up lying in the snow while reindeer and pulk disappeared into the distance. Question: "What is a pulk?"

I walked into the local Sami museum, and there right in front of me was a model of a Sami man in his bright blue traditional costume, decorated with red and yellow braid. He was leading a reindeer which was harnessed to a long, narrow object, a cross between a shallow canoe and a sled. This was a pulk! I stood there, looked at the pulk, and could understand my ancestor's difficulty. Once he had the reindeer running in the right direction, it would have been a major athletic feat to jump into the pulk as it zipped past without falling out or tipping it over. He learnt, in the end, but I'm sure he got quite wet and bedraggled in the process.

Leaving Karasjok, the plan was to cycle up Route 93 which follows the Karasjohka River to the Suossjavri Lake on the high plains, then stay in a cabin in Suossjavri village. The weather forecast showed a cold front passing through. It was going to rain and maybe even snow. In hindsight, we should have stayed in our warm cabin and refused to move until the weather cleared again.

It started to rain soon after I set off, not a heavy rain but a steady soaking drizzle. After forty kilometres the rain turned to sleet and then it started to snow. I arrived at Suossjavri where I had agreed to wait for Jacquie and Mark. There was only one place with a few cabins which were all locked up and unoccupied. There was no-one around. I found a cabin with a small veranda attached. The cabin had some phone numbers written on the door, but I had not organised a SIM card for my phone, so it was effectively useless. I set up my stove on the veranda, made myself a cup of hot chocolate, and settled in to wait for the others. They rolled in some time later, just when I was starting to shiver and get really cold.

Jacquie rang the owners and got permission for us to stay there. We switched on all the heaters, Mark lit the wood fire and soon it was all very warm and cosy. There was no running water in the house. The bathroom was in another building and the toilet was a wooden seat with a hole in it. The excrement landed on a pile in the open air below the seat. Having the cold wind blast past my privates while I sat on the loo was definitely a new experience. I only went to the toilet when I really needed to. Even so, we were so happy to be there. We were snug, warm, and out of the wind, the rain, and the snow.

That evening, Jacquie told me that they were not happy with my habit of riding off by myself. They were concerned that I might fall into a ditch and be unable to call out to them as they rode past or that I couldn't help if one of them got into difficulty. I could see her point so decided that I would ride with them for the foreseeable future. Riding as a threesome would curtail my independence but the safety and security of all three of us was more important.

Breakfast the following morning was a cold affair. We wanted to make sure the fire was completely out before we left the building so had let it burn out some time in the night. Compensation for this was the sighting of a moose. It was grazing in the scrubby marshland at the edge of the lake a long way away. Jacquie and Mark could see it reasonably well but for me it was just a little brown blob in the distance. I zoomed in on my phone/camera, at which point the little brown blob became a fuzzy brown blob jumping around erratically in my screen. Still, we saw a moose!

The skies were still overcast but the rain, sleet and snow had stopped. It was quite cold, under four degrees. I dressed in all my glorious cycling gear for cold weather. On my head: a beanie to keep my ears warm, a bike helmet with a high-vis shower cap for safety, a neck warmer which was often lifted over my nose and mouth, and sunglasses to keep the wind out of my eyes.

On my body: a bra, a long-sleeved thermal top, a T-shirt, a cashmere jumper from Mongolia with a hole in one elbow, and a waterproof, windproof jacket. On top of all that I wore a bright yellow high-vis vest so that motorists and stray reindeer could get a good look at me before they raced past or ran away in fright.

On my hands: a pair of short-fingered gloves with an odd pair of long-fingered gloves over the top. I had originally had two pairs of long-fingered gloves but had managed to lose the right hand of one pair at the North Cape and the left hand of the other pair somewhere unknown. Not only were the gloves an odd pair, but they were of different sizes too. I had originally bought one pair to fit snugly and a larger pair to go over the top. With only one glove of each pair left, I had one snug glove and one very loose one. Still, it could have been worse – I could have been left with two right-hand gloves of different sizes.

On my legs and feet: a pair of long thermal pants under a pair of Daddy-Long-Legs which are tight but very warm pants. I wore a waterproof pair of pants over the top in the rain or exceptionally cold wind. My feet were kept warm with one pair of woollen socks, my leather shoes, and a pair of over-boots which were not waterproof but did keep the wind out.

Of course, there was another advantage to wearing so much clothing. What was worn on the body did not need to be lugged about in a pannier.

Leaving Norway, I appreciated all the different road signs I had seen so far on the way. The place names were sometimes so long that I wondered how anyone could learn to say them, let alone write them correctly. The sign for Govdavuohppenjárga needed three posts to support it. Many signs were also written in the three local languages – Norwegian, Northern Sami and Kven. Apart from the standard road signs, there were also directional and distance signs for snow mobiles. The tracks and signs for these nifty machines didn't follow the road but took the "scenic" route disappearing into the forest and reappearing again when they felt the need. My favourite signs of all were the little ones which were placed on a post every five hundred metres. The numbers on these signs told me exactly how far that post was from the beginning of that particular road. From that, I could entertain myself with some mental arithmetic. How far had we ridden and how far did we still have to go?

# | 11 |

## Finland is Forests

### The Norway/Finland Border to Tornio,

#### 425 km

Once we left Norway, the weather started to warm up. It was a massive eight degrees Celsius as we cycled over the border and I felt positively warm! The only annoying thing was that the wind had turned. Riding south, we were cycling head-on into a strong south wind. It was very frustrating. Then I realised that the very annoying strong south wind was bringing the warmer weather with it. That realisation brought a challenging dilemma. Would I prefer a cold north wind to give me a push from behind or a warm south wind to warm me up but slow down our progress?

We arrived in a small outpost blip which included two tourist shops, one of which had the only tax refund office for Norway on that road. I dug out my receipt for a Sami knife which I had purchased back in Karasjok. While going through the paperwork for my refund, I saw a rather lonely looking moose on a keyring. He was obviously an orphan in need of love, attention and rescuing so I purchased him from his owner with my refund money. I decided to call him Mouse, Mouse the Moose. The first thing we did together was to free him from the keychain clip which he was shackled to. He rode proudly, all the way to Malta, at the front of my bike, from where he had a great view of the world as it passed by.

Arriving in Mounio was a good excuse for a rest day. I wandered over to the Swiss Café which was a bit of a highlight of this town. The lady who ran it spoke fluent German, Italian, English and Finnish. She could also read, understand and have a good crack at Norwegian and French. It was so cosy and civilised that I had my morning coffee, lunch, and afternoon tea in the café. Lunch was reindeer pie with berries.

I had been pondering the importance of reindeer in the lives of the locals and whether this was reflected in their languages. The Swiss Café provided a partial answer to this with a booklet about the reindeer industry, including a glossary. Having grown up in a dairy and beef farming family, I found this stuff quite riveting. The following words are all in Finnish, but they still illustrate the importance of reindeer for the Sami people.

- Hirvas: a male over three years old
- Härkä: a castrated male
- Kalppinokka: a reindeer with a white muzzle
- Kesukka: a tame reindeer
- Kulvakko: a male over three years old which is exhausted by the rutting season
- Luostakka: a white-sided reindeer
- Maanija: a timid reindeer which avoids people
- Mutsikki (Musikki) a dark coloured reindeer
- Nulppo: a reindeer without antlers
- Pailakka: an untamed, untrained reindeer
- Peura: a reindeer without an earmark
- Raavas: a fully-grown reindeer
- Rusakka (Russako): a brownish-yellowish reindeer
- Takkahärkä: a castrated male which carries a load
- Vaadin: a female over three years old
- Valkko: a white reindeer
- Vuonelo: a female in its second year

Earmarking the calves seems just as complicated. Each calf needs to be earmarked soon after birth to identify which reindeer herd it belongs to. All herders have their own earmark for their reindeer which are made by small cuts in both the left and the right ears. There are twenty-one different types of cuts made which combine in a multitude of ways to make up the twelve thousand different earmarks in use at any time. New earmarks are made up when needed and old ones can change owners. Earmark descriptions start from the tip of the right ear when looking from behind. The most important cuts are described first followed by the lesser cuts.

Back home on our farm in Australia, we used to clip a brightly coloured tag onto the right ear of our cows and calves. Each tag had a number. It wasn't an issue if an animal lost its tag because we never had more than 150 head of cattle at any time and we knew them each as individuals. A reindeer herder with hundreds or even thousands of reindeer would need a much better system, one which cannot be lost or destroyed. It made sense to me.

For the first few hundred kilometres, Finland was forest, forest, and more forest, interspersed with trees, trees, and more trees. The trees in the area were already much bigger than those stumpy little things in the far north. The silver birches were giving way to mixed forests of birches and conifers. The wildflowers, the heather, and the small shrubs were preparing to stun the world with their splendour. Yellow, white, purple, and pink flowers livened up the light green of the birches and the darker green of the conifers.

Every now and then we zipped over a gurgling stream as it raced to join a river or lake. There were huge stretches of swampy marshland which must be a haven for the wildlife, heaven for mosquitoes, and absolute murder for those people who live in the area. I was told the mosquito repellent in the north has to be so strong it almost has nuclear qualities.

We eventually arrived at the Torne River and prepared to follow it all the way down to Tornio where it empties into the Gulf of Bothnia. The main advantage of following a river is that if it is big and slow enough, the gradient is usually quite gentle, and it always goes down-hill. The most significant part of this section was all the intermittent roadworks which we had to ride through for at least thirty kilometres. Long stretches of STOP signs; trucks and heavy machinery coming and going; dirt, gravel, and stones; bosses and drivers standing around campfires, holding steaming cups of coffee; and three cyclists slowly weaving their way through the mess. Mark scored the pun of the day with his comment that all the roads were un-*finn*-ished!

At Kolari, we crossed the Torne River into Sweden. We could see that the road on the Swedish side followed the river closely around a leisurely bend while the road on the Finnish side went straight through the wilderness before coming back to the river. The Finnish road would have been shorter, but it looked like it would be much hillier. The Swedish road was well maintained and wide with little traffic. It was a gentle descent, as expected. We zipped along at an average speed of eighteen kilometres for the whole day. Those sorts of days, where the cycling was easy, the weather was co-operative, and the surrounding environment was calm and relaxing are the closest thing to heaven for a cyclist like me.

The constant forest was broken up by many cabins and a few farms. We passed some horses, some ploughed paddocks, and even a dairy farm. Some sections of the forest were being harvested. The smell of pine resin as we rode past piles of logs was a delight for the olfactory glands. The cabins seemed to be just parked in the centre of a patch of grass. There were no gardens or fences, just a driveway with a row of letterboxes at the roadside and a cabin or five at the other end.

We found some cabins to overnight in at Pello but the owner insisted we rent his father's house instead, for the same price as two cabins. The house was quite cosy, with all the mod-cons, and a washing machine which I fell onto with great delight. Our landlord was a man of many occupations - auctioneer, antique dealer, football coach, landlord, and occasional helper in his wife's cafe.

We had often seen people in small rowboats fishing on the river and wondered whether they were fishing for salmon. Our host seemed to be an expert in his region and was keen to talk so we asked about local fishing practices. It was the main fishing season because the salmon were migrating upstream to their breeding grounds in the headwaters of the rivers. Fishing for salmon or trout with a fishing rod was only allowed for three months of the year from the start of June until the end of August, but not from Sunday evening until Monday evening. Most fishermen rowed a boat upstream, trawling for the fish as they went. The catch was limited to one fish per day. There was a long list of other rules to do with fish size, boat motors, fishing gear and areas available for fishing. It was reassuring to know that not only were there regulations to ensure the continuation of the species but also that the local fishermen were well aware of the rules, and hopefully, willing to abide by them. As an afterthought, we learnt that it would be easy to buy a cabin in this area for 35,000 euros. It was very tempting, except I'm not into fishing.

We crossed over the Arctic Circle again just after Pello. I was quite sad to leave the Arctic Circle as it is such a unique environment and my chances of returning to experience it more are rather slim. On the other hand, I was very happy to be south of the line, it meant that the climate (and us) would be getting a little bit warmer every day.

Our host in Pello had told us about a restaurant which we would be passing on the way south. It was the site of some sort of salmon count-ing technology. The previous year, 100,000 salmon had passed that point on their way upstream. Usually about a thousand passed through every day but at the height of the season six thousand were counted on one day. We pulled up at the restaurant which had a large glass window overlooking the river as it churned and tumbled downstream. I couldn't see any salmon, but I made sure that I had a close encounter with one on my plate. I love salmon anyway, but this one was absolutely superb, grilled to perfection with a crisp skin and succulent meat, served with warm potato salad, sour cream, and a slice of lemon.

During the preceding days, it had become clear to me that Jacquie and Mark's aims for our trip were very different to mine. We hadn't re-ally discussed this during our trip preparations as it never occurred to any of us that this might become an issue. They had commitments and responsibilities at home, they had employment to go back to and a set period of time available for holidays. They needed to cycle down Finland as quickly as possible so that they could catch a train and ferry to get to Germany and then to cycle to Switzerland by a certain date.

I, on the other hand, was retired, with no time limits, no responsibilities and nothing else demanding my attention. I am a slow traveller. I wanted to slow down, to spend more time exploring each area as we went through it. I was always aware that I would most likely never have the opportunity to see any of these places again and I wanted to see everything of interest. I found the tug between their need for speed, and my own desire to see and experience as much as possible en route, a little frustrating.

By the time we pulled into Ylitornio, I was physically tired and socially exhausted. I wanted an afternoon off to rest, to collect my thoughts, to sort out my photos, and to catch up on my writing. I decided to continue on this journey by myself, so without further ado, I said goodbye the next morning and wished my friends well for the rest of their trip. My decision was rather abrupt. In hindsight, I should have approached the issue in a very different manner; but then again, if we were all perfect, we wouldn't have anything more to learn. Jacquie and Mark made it to Switzerland with one day to spare and returned to Australia before I even managed to leave Scandinavia.

I cycled off alone, following the Torne River to its mouth and cruised into the campsite in the town of Tornio in the early afternoon.

# | 12 |

# A Language of Ks

## Tornio to Pietersaari, 382 km

The twin cities of Haparanda (Sweden) and Tornio (Finland) sit on either side of the Torne River at the northern end of the Gulf of Bothnia. From there, I planned to follow the west coast of Finland all the way south until the Åland Islands. At least the navigation would be easy. I just needed to head south and stay out of the water.

On my second day of solo cycling, I spent most of the day on the E8 which runs down the west coast of Finland. The traffic was absolutely dreadful. The E8 really needed to be a four-lane freeway; instead, it was a two-lane life-threatening disaster. Some sections had bike paths and there was one long stretch of small country road which was absolute bliss to cycle along. For the remainder of the time, I wavered between absolute terror, confidence that the local drivers were clever enough to avoid me, and a state of resignation - "whatever will be, will be." At one stage, a very sick reindeer staggered drunkenly along the centre of the road. The stream of cars, trucks, buses, motor-vans, and motorbikes all slowed down and swerved gently around it. I hoped someone had the sense to contact the local authorities to get the situation sorted out for the safety of all the road users, including the reindeer.

It always takes me a few days to get used to the idea of being a solo traveller again, but I was aware of this and didn't let any negative thoughts disturb my equilibrium. By far the hardest part of any long-distance cycling or walking tour is the mental aspect. Other solo cyclists tell me that they have the same issues. Constant walking or cycling leads to constant thinking and self-talk which has the potential to become negative and self-defeating if one doesn't have good mental health and discipline. I made a point of focusing on the beautiful scenery, the interesting architecture, the friendly people, and the wonderful food so that by the third day, I was starting to feel quite chirpy about being alone again. I thoroughly enjoyed the freedom of cycling as far and as fast as I wanted, stopping when I wanted, and planning my own program; or not planning anything at all if I didn't feel like it.

I was cycling past Haukipudas, a village twenty kilometres before Oulu when I saw a small church peeping over the trees in the distance. I went over to have a look because it was very early in the afternoon and I had ample time available for diversions such as this. I was stunned to see over one hundred and seventy graves in long lines in the churchyard, each with a small tablet, and planted with a fuchsia bearing red flowers. Many of the graves were from November 1939 to March 1940, the period of the Winter War when Finland fought off an invading Russian army. It was so sad to see so many young lives lost in such a short period of time. The rest of the graves were from 1941 to 1945. This graveyard really brought home the dreadful cost of war, the sacrifice made by the young men, and the suffering borne by the ordinary people. To think that this sort of violence is still going on around the world is absolutely heart-breaking.

Afterwards I rounded the corner of the bell tower and nearly had the living daylights scared out of me by a man leaning against the wall He was a wooden "pauper statue." There are about 145 of these statues in Scandinavia, mainly in this area. Way back in 1629, the Swedish Queen, Kristina, ordered that money collection logs be set up next to churches in the area. Their purpose was to collect money for the local poor people, many of whom were ex-soldiers who had been wounded and subsequently disabled during one of the many interminable wars in Europe. Over time, the logs morphed into statues with a coin slot and collection box built into the pauper statue's chest. So, the man who had given me such a scare was really an early version of the Finnish social security system.

I originally planned to spend a whole day sight-seeing at Oulu, but I got there so early, and I was so energised from cycling that I went into town in the afternoon to have a quick look. The market square in Oulu is right on the water's edge and it was really hopping with life. Oulu is a student town and it seemed the students were all out enjoying the sunshine, the waterfront, numerous beers, and each other's company. Some old boat sheds, all painted in the traditional oxide red colour, had been re-incarnated as boutiques, but they didn't have too many customers. Maybe the students were too poor or maybe they were too busy hanging out with their friends. Further on was a great statue of a short, chubby and very friendly looking policeman. I parked my bicycle in front of him so he could check it out to see whether it was roadworthy. Then I took a photo, of course!

I left Oulu early the following morning, managing to get rather lost on the way out of town. I started asking people for directions and ended up stuck in a no-through street in an industrial estate. Generally, asking the locals for directions works best when the proposed route is only one or two turns away. Anything more complicated than that has me confused before I've even started! I pondered whether I should just buy a SIM card and use a navigation app in future. I hadn't considered it until then because finding my way had been quite simple. I had just used a standard small road map and headed towards the sun.

My daily routine was beginning to settle down. I planned the next day's ride, the route, and the accommodation the evening before. I also checked the weather forecast and the terrain so there were no nasty surprises. I got my clothes ready accordingly. My rain gear and jacket were always packed in my orange bag at the back of the bicycle where I could grab them quickly if I needed them.

I usually got up at about 7.30 a.m., organised myself, and then had a leisurely breakfast. I found that if I started to pack up before I had got myself ready for the day, I tended to waste a lot of time looking for an all important item which I had already packed away, or I discovered that I had forgotten to pack something which had to go at the bottom of a completed bag. So, the routine was:

1– organise self

2 – eat breakfast

3- dress bike - hang helmet and gloves onto handlebars, fill and attach water bottles, unlock security locks

4- pack panniers but leave them open until the very end, stand them in a row next to the bike

5 – dismantle and pack tent

6 - close panniers, attach to bike

7 – check campsite for forgotten items.

This routine may seem pedantic, but it actually saved a great deal of scrabbling around in confusion and disarray.

I would cycle out of camp around 9 a.m. and set a first target of about twenty to twenty-five kilometres away. I usually aimed for a small town with the possibility of buying supplies for lunch so that my morning break also became a quick shopping stop. I would then eat a snack; a muesli bar, a banana, a yoghurt, a hard-boiled egg, or any combination of these. Later on in the trip, as I lost weight and started to get much hungrier, my morning snack invariably included some sweet pastries bought on impulse from a bakery, as well.

Lunch break was after another fifteen to twenty-five kilometres depending on the terrain, the weather, the daily target and the scenery. I preferred to have a picnic stop in the countryside, along a stream or on the edge of a forest. Lunch was usually a bread roll or two with slices of cheese, a yoghurt or a piece of fruit, and a Fanta or an orange juice to drink. I got a bit tired of only drinking water and I was craving sugar, so I rewarded myself with one sweet drink per day. Since then, I have realised that I always crave sugary drinks when doing a long ride or trek. This need usually disappears about three days after I have completed the trip and I'm not pushing my body so hard anymore.

After lunch, I only had very short breaks to fuel up or to catch my breath if needed. I stopped whenever and wherever I felt I needed a break, once again depending on the weather, my target for the day and my overall progress.

In general, I found that my cycling in the morning was relatively lethargic. I cycled smoothly and evenly but found it a challenge to get any great speed going. I didn't worry about this, I just rode as it felt comfortable. After my morning break, however, my legs and brain co-ordinated much better, my speed picked up dramatically and I often found myself churning through the kilometres in a type of cycling trance. The monotonous landscape and the ease of navigation certainly helped with this. I could get into my cycling rhythm and not need to slow down to turn a corner or stop to look at a curious sight. I lost a lot of weight in those weeks, to the point that I had to hold my pants up when walking or they would fall down around my knees. I never got around to buying a belt.

When I rolled into camp in the late afternoon, I first had a coffee or an ice-cream. I would wander around, check out the facilities, locate sources of food for dinner and decide where I would pitch my tent. I had much more energy for doing everything that needed to be done if I gave myself the time to slowly relax and morph from flat-out-cycling mode to camping-and-not-moving mode. When all had been organised and the washing had been done, I would hunt down dinner and then the whole business of preparing for the next day would start all over again.

I have commented before that Finland is all about trees and forests. I was wrong! It's also a land of rivers, rivers, rivers and lakes. The Finnish word for "river" is "joki" and I passed through numerous towns with names ending in "joki". In two days, I went through Lumijoki, Pattijoki, Pyhäjoki, Kalajoki and many more. It was becoming quite a "jokie." Having said that, every river I crossed was absolutely gorgeous. I took dozens of photos of boulder strewn streams, rushing rivers, thickly vegetated moorlands and lakes sprinkled with islands and colourful rowing boats.

I was fascinated with the Finnish language as a whole as it is quite extraordinary. My interest comes from having dabbled in linguistics while in my first year at university. My observations, while being very amateurish, went thus:

- They have lots of long words such as "Kuljettajantutkinto" and "Hovioikeudenpuistikko" (the name of a street)
- They have lots of double letters as in "nappaamaan" or "viatto-muuttaan"
- They sprinkle umlauts around like confetti as in Vähäkyrö" or "pääseväni."
- There seem to be very, very few place names starting with the letters A to G. When I first looked in the index for camping sites, I thought I was missing some pages. Then I realized that Alavus, Enontekiö and Espoo were the only A – G place names in the book. The next one was Hamina.
- They love the letter K as in "Kurikka". 20 % of the place names in my camping guide started with the letter K. One road sign I saw had the names of four towns on it: Koskenkylä, Kokkola, Karleby and Karhi.

This area, along the coast, has a large percentage of Swedish speakers so the town names were often in Swedish as well as Finnish.

I rode on to Jakobstad (Swedish), also known as Pietersaari (Finnish). The weather was forecast for rain, wind and generally freezing conditions so I opted to stay in a cabin in the campground for two nights, to have a day's rest, and be a tourist.

# | 13 |

## Meeting the Friendly Finns

### Pietersaari to Pori, 345 km

The Skata, a neighbourhood of Jakobstad/Pietersaari consisted of old wooden houses dating back to the early 1700's when it was home to the town's seamen and their families. There were still over three hundred of these traditional wooden houses to be wandered past, all in excellent condition. The area had a lovely, comfortable ambience, the houses were all painted in a variety of pastel colours: red, green, blue, or yellow. Most of them had the wooden boards going vertical but some had horizontal boards and a few even had horizontal cladding below floor level and vertical cladding above that.

Back at camp, I met another camper, Markku, an advertising producer. He was accompanying a woman who was walking through Finland as a charity stunt. Markku's job was to create enough video footage of her for her charity to be able to use it in their fund-raising program. He sat with me and went through the best route to travel down to Pori in quite some detail. Markku had lived there for twenty-two years and was keen to explain where I could try some smoked fish, where there was an old fishing village, which roads were the most scenic, and so on. He told me the story of the cemetery at Ii which I had ridden past between Merihelmi and Oulu. Long ago, the cemetery had been put on an island to keep the bodies safe from bears and wolves. When the ice on the river was too soft though, it was too dangerous to try to cross over to the island, so any deceased persons had to be put into cold storage until the ice had frozen over properly. There's a bridge there now.

Having spent a full day at Jakobstad/Pietersaari, it was time to move on. The weather was still quite bad - raining and with a strong north wind. I had to get dressed in all my wet weather gear before I even started out but, at this stage, I was getting quite inured to cold and wet conditions. I found that every time I had an excuse not to cycle, if I just gritted my teeth and cycled anyway, the excuse invariably disappeared. My main concern was usually the strength and direction of the wind. I much preferred a north wind which would push me from behind, even if it was much colder than a south wind. By the afternoon, the weather had cleared, the sun came out, the wind died down, and I arrived in Vaasa dry and happy.

I also very quickly found that the best part of travelling alone was all the people whom I met. Cycling from Vaasa to Tjärlax, I had three interesting encounters with local people. I was having my picnic lunch on a lawn next to a café when a woman passing by decided to stop and have a chat. She, of course, wanted to know all about my trip; where from, where to, how long, was I all alone, was I not scared?

Later, I was cycling along the road, coming up to a roadside parking stop when a man stepped to the roadside and called me over with: "It's coffee time! Would you like a coffee?"

"Yes, please!"

He was a cyclist too. The previous year he had ridden from Alicante in southern Spain to his home in Jakobstad. It took him three months. He usually rode about seventy to eighty kilometres per day but on the last day he was so keen to get home that he rode 240 kilometres. His wife poured me a coffee, gave me a delicious triangular donut type cake and was so very proud of him. They both studied my bike and were keen to hear the "where from, where to, how long?" The man was very positive about cycling through France and was considering a cycling trip in Japan. They gave me a bottle of sparkling mineral water and we went our separate ways. It was lovely! He had explained that the Finns are very reclusive and difficult to talk to but that hadn't been my experience at all.

I found my way to the Tjärlax campground and was enthusiastically greeted by a group of locals who were sitting outside their vans, enjoying life together. None of them were confident with English but with a great deal of laughter and Finnglish, they managed to point me to an older gentleman who ran the campground. He spoke quite good English which he had learnt in the sixties from listening to The Beatles, The Rolling Stones, and others. My campsite cost me ten euros for the night, with basic but clean facilities, steaming hot water, and a beautiful setting on the shores of a large lake. The water was quite cold, but I went swimming anyway. There are some things in life which just need to be done. Swimming in a freezing lake in Finland is one of them.

By this stage, I was covering about ninety kilometres per day. Navigation was still quite easy, along the lines of "cycle on this road for forty kilometres, then turn left." I still hadn't bothered with getting a SIM card and internet access for my phone. There was just no need.

I cycled from Tjärlax to Merikarvia, a distance of about eighty-five kilometres but for the first time, managed to add an extra ten kilometres to the distance. This may not seem much, but at the end of a long, tiring day, any extra distance becomes a huge hurdle to overcome. I had wanted to follow Markku's route plan along the smaller roads but ended up getting in a muddle, missed a vital turn-off and rode further than I needed to. Maybe it was time to rethink the whole SIM card, navigation, internet situation.

Merikavia was the fishing village where Markku had told me about a smoked fish stand which had been in the same family for four generations. I looked for, and found, a smoked fish shop although I had no idea whether it was the right one or not. I tried to purchase a small fish as a taster, but the old lady wouldn't let me pay. I ate it, carefully avoiding the many bones. The locals might have loved their smoked fish, but I wasn't going to get fat on them.

The ride to Yyteri/Pori was a lovely saunter of under fifty kilometres along the coast with numerous small islands. It was a day of marshes, bridge crossings, and little surprises around every corner. The sun was shining, the sky was a clean-washed blue, and I felt really relaxed and happy. I *almost* started singing.

Then, ominously, I began to hear strange clangings and bangings from my front wheel. I stopped and checked everything. I rode off again, no improvement. I stopped again, found a loose screw, and tightened it. Still no improvement. I stopped twice more, checked every screw, fastening, and spoke but still couldn't find anything wrong. The clacking kept on, but without any logic to it. Peddling or not peddling made no difference; the road surface, whether tarmac or bumpy gravel also made no difference. Every now and then I wondered if the noise was coming from the back wheel, so I stopped and checked all of that too. I couldn't find anything obviously loose or out of place. I was getting quite worried, particularly as I was cycling a narrow, winding road through forest with very few houses and no traffic. What would I do if something serious broke?

I decided to leave it to fate and stop worrying. I pulled over to have a drink and brush my teeth because they were feeling feral. In unstrapping one of the back panniers to get out my toothbrush, I noticed that I had forgotten to do up the cross strap on the other back pannier. Part of the strap with the attachment on the end was hanging down loose next to the spokes. It would have been bouncing around, clanging and banging as I rode. Duh!!!!!! Problem solved.

Being able to relax again, I made the effort to enjoy the scenery and made a small detour to an old fishing village for a coffee and cake, Markku's recommendation again. The village was full of the old painted wooden houses which were so common in the area. I had my coffee and cake in a house painted a soft buttercup yellow. It glowed in the sun. Very nice!

It was in this village that people were said to be buried in foreign soil when they died. How was that possible? Well, in the last two hundred years, during the days of mass emigration, many ships left Finland loaded to the brim with emigrants. The ships' captains often couldn't find enough goods in the Americas, Australia or other foreign places to return home with, yet the ships needed ballast to stop them capsizing in stormy seas. The solution was to fill the hold with sacks of soil and bring them back to Finland. Once home again, the soil was unloaded and somehow ended up in the cemetery, covering the recently departed. Would that have made the locals happy? Would they have enjoyed knowing that they would be chewed up by worms which were bred in America or Australia?

The church had a memorial graveyard for soldiers who had died fighting against the Russians and in WWII. Many died on the same day, 12.09.1942. I think they were all on a ship or submarine which was destroyed. Once again, I was appalled to see how many young men lost their lives in such a senseless and brutal fashion. To take young men who have so much to live for, a future of so much excitement and possibility, and then to cut their lives short on the battlefield, for what? It's just dreadful!

I arrived in Pori twenty-seven days after leaving the North Cape; that included four days of resting and sightseeing in Karasjok, Mounio and Jakobstad. I was quite pleased with my progress, but it was going to be interrupted for at least four weeks. One of my cousins was quite keen to go cycling with me but, being short of time, she only wanted to cycle in Germany and Poland. So, I caught a bus from Pori to Helsinki and spent a day relaxing before I caught a ferry for the 24-hour journey to Travemünde in Germany.

# | 14 |

# Walking Through History

## Pori to Kustavi 197 km

Four weeks later, I disembarked from the ferry in Turku and took the bus back to Pori where I reloaded everything on to my bike to set off on the first day of the next leg of the journey. The aim (or hope) was to get to Berlin before I had to go back to Australia by the end of October.

While in Germany, I had discovered that the mobile phone networks in Europe had been re-organised so that it had become possible to take a mobile phone with its SIM card from one country and to use it with a partner telco in another country within the EU at no extra cost. I had seized this opportunity to get a SIM card which I used initially in Germany and in Poland. I was planning to use it as long as it lasted in Finland.

Having a SIM enabled me to navigate the smaller roads now that I was heading into more densely populated areas. In the far north, the road network was not so complicated. Once out of town, it was usually a matter of following the main road south with an occasional turn to the right or the left. I had to stay near the coast and not ride into the sea. It was easy. The further south I rode, the more complicated things got. If I missed a turn-off and tried to find my own way, I invariably got lost. I made sure to practice using Google Maps while cycling in Germany and felt reasonably confident that I knew what I was doing.

I was so excited to get back on to my bike, yet reality hit with a thud when I realised how much fitness I had lost just in the previous four weeks. It was really hard work! Stupidly, once I had got out of Pori, I decided not to look at my Google Maps again for quite a while. I stopped for a coffee at Eurojoki, looked at the map and discovered I need not have been cycling along the terribly busy E8 for the last three hours. The app had told me to turn off and go along quiet country roads, but I missed all of that, yet another learning experience.

I cycled along quieter roads for the rest of the day and enjoyed the scenery so much more. Nature was already preparing for autumn. Many fields were golden and heavy with grain although the leaves on the trees hadn't started turning yet. I saw many farm sheds made of wood on a base of massive slabs of stone. One very long shed was slowly sinking into the ground. It looked so picturesque in a quaint naive way, but I doubt that the farmer saw it that way.

My first night on this stage of my tour was spent in a lovely campground in Rauma. I set up my tent amongst trees and rocks on a small hill which sloped down to a bay. A jetty at the base of the hill held a few boats captive as they quietly bobbed about in the water. There were only a few other tents, so it was not at all crowded. On the other hand, this blissful and scenic campground was somewhat marred by a cantankerous, screaming toddler in another tent. She screamed over breakfast, she bawled when they were setting off on a walk, and she was still blubbering when they came back. The child howled over her supper and went sobbing to bed where she continued to wail, until she fell asleep later. I don't know how the parents managed not to throttle her, but they were incredibly calm and patient with the little horror.

Even though I had only been cycling for one day, it was time for a two-day break. I had always planned to spend a full day in Rauma which is a UNESCO recognised town. There was also a stone age burial site twenty kilometres away which I was determined to see.

I cycled into Rauma in the morning and completed the walking tour by bike. I not only wanted to see this heritage town as a tourist, I also wanted to see whether I could find any clues as to whether it had been part of the Hanseatic League in late medieval times.

The Hanseatic League was a trading confederation of cities and towns across most of northern Europe. The League dominated commerce in the area from the thirteenth to the fifteenth centuries, becoming so powerful it raised its own army and fought against neighbouring nations on at least three occasions. Lübeck, known as the Queen of the Hanse, was in the geographic centre of this league and hosted annual meetings of the major Hanseatic players. It was also my mother's hometown which partly explains my fascination with the topic. For the rest, I'm just a history nerd!

Many of the cities which were important centres of trade in those days still reflect proudly on that part of their history. There are elements of Hanseatic history on display all around the Baltic area if one knows what to look for. Rauma was a port, had been an important trading centre. It would have been a member city of the Hanseatic League. Would I find any evidence or clues in the town?

There were over six hundred wooden houses in Rauma, each one painted a different colour from a palette of traditional colours – ochre, butter yellow, dusky blue or a soft mint green and so on. The streets were all cobbled which was awful for bike riding but added to the ambience of the town. The Church of the Holy Cross had paintings from medieval times on the ceiling. A woman sitting in one of the pews was totally absorbed in her hymn book, it was only as I walked past that I realised she was actually a life-size mannequin doll dressed in her Sunday best, a piece of very realistic artwork. And to think that I was going to go up to her for a chat!

Of special interest for me was the "Marela," a ship owner's home. Most of the buildings of interest in Rauma date back to the nineteenth century which is a bit late for the Hanseatic era, but I thought I would check it out anyway. The house belonged to the Granlund family from 1873 to 1907. Gabriel Granlund had been the richest man in Rauma, with the biggest ships, but he was a well-known miser too. After he died in 1901, the family spent up big on a long list of renovations and additions to the house, but they can't have been terribly clever because they were declared bankrupt in 1907 and the house and all their possessions had to be sold to pay their debts. I was intrigued by the really short beds, for dwarves? I was told they were extendable beds which could be pulled out to regular length when needed. Thinking about it later, I wondered about the mattresses. Were they extendable too?

Then, I saw an amazing sight! On the wall in the best parlour were three old pictures of towns, each with a harbour. They caught my eye because they were so similar to our pictures at home of Lübeck; long, narrow copies of prints in black and white, showing the whole town from a distance complete with church spires. I looked closer and realised the description below the central picture was in German. Further investigation revealed that they were pictures of Hamburg, Lübeck and Rostock, three very close friends within the Hanseatic League. There were no other similar pictures of any other places in the house. Every other picture was a coloured print of a sailing ship or a photo of Gabriel Granlund and his family. The house was built and decorated long after the Hanseatic League was past its prime, so it was a long shot to talk about a connection with the Hanse; but it was certainly interesting.

Later in the day, I found a shop which specialised in printed T-shirts. I like T-shirts as a souvenir, provided they are not slathered with the name of the place in a way which boasts about the wearer's travel history. In this shop, I was able to choose my own design and get it printed on a colour of my choice. I had fallen in love with the many reindeer which I had seen up north, so I looked through the pattern book for some reindeer pictures. A page of white reindeer of different sizes caught my attention, I chose three and the proprietor arranged them to march across a sky-blue T-shirt for me. I'm notoriously un-artistic so I was happy to outsource this part. I handed over my twenty euros and became the contented owner of three reindeer trotting across my torso. I still treasure this T-shirt to this day. After all, it's better than being trampled by the real thing!

Wearing my new T-shirt and full of love for life and the world in general, I rode back into town later to find some supper. My happiness was somewhat marred by a gentleman who told me off for riding my bicycle in a pedestrian zone. What is it with these people? It was after 8 p.m., the street was completely deserted, and those very picturesque cobblestones were keeping my speed down to a relaxed walking pace. I was going so slow it was a wonder that I hadn't already fallen off. I was so astonished that I actually dismounted and left the town, walking, pushing my bike, and fuming over the stupidity of some people, including me, for listening to him.

Sammallahdenmäki was calling. (I challenge any non-Finn to learn how to spell that one!) At twenty kilometres away from Rauma, it was perfect for a day's jaunt without carrying luggage. I did a complete set of stretches for my knees then set off. I made sure that I checked the route before I left, just in case there was no internet access out in the wilderness. Seven kilometres out of town, I turned off the main road onto a quiet country lane. The rest of the route was a standard country scene of southern Finland; fields, forest, houses, and sheds. I rounded a corner of the road and gaped at the beauty laid out before me. Golden grain glowed in the sunshine. The field rippled and flowed around piles of boulders, over small hillocks and into curving swales before disappearing into the distance through a break in the trees. Where was Van Gogh when he was needed?

Cycling into the forest, I marvelled yet again at the rocks under the trees, the moss, lichen, heather, and other low growing shrubs. I could see so much life at ground level of a pine forest in Scandinavia compared to our pine forests in Australia. Scandinavian pines are an integral part of the ecosystem. At home, they're imported weeds farmed as a resource for paper and timber.

The site, Sammallahdenmäki, was an area of thirty-six heaps of stones which were piled together during the Bronze Age and early Iron Age, (1500 – 50 BCE). Archaeologists have excavated some of the piles and found a few bone fragments as well as a piece of a metal bracelet. They concluded that these were burial mounds. The largest mound was almost a quadrangle and had an even surface, so it was named "The Church Floor." The other mounds were all circular. I noticed many had a depression in the centre although I couldn't establish from the information boards whether they were like this originally or not.

As I wandered around, I was amazed to think that people with so little technology to help them would expend so much effort to create something for their dead family and friends. How much time did it take to carry enough stones from around the area to create the "Church Floor" mound? Why? What did they think they would achieve?

In other cultures, the local people would have raided the site for the resources there, rocks for building already gathered and heaped up ready to be loaded on a cart or a truck and taken away. I was impressed that this particular site had remained relatively untouched and kept protected for so long.

I was also taken by the natural beauty of the site. The quiet of the woods, the boulders, rocks and stones scattered about, the multitude of yellow, white and mauve flowers, the pink heather, and the mosses and lichens in every colour of green. It was the loveliest scene and I could truly understand why so many Finns love being outdoors in summer.

The ride from Rauma to my next stop, Uusikaupunki was one of those days – it started off quite ordinary, just another day, but soon changed into just perfect.

I had had a rough night. It was quite windy, the tent was flapping and carrying on, but I fell asleep anyway only to be woken in the middle of the night by someone tugging at my guy ropes and banging on the tent pegs with a rock. I don't know who it was, but I suppose I should be grateful. I was woken again in the early morning by the screaming toddler in the next tent. She was still wailing by the time I left three hours later.

I dragged myself out of my cocoon and checked my tent. Some unknown creature had bitten or clawed two holes into my tent inner just where it was connected to the guy rope that the mysterious person had tightened in the night. Suspicious! The same critter, or maybe another one, had grabbed my rubbish bag, scoffed all the old bread and food scraps in there, then spread my plastic rubbish far and wide for me. My first job of the day was to clean up the mess.

From then on, it got much better. I rode off into strong winds which settled to a slight breeze during the day. The sun came out and all was well with the world. I found alternative roads to the E8 and spent the day cycling about forty-five kilometres on small country roads, winding through the fields and the forest. Much of the time I was on a fairly new cycle path; three metres wide, smooth black asphalt with no cracks, bumps or potholes. As I rode, I reflected how it was the small things which I saw which were so enjoyable; the bicycle decorated with flowers, the long line of mailboxes indicating there was a community hidden in the trees, a boat pulled to shore on the river bank, the smell of freshly cut grass drying for hay, the way the farmers ploughed and sowed their fields in straight lines while those same fields had such sinuous edges which wound around piles of rocks and patches of trees.

I zipped past an elderly gentleman on his bike. I smiled and said "Hello." He just looked astonished. When I stopped a kilometre further on to check my map, he pulled up next to me to help me out, in Finnish, of course. I crested a hill to see a local lady slogging up the other side. I waved, she smiled and waved back. A young man on a weird bike with super fat tyres sped past me. Those tyres must have made the bike so hard to peddle but he was going like a man on a mission.

Then there were the signs. The 196 sign was popular, it kept telling me I was on the right road, but even better were the elk signs; just at the right angle and height so they were incredibly difficult to photograph because of the bright sun which told me that I was definitely heading south. One sign warned of elk for the next 1.9 kilometres. Why 1.9? Why not two kilometres? What was going to happen at the 1.9 mark so that no elk would be found further along? There was no elk fence there, merely another sign warning of elk for the next eight hundred metres.

A mid-afternoon pick-me-up of coffee and a delicious piece of cake called Valkosuklaapuolukkakakku, in the town of Uusikaupunki followed. I was finding the cake in Finland to be quite dangerous. I would walk into a coffee shop for a quick pick-me-up and there would be a piece of cake on display just begging to be sampled, just screaming to be appreciated. How could I resist? I had already lost so much weight that I could easily slide off my pants without undoing them, so I figured that the cake was quite right in its demand to be eaten. After all, who better to appreciate good food than a hungry cyclist? The problem was going to be when I eventually stopped cycling. I would have to work out how to get around town without going past any cake shops.

My coffee and cake set me up for a visit to the Tourist Information Office to get information about the Åland Islands. I was looking for a map with campgrounds and ferries. The lass there spoke excellent English and armed me with so many pamphlets that it took me forever to sort through it all. The main objective was to work out a route from Finland to Sweden, island hopping all the way. I needed to identify where the campgrounds were and at what times the different ferries left each port. A local had told me a few days previously that the main ferries needed to be booked in advance, which concerned me. The lass couldn't answer the question about pre-booking tickets.

One of the best aspects about cycle touring in northern Europe, apart from all the cake which one is allowed to eat, is that cyclists usually do not need to book ferries in advance. Tickets for vehicles and their passengers generally need to be booked beforehand, while cyclists and foot passengers usually purchase tickets on the spot. For me, it was perfect as I couldn't possibly plan my travels four weeks in advance. I had a good idea of the general direction in which I wished to go, south, but no idea as to timing. I wanted the freedom to move or to stop whenever and for as long as I wished without having to worry about a ferry booking.

I headed off to the campground, which was a pleasantly treed, grassy spot next to the bay. It was very quiet there with only two campervans and no other tents. I hoped it would stay that way, particularly as I had found an unused power-point in a small room in the corner of the recreational building. As long as there were not too many people around, I felt it was quite safe to leave my phone and other devices there for charging. If more people arrived, I would feel more nervous about that.

My phone, in particular, was so important to me for the success of my journey. It was not just a phone, it was also my camera, navigator, contact point with my children at home, provider of data for my laptop and website, translator, bank account spy, my encyclopedia, my thesaurus and dictionary, holder of dozens of library books and of a series of Lonely Planet guides. My phone was *Life Itself*! I couldn't risk having it stolen.

Some people wandering through camp spoke to me in Finnish and when I replied in English, the older lady perked up and came over for a chat. She was originally from Finland but had emigrated to Canada as a young woman and was on a four-week trip around Finland with her daughter, son-in-law, and grandson. When the daughter heard I was an Australian, touring with my bike, she immediately came over too to find out all about my trip. It was lovely to have an uninhibited conversation with some native speakers. We chatted for half an hour, discussing my bike, my route, and my camping gear before comparing notes about healthy fast food options in different countries. You can always buy soup in Germany, but Denmark mainly has hotdogs, pizzas and hamburgers while Finland has the most wonderful hot buffets for only nine euros.

Another fifty or so kilometres took me to Kustavi where I dropped into the tourist office and requested that the young man there earn his money for the week. I asked about the necessity of booking the ferries for foot passengers with bicycles as the brochures had been unclear on this. All the information was for cars and caravans. He thought I wouldn't need to book but I, very politely but insistently, asked him to check with the ferry company which he did. There was no need to book.

# | 15 |

# Across the Åland Islands

## Kustavi to Eckerö, 121 km

The ferry timetables in the Åland Islands were not very cyclist friendly. They went three times a day; very early in the morning, sometime in the afternoon and late in the evening. Given that the campgrounds were often ten or more kilometres from the ferry wharves, it made catching the early or late ferries a bit difficult. I could see that I would have to organise my time well in order to not miss the ever so important afternoon crossings.

Leaving the mainland for my first day on the Åland Islands, my day was arranged around the ferry leaving Vuosainen-Osnäs at 1.30 p.m. I didn't want to get to the ferry landing too early as I knew there was nothing to do there except to twiddle my thumbs and to wait with good grace and patience, which would be quite a challenge for me. Conversely, I didn't want to miss the boat either, so timing was of utmost importance. Mid-morning, I cycled the four kilometres to the first ferry which took me onto the first of the islands. This was a small ferry which travelled back and forth all day, whenever enough cars or passengers had assembled, so waiting time was minimal.

The route across the next island was only about eight kilometres but I did a detour to an old schoolhouse which had been converted into a café/gift store. This was suggested by the young man at the Tourist Information Office the previous day. The old school was set in the forest off a small road. It would have been wonderful for the children to learn and play in such an environment. In modern times, it serves coffee to passing travellers in the know.

After coffee and a huge donut, I cycled on past two unusual sights, the type which I enjoyed looking at so much. The first was a row of sixteen mailboxes and one letterbox. There were obviously at least sixteen homes hidden in the forest further up the side road, yet I couldn't see any at all. More intriguing was the letter box. We often have rows of mailboxes lined up at specific points on the road at home, but I had never seen a letterbox where the inhabitants could post their letters at the same time as they collect their mail.

The second sight was a garden gnome being challenged by a model reindeer, very like the young girl staring down the massive bull on Wall Street in New York. The reindeer was so much bigger than the gnome but he, the gnome, just stood his ground and glared up at those huge antlers in his face. It was hilarious and told me that some Finns do indeed have a sense of humour.

I arrived in good time for the afternoon ferry at Vuosainen-Osnäs and was pleasantly surprised to learn that my passage would be free. I only had to pay six euro for my bicycle and even that was a once only cost. The ferry attendant explained that the ticket covered all my travel on all the ferries across the islands, as long as I kept going in one direction and didn't meander off on other routes. I was impressed!

I was fascinated to see how much care and attention needed to be taken to load the cars, bus, trucks, motorbikes, bicycles and passengers onto the ferry. The cars went on one side, on two levels. The centre and the other side were for the two big trucks and the bus. The last truck fitted with only inches to spare. The four motorbikes and six bicycles just went anywhere.

Having arrived on Brändö Island at 2.10 p.m., it was a twenty-three-kilometre cycle to the next ferry at Torsholma which was going to leave at 3.15 p.m. There was no way I could make that, even without the delay in getting off the ferry (bicycles were let off last) and the very strong southerly wind. I considered cycling the thirteen kilometres to Brändö campground, staying the night, then cycling the next ten kilometres to the next ferry which would be leaving at 8 am. When I arrived at the campground at Brändö, I thought it was ridiculous to stop so early in the day so I kept going, hoping there would be some accommodation in Torsholma. The map showed that there would be cabins there. When I arrived, there was nothing.

I was faced with three choices – I could take the 8 p.m. ferry to the next island which would arrive there at 9.40 p.m and hope I could find accommodation at that hour, but I don't like arriving somewhere so late. I could go back to the campground at Brändö, or I could camp in the forest down the road somewhere. Wild camping was not only allowed, but actively encouraged in Finland so I wasn't worried about the legalities of pitching my tent in the forest.

An hour later, I was sitting snug in my tent in a pine forest a short way off the road, about two kilometres from Torsholma. I could hear the wind soughing in the treetops but down at ground level it was very still and quite warm. I had made sure that I was far enough from the road that no-one could see my tent but did get a bit spooked when I heard voices nearby. Who were they? Had they seen me? The voices slowly moved on and faded into the distance. The only other sounds in the night were the rustling, of dried leaves and the scrabbling of tiny feet. It was all good.

In the quiet of the night, I reflected on the day which I had just enjoyed. Cycling across Brändö had been a lovely experience apart from the wind which was so strong that I did wonder whether turning around and trying to cycle backwards might have been quicker. The road was well made, bitumen, with no cracks, potholes, or the constant repairs I had seen elsewhere which can make cycling at speed a fairly hazardous enterprise. It was very quiet, only three cars had passed me. The road wound through the forest and fields, (nothing new there), over and around small hills or mounds of rocks. There was the usual collection of lichens, mosses and heather but what was different were the great walls of rock cracked by water and cold into giant building blocks. The large boulders on the mainland were usually standing alone or tumbled about in the forest. The rocks on Brändö had been carefully placed by giants to line the roadside and provide a flat surface for passing tourists to dance around on.

Brändö is not one island but a natural grouping of over a thousand islands, ten of which are connected by bridges or ferries. Cycling across these small islands was a constant symphony of change; forest, fields, water, bridge, sheep in a field, forest, water, bridge, chickens in a field, farm shed, water, forest, water, bridge, village, horses in a field, water, bridge, ferry. It was all very scenic, quite distracting for photography nuts, and a lovely memory to ponder over as I slowly drifted off to sleep in my tent in the forest.

Some days were "almost but not quite" days where I started a number of different things, but nothing got taken to its logical conclusion. We all have those days, which can be quite frustrating. My day on the next island was one of those days.

I rolled out of bed early enough to be on the road by seven, taking numerous photos as I went. The ferry left at eight, so far so good. Once on board, I plugged my spare battery in to a power-point near my seat. I disembarked at 9.05 and was happily pedalling towards my accommodation, a guesthouse on an organic farm when I realised that I had left the battery and charger on the ferry. Luckily, there was a young lass working on the farm as a volunteer. She lent me her charger for the day, so I was able to get enough charge to get me through that crisis for the time being.

In the early afternoon, I cycled into town, found the one and only shop, purchased some ingredients for dinner, and went in search of touristy things to look at. I found a distance road-sign which used a different measure, the verst, which could be divided by twenty. According to the sign, the distance to Brändö was 23 and 3/20 verst. I found the church which was from the fourteenth century. I walked around the graveyard and noticed an unusual date system: 19 14/7 35 which, I think, meant 14 July, 1935. The church, theoretically, had magnificent paintings in the interior but it was locked, it was only open for a few short hours on some days during the high season. (First "almost but not quite")

I had a strong desire to go for a walk, so I set off on the marked trail down to the harbour but ended up at the main road, not the harbour. (second "almost but not quite")

When I arrived back at the church, I saw a mailbox with "Map for Trails" written on it. "Goodo," I thought. "I'll follow the map." There were no maps in the box. (Third...)

I noted the box was painted in blue and yellow stripes. A rock on the roadside also had a blue and a yellow stripe. I rode past it, saw another rock with blue and yellow, then a tree, and so on. At some stage the yellow patches disappeared but the blue kept going until I found a wooden ladder, painted blue, which went up the steep bank on the side of the road. I ditched the bike and went up the ladder, across some rocks, and through the vegetation; following blue patches as I went. I had found the trail. It went over a rocky area and down to some paddocks, turned sharp left and followed the edge of one paddock. I've walked enough paddocks in my life, so I turned around and went back. (Fourth...)

"Stuff this!" I thought. "I want to see the harbour where the path is supposed to end up." I hopped on my bike and rode there instead, about four or five kilometres. There was a restaurant, so a coffee was called for. Sipping my coffee, looking over the harbour to the islands beyond, I realised that I was only a stone's throw from Snäckö. Now it's not possible to be near a place with a name like that and not go there, so off I went. I have a selfie of me in front of the recycling shed to prove it. Why the recycling shed? It was the only name sign I could find on this tiny blip of an island. Wow! A task completed! I never did find the other end of the path from the church to the harbour which I had been looking for.

Some minor miracles needed to happen to get rid of the "almost but not quite" jinx. I arose at 7 a.m. (first miracle), was packed and on the road by 8 (second... ) in order to catch the first ferry of the day at 9.10 a.m.; the exact same ferry as I had used the day before. Then a major miracle occurred. On boarding the ferry, I raced up the stairs to see whether my battery and charger were still where I had left them, and there they were; blinking happily to tell me the battery was one hundred percent full! A very happy moment!

My bike, battery, charger and I all disembarked together and cycled off in joyous unity. I crossed a few channels in hopping from island to island. Mostly the islands were connected by bridges, but one channel had a ferry. I had been wondering what my guidebook meant by "cable ferry" and suddenly realised I was standing on one. The ferry was moving along a cable which stretched from shore to shore.

All the smaller, cable ferries were free. People just drove up to the ferry landing, parked and waited, drove onto the ferry, sat tight while they were being shuttled across, drove off, and disappeared into the distance. There were three lanes on the ferries. Drivers manoeuvred their cars into the correct lane according to a traffic light system. The ferry driver sat in a cabin at the top of a tower and kept an eye on everything but otherwise had no contact with the passengers. All the small ferries I used were painted bright yellow.

The larger ferries were free for passengers but there was a charge for vehicles. I had to pay six euros for my bicycle, but this was only charged once at the start. I was required to keep my ticket with me because the same ticket was used for all three legs traveling in the same direction. My route was the "Northern Route." There was also a "Southern Route," a "Transverse Route" which joined the Northern and Southern Routes, and lastly there was the "Föglö Route" which went to the Föglö Islands.

An interesting side effect of the ferries was their impact on traffic. If the ferry landing was at the end of a road, I would wait to be the last person off the ferry, then I could tootle along the road at my leisure knowing there would be no traffic sneaking up behind me. Sometimes, I would be riding along, listening to the wind, minding my own business, when suddenly there would be three, or up to thirty cars, trucks and buses pass me in a long procession. Yep, a ferry had just arrived. At other times, I would notice a number of vehicles coming towards me and heading in the other direction, the last few would be racing to get somewhere ten minutes ago … hmmm, ferry leaving soon.

Crossing the bridge onto Bomarsund, there was quite a strong head-wind, as usual, with sudden bursts from the side which had the potential to push me across the road into the path of following traffic. I was concerned that I might be tossed around as I was crossing the bridge, so I started pedalling in the very centre of the right lane. A car came up behind me, but the driver stayed well back so I felt comfortable enough to stick to the middle of the road and got across as quickly as I could. Once off the bridge, I cycled on the road's edge again. The car drove up, a quick toot, a wave and a smile and he was off into the distance. The courtesy of the drivers in Scandinavia just astounded me!

I stayed overnight in a cabin in Bomarsund. The wind had just been too strong all day and even though I hadn't cycled very far, I was still quite exhausted by the time I got to the campground. I noticed a few other cyclists arriving, all of them slept in their tiny tents but part of the deal which I made with myself at the beginning of this journey was that I would not camp unnecessarily in wet, cold or windy weather. I used to do that when I was younger, but it's no great surprise that age has turned me into a fair-weather camper.

Leaving Bomarsund, the rain had stopped but the wind was still ferocious, not just very strong, but constantly blowing directly towards me and making cycling a very slow and tiring form of travel. I cycled past Kastelholm Slot, the ruins of the only medieval castle built on the Åland Islands. Later I crossed the bridge to Godby where there was a viewing tower and a café. The freshly baked pastries smelt so wonderful that a stop there was mandatory.

I was interested in the three flags flying at the café - Swedish, Ålandic and Norwegian. The Ålandic flag had prime position, in the centre, reflecting the locals' insistence on the Åland Islands being as independent as possible given their important geographic position in the Baltic Sea. Officially, the islands belong to Finland, but the dominant language is Swedish. The islanders have their own parliament, flag, stamps, number plates and even their own agreement with the EU which allows them to be a duty-free zone between Sweden and Finland. They live on tourism, agriculture, fishing and pretty well anything that can be done on the web. Internet access everywhere was brilliant. I was able to access very fast wi-fi at every campground, much better than anywhere else I had been up to that point in northern Europe.

Later in the day's cycling I found the Kattby church with its thirty-two iron-age burial mounds. The church was set away from the village, a phenomenon I had noticed before. In medieval times, the churches were built on top of pagan holy sites which were always some distance from the village. A village couldn't be too close to a holy site, it would have been far too scary at night! Whenever I saw a church spire it meant that there was a village somewhere nearby. The Kattby burial mounds were fairly non-descript, hidden under long grass being grazed by a flock of sheep. Some things are only interesting to those in the know, the rest of us just see mounds, grass and sheep.

I finished the day's cycling at the Sortby Post and Toll Building which was built in the 1800s. Nowadays it is used as an artists' work-shop/gallery and café space. There was a display of artworks about the Kalevala – a Scandinavian epic saga about the Creation and their history written in fifty songs. The artworks were of every form imaginable - textiles, pottery, sculpture, jewellery, and so on. I particularly loved a print of a horse and also a painting of a red boat. I felt it would be worthwhile to read the saga so as to learn enough of the story and to be able to appreciate these artworks properly.

Over a coffee, I mulled the constant dilemma of a long-term traveller. Should I slow right down and explore each culture in depth as I travelled through it? In that case I should have spent much more time on the Åland Islands, I should have gone to the capital, Mariehamn, I should have gone into Kastelholm Slot, and I should have seen some museums. Or should I just focus on the cycling and just cherry-pick the most interesting cultural aspects, knowing full well that I was not doing that particular culture justice at all. Having spent almost a week crossing the islands, I felt the need to move on, preferably at speed, but couldn't help feeling a bit sad that I was also missing out on so much which was worthwhile and interesting.

Keen to get out of the Åland Islands and move on through Sweden, I made it onto the early ferry which left at 8.30 in the morning. The trip took almost two hours and cost a whole 7.50€. At that price, the trip was marginally more expensive than breakfast and cheaper than the two rolls which I bought for lunch. Due to the change in time, the ferry arrived in Grisslehamn, Sweden, shortly after 9 a.m. so it saved me an hour of time as well.

# | 16 |

## A Rocky Start to Sweden

### Grisslehamn to Södertälje, 165 km

My first day of cycling in Sweden was easy. Quiet country roads wound up and around small undulations in the landscape. I saw all the ffffs - fields, forest, farms, flowers, ferns, and rocks. The road signs were blue and yellow, the colours of the Swedish flag.

I arrived in good time and good condition at the camp site in Norrtälje to discover that there was no-one at reception. This was my first experience that, according to the Swedish, the season was over. In other words, their major summer holidays had finished, most people had gone back to work, and most tourist services were on very restricted timetables or even completely closed. They completely disregarded all the older people, singles, couples without children, and families with very young children who were still travelling around and wanting to avail themselves of all the wonderful things which Sweden had to offer tourists.

The man mowing the lawns rang the owners who took my details over the phone and charged me 185 Swedish kronor for the pleasure of camping for one night. The wash facilities were okay and there was a reasonable kitchen with power-points, but the laundry was locked and the wifi didn't seem to be working. Of course, there was no-one available to ask about these things.

To make my introduction to Sweden even worse, the following day's cycling was just awful. I rode all morning along a very busy road with no bike lanes. The afternoon promised to be much better; I had a fantastic bike path for eleven kilometres, but this was followed by a truly dreadful stretch of ten kilometres of narrow road with no shoulder, but with frantic traffic. Some of the hills had overtaking lanes on them but most of the way there was no such thing so that cars had to swerve into the opposing lane to pass me. Whenever I saw a line of cars behind me or a couple of big trucks, I pulled over onto the grass and let them all pass me safely in one go.

There was no-one at reception when I arrived at 4.30 p.m. The manager had just left for the day, even though most tourists arrive at a campsite in the late afternoon or early evening. Everything was locked; the laundry, the kitchen, and the ladies' facilities were all locked. Whenever I wanted to use the facilities, I had to hover around the door and wait until some-one else came to use them too. The men's facilities, strangely, were not locked. I rang the manager who promised to send someone to give me a key. Nobody came. Three or four more camping parties arrived but left to look for other options. They were travelling in vehicles so finding an alternative was much easier for them than for me. It did cross my mind to pack up and leave the next morning without paying but my conscience got the better of me. I did refuse to pay full price though, even paying half price for a patch of grass with no facilities was a bit of a stretch.

The ferry for Stockholm took just over an hour through waters which were so busy with boats of all sizes, from little yachts to massive ocean-going vessels, that I was amazed that we didn't run into anyone. Before I knew it, I disembarked in the centre of one of the world's most beautiful cities with canals and bridges in every direction. I had spent a few days previously in Stockholm so didn't feel the need to stay and wander through the standard tourist sights.

I entered my destination for the day into Google Maps and set off past numerous stately old buildings and over romantic bridges. The footpaths were cluttered with locals hawking their wares, and awestruck tourists taking selfies. The bike lanes and traffic lights specifically for cyclists kept me safe as I very slowly navigated my way out of the old town. I thought that once I arrived in the suburbs that the distances between traffic lights would lengthen, and that the cycling would have less stops, starts, turns and confusions, but I was wrong, very wrong! Google Maps took me on a long, laborious meander through the outer suburbs. I rode over bridges, under bridges, down a corkscrew path, along a lake, past numerous other lakes, on tarmac, cobblestones, bricks and even a narrow sandy track through forest where I was absolutely convinced that I was lost. It took me all day to cycle the thirty-five kilometres to the next campground.

Apart from the city and its traffic, another challenging aspect was the navigation app itself. I was still not terribly good at using it properly. It kept closing down on me, zooming in or out at will and changing the route. I had to stop dozens of times to work out where I was, where I was going or to get the app started up again after it had shut itself down. It may have been an issue with the settings or maybe the app was just having a bad hair day. Either way, I was convinced there must have been a better, less complicated route to follow, if only I knew where it was! Despite all my complaints, I wouldn't have managed even one kilometre without Google Maps. Unlike bike paths in Germany and the Netherlands, the paths in Stockholm had hardly any signposting at all so getting around without a navigational aid of some sort would have been rather difficult.

I rode through some new estates in the suburbs and outer towns. The apartment buildings were no more than three or four storeys high; spread apart with gardens, lawns and walking paths between, with playgrounds, and with meeting places and seats in the sun. I followed a path which had a dividing line down the centre like on a road, except the line meandered all over the path and even did some swirls in places. The path ended in a playground which had a multi-humped camel for the little children and a soccer field with a difference for the older children. The field was an area of mounds, valleys and curving line markings which would make playing soccer there totally unpredictable. The goal square was a painted, whirligig of posts. Imagine kicking a ball, straight and true, to the goal square. The ball lands short, bounces on the side of a mound and then veers off on a 45-degree angle like a hyper-active dragonfly. It must be great fun to play on.

The campsite at Södertälje was a large swathe of grass at the edge of a lake and sprinkled with trees. The manager and her partner had been living there for the previous nine years. They lived in a caravan but unlike other long-term residents in other campgrounds, they had no garden, fence, permanent annex, or little dogs. They claimed that they didn't get cold in winter. I could imagine spending a great deal of time in this lovely park, but over **winter**? With all that ice and snow? Having to walk two hundred metres at night to go to the shower or to the toilet? The café was closed because "The Season Was Over" but the manager took pity on me; I must have looked terribly hungry and exhausted! She took me in her car to buy food at the local shopping centre, about six kilometres away. Now that was service!

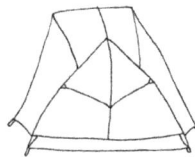

# | 17 |

# When Things Got Much Better

## Södertälje to Söderköping, 171 km

Navigating my way out of the town and into the countryside was not nearly as stressful as it had been the previous day. I only had to stop to check my app about ten times and I was mightily relieved when I met the Nyköpingsväg, the road to Nyköping, which promised to take me almost all the way to my destination for the day.

I pulled in for a coffee at a service station. The young attendant had been in Melbourne for a month earlier in the year, so he was quite pleased to be able to sell me a hot drink and a sweet bun, all the while chatting about his experiences "Down Under." He cleared up a bit of a mystery for me. There were any number of towns called …köping in the area. "Köping" means "town" so Nyköping really means "New Town". Adding to that, the "k" is pronounced as "sh" so Nyköping is pronounced as "Nyshöping."

The countryside was beautiful. Large sweeping fields of golden grain being harvested, an occasional horse stud or dairy farm, a few patches of forest, and every now and then a view of a lake. The road was excellent all day with a verge for cyclists, sometimes narrow but often quite wide, broken by stretches of actual cycle path. I had a picnic lunch by the roadside with my back to the road. Some instinct made me look around to see another long-distance cyclist disappearing over a hill, the first such creature I had seen for a long time.

Seven kilometres after lunch was decision time; turn left for about ten kilometres to Trosa which, according to the reviews, had a splendiferous setting but a fairly tired campground or turn right for fifty-three kilometres to Nyköping. I checked Google Maps and saw the Nyköping campgrounds, about three of them, were all at least ten kilometres on the other side. That decided me. I felt that I was too old to knock myself out trying to rush things. I turned left.

My energy levels plummeted; it was time for my afternoon coffee. I stopped at a café in Trosa before cycling further to the campground. There were two women and a young man sitting outside and eating ice-creams. One of the ladies was very interested in my bike tour and asked all the usual questions. She dreamt of being a free spirit and just wandering wherever fate took her. At the time. she was building an eco-home with the young man, her son. The home was being built of short lengths of wood stacked horizontally with the ends facing inside and outside the walls. The wood was held together by a cement made of clay and horse manure along with a few other ingredients. The walls were then going to be clad with more clay. Fascinating stuff. In hindsight, I should have peppered them with questions and maybe they would have taken me to see it. The house was being built in some sort of eco village nearby. Hindsight is a wondrous thing.

The campground at Trosa was indeed in an idyllic setting. Set on the tip of an island, the beach and water were just over the bump, a short walk away. I had a swim and found the water to be cold as well as wet. The beach was set up for all ages; the sand sloped gradually into the water with a slide for the little children to slip and slide into the shallow water. There were two parallel sets of bars also going into the water, ideal for the elderly who might be a bit hesitant about their balance. There were three piers, one with a platform at the end for people to mill about and jump into the water. The other piers had ladders and higher platforms for more ambitious divers.

Back at camp, the tent pitches were smallish, flat grassy patches between the rocks and the trees. There were picnic tables, a couple of Adironack chairs, and even a hammock spread around for people to use. The facilities were basic but clean; nothing to complain about. The power points in the kitchen all had thirty-minute timers on them but being the intrepid traveller I am, I found one in the gap between the refrigerator and the wall which had no timer so I was able to get my phone and laptop charged without any problems.

It started to rain as I was packing up to leave Trosa. First it was just an annoying drizzle, but before long the rain was coming down in a very serious effort to drown me. I was fairly well set up for rain. When cycling, my jacket and over-pants did an excellent job of keeping me dry. The only problems were my hands and feet which still got wet and cold in such torrential rain.

My cycling bags were all waterproof. I found out how waterproof one day when I accidentally spilt water in one of them. I opened the bag up and thought it would dry out by itself. It didn't. Waterproof means that water can't get into the bag, but it also can't get out! I had also thought up a system where I put all the different parts of my tent into separate waterproof bags so that each part couldn't make anything else wet. Isolating any wet items like that worked brilliantly. When the rain came out and the sun shone again, I could take each item out, one at a time, and deal with it before worrying about the next item so I was never confronted with a whole mountain of wet, soggy mess.

The scenery throughout the day slowly changed to big farms and low rolling hills with many bays and inlets. Navigation was easy, so I was able to focus on observing my navigation app in action. It definitely did do route changes even though I hadn't gone off the proposed route or requested any changes. Part of the problem could have been that every time I hit a bump or left the phone untouched for a few minutes, the app either shut down, zoomed out or went somewhere else. The good news is that I learnt how to save a route, and how to put a shortcut to it onto the opening screen of my mobile phone so that I no longer had to type the destination in multiple times during the day.

I arrived in Nyköping early enough for a coffee in a café. I took out two thousand kronor at an ATM and started getting seriously annoyed. The ATMs didn't allow me to withdraw any more than that, which only lasted me three or four days. I preferred to take out at least twice that amount to save on wasting time looking for an ATM every few days and also to save on those horrendous ATM and bank fees. Obviously, the locals could get around for a long time with less cash as they paid nearly everything by card. The card culture was so strong in Sweden that shop assistants were often genuinely astonished when I wanted to pay with cash, even for something as small as a coffee.

The campsite at Nyköping was in yet another stunningly beautiful place with trees, an inlet, noisy geese and ducks. There was no internet reception at all and the wifi was too weak to be of any value. I compensated for the lack of technology by going for a gentle stroll along the water's edge. As most evenings, I could hear and see dozens of geese flying south. They usually flew in V shaped formations. On this evening, one flock had a very lopsided V with four geese on one side and about twenty on the other. Another flock couldn't get their V sorted at all, a number of geese kept wobbling from one side to another, maybe they hadn't been paying attention when their parents explained the theory of flight to them.

The weather was getting colder at night. I took a cabin as a bit of luxury and so I could dry my tent properly. The heaters in my cabin and in the shower-block were on. It was so nice to feel warm and toasty after having spent most of the day being hot and sweaty inside my waterproof clothes but with chilled hands, feet and nose.

The first thirty kilometres from Nyköping went in a flash, through a large agricultural area. The next section followed an inlet shore with numerous small hills and on a narrow road with forest and rocks on each side. A few other cyclists on racing bikes zipped past me as I struggled and sweated up each hill before freewheeling down the other side.

By noon, I was at the river crossing waiting for the ferry. I chatted with a young Dutch lad who had passed me on the hills. He was about to start a semester at the university in Linköping and was spending his last week of freedom cycling through the countryside, learning Swedish as he went. He was on a racing bike with very little gear – a small tent, a light sleeping bag, one spare sweater and not much else. He was amazed at how much I was carrying, but I was amazed at how he could survive with so little.

The last thirty kilometres were a bit more of a slog, only because I was starting to run out of puff. There was more agricultural land with farmers ploughing up huge fields. I arrived in Söderköping by mid-afternoon to find a Medieval Week in full swing. The town was packed out with peasants in sackcloth, children waving swords and food stands everywhere. Toffee apples seem to have been popular in the Middle Ages. I ate a flat bread roll filled with wild boar and cabbage. There were no starving peasants on that day!

Through the course of the day, I had kept feeling some discomfort in one of my molars and I suspected that I had developed a tooth issue. The tooth was still in one piece, so it was possible that I had an internal hole or an abscess, the gum was also very sore. It was a Sunday so a visit to a doctor for antibiotics wasn't practical. This is one of the negative aspects of long-term travel. My doctor and dentist who have my medical and dental history at their fingertips are always too far away to be of any use. To go to a strange doctor, dentist or hospital in a strange country with a vague ailment like a toothache is daunting at the best of times and twice as bad when I'm on my own and feeling unwell. The nearest hospital was in Norrköping and I couldn't be bothered with the effort of going there so I took some painkillers and hoped it would all go away, which it did.

I went into town the following day to have a slow stroll through the medieval fair. The market was quite impressive with over a hundred stalls selling reed baskets, leather wares, wooden items, bows and arrows, pottery, metalwork, silverware, and so on. Everything looked quite authentic and well made; the creators were often at work at their stalls. The bows were made of wood and leather, no plastic at all, but the bowstring was some modern carbon fibre. Most of the people were dressed in medieval costumes; two toddlers lay sound asleep while being pulled around in a handcart.

After a while, I ventured into the old church to discover a female choir at practice. I sat down to listen and was told there would be a concert later, so I stayed. The program was written in Latin and was of pieces composed in medieval times. Pieces by Hildegard von Bingen and Wolfgang von der Weide were included. I thoroughly enjoyed sitting there listening to all those lovely voices singing the Lord's praises.

The late afternoon saw me practising my bicycle maintenance skills. The chain had been rasping and grinding for a few days, so I tipped the bike over and checked all along the chain to see where it had been rubbing. I couldn't find any friction points and it didn't seem terribly dirty, so I just oiled it instead. When I hopped on my bike the following morning to get some supplies before leaving town, I was pleasantly surprised by how quiet the bike was travelling. There was no rasping or grinding at all, just the quiet whisper of tyres on bitumen. It was so good!

# | 18 |

## Along the Göta Canal

### Söderköping to Vadstena, 100 km

The Göta Kanal is 190 kilometres long, and, with its fifty-eight locks, it is to this day Sweden's most impressive engineering project. The canal was first dreamt up in the sixteenth century as a way of connecting the Baltic Sea directly to the North Sea and thus bypassing Denmark with its thousands of islands, very narrow waterways and high tolls. By shortening the route to the North Sea, the canal had the potential to dramatically speed up and transform Sweden's trade with the rest of the world. The proposed route began at Mem on the east coast and "lake hopped" across Lake Asplången, Lake Roxen, Lake Boren, Lake Vättern and Lake Vännern with all the lakes joined by the canal. Lake Vännern was already connected to Gothenburg on the west coast by the Trollhättan Canal with four locks bypassing a set of wild waterfalls.

Nothing happened with the Göta Canal proposal for three hundred years until Sweden lost Finland to Russia in 1809. With Stockholm lying on the east coast, suddenly, the Russians were right next door, just a short sail away. The king decided that there needed to be a quick and efficient escape route into the safer inland areas for the military, the royal family, the parliament and the country's gold reserves. The Göta Canal project was dusted off and begun. It was built over the next twenty-two years.

The canal was planned, surveyed and engineered under the leadership of Baltzar von Platen who unfortunately died three years before the its official opening in 1832. At the time, the English were recognised as the world's foremost experts on canal building so a number of them were imported to work as foremen and engineers. The rest of the workforce consisted of 58,000 soldiers from the Swedish army, including a company of two hundred Russian deserters. The men dug eighty-seven kilometres of the canal by hand using iron-tipped wooden shovels and working twelve-hour days. Their rations included enough schnapps to keep them happy when the winter weather turned fingers and toes blue with the cold.

The canal never became as important in Swedish commercial or defensive life as initially planned. Road and rail transport options improved so dramatically within a short period of time that the canal quickly lost its importance. Nowadays, it is one of Sweden's biggest tourist attractions with a never-ending stream of boats sailing in both directions over summer, and cyclists peddling the tow paths as well.

I pointed my bicycle west and set off along the tow path. I planned to follow the canal for as long as I could, all the way to the west coast, if possible. I hoped to be able to take ferries across each of the lakes as I came across them.

Beginning at Söderköping, the first five or six locks had a boat or two in them, going up or down. It seemed very busy. For the first section along the canal, the path was flat and of gravel but still acceptable. I figured that the horses which towed the boats in the days before motorised transport would have preferred gravel to bitumen.

After Snöveltorp, the canal turned into Lake Asplången, no horses would have been necessary, and the path headed into the hills. Over summer, there were boats available to ferry cyclists and other tourists from one side of the lake to the other. I rang to ask about availability, times and prices only to learn that the boats were not sailing anymore because "The Season Was Over."

I had to take a path into the steep hills instead. It wound up, down, and around corners, but the worst part was the road surfacing. It was a deep covering of unstable blue stones and it was absolutely awful! I had to walk considerable stretches because I couldn't ride up the hills, the back wheel of my bicycle kept slipping. I couldn't ride downhill because the front wheel slid around, and I couldn't control the bike. I tried to roll down one section and immediately slipped over in the gravel and fell off. There were no other cyclists, no traffic at all and deep forest all around. I didn't want to injure myself, so it seemed much wiser, even if much slower and infinitely more frustrating, to walk along, wheeling my bicycle until I eventually found myself at the canal again.

Once at the canal, the path became a lovely flat gravel tow path, and all was well except the water looked very green and there were no boats at all. Seven kilometres of uneventful cycling took me into Norsholm where I was standing at an intersection looking confused when a gentleman on a bike came over to me. He seemed to want to help but looked a bit unsure whether he should offer assistance or not, so I asked for his help instead.

The gentleman was a local. He was going part of the way towards Linköping, so he offered to guide me on a better path than the one which my navigation app was suggesting. We slowly cycled along a quiet country road for twenty minutes together then he pointed to a little yellow house, explained it was his and invited me in for a coffee. His wife soon came home, we sat outside in their covered and glassed-in veranda, drank coffee and chatted. They had two children and five grandchildren living nearby. They were both retired, she had retired only two months previously from her work as a school cleaner. He had worked for twenty years as a farmer and then in various jobs in workshops. They sometimes saw moose, had had one the previous year eating apples in their garden. The latest sighting had been in a paddock nearby, only a day ago. The moose wander through at night on their way to have a drink at the lake. They have to leave the forest, cross the highway, the railway line, and a few smaller roads to get there; quite an undertaking for a moose.

From Linköping, the Göta Canal kept going west to Borenberg where it entered Lake Boren. At the village of Berg, there were seven locks all in a row. One of the locks had a road crossing over the top. When that lock was being used, the bridge divided in half and each half lifted, standing in salute as the boats sailed through the centre. Four sailing boats and a passenger vessel were negotiating these locks and bridges to slowly move up the canal. Further on from Berg, smaller roads crossed over the canal on bridges. When a boat came up, the traffic lights changed colour and the bridges slid back into the canal banks like a SIM card slot in a mobile phone.

At one stage the canal was high above the surrounding land, there was a lake on my right which was about ten metres lower than the canal. Canal and natural waterway were completely separate. The canal was engineered that way because it was considered too difficult to control water flows in a natural system. It felt rather strange to be cycling along one stretch of water while looking down at even more water far below.

It was along this part of the canal that I discovered that I could easily cycle faster than the boats could motor along the canal. However, I stopped so often to enjoy the scenery that the boats and I kept leapfrogging each other along the route. Three of the four 'captains' (each boat only had two to four people on it, so the captains were usually Dad/ Husband) got so used to seeing me that they started waving and saying hello every time one of us passed the other. It was quite a sight to see four boats motoring in procession down this beautiful canal.

At Borenberg, I turned south west and hit a challenge of the type which turns boys into men and this particular cyclist into a shaking, snivelling mess. The problem was the wind, a really shocking south wind which belted and buffeted me until I begged for forgiveness even though I had no idea what for. A sudden gust pitched me off the road into the ditch where I landed all tangled up with my bike and panniers. It wasn't a beautiful sight and I swore, quite loudly, until I realised it was better to be pushed into a ditch than into the path of an oncoming bus. I arrived exhausted at Vadstena, at which point I was so fed up with the wind, which was still belting me around the ears, that I took a cabin for the night in disgust.

# | 19 |

# Two Women of Vadstena

I was still quite fed up with the strong wind which had not settled by morning, so I decided to spend a full day being a tourist at Vadstena. I had read that the town had both a monastery and a castle, and, being an unrepentant history nerd, I put them both onto my "to do" list. I was intrigued to discover the fascinating stories of two women of Vadstena. Neither was born or had lived here but both had had lives which were greatly impacted by their association with this town.

*St. Birgitta was a noblewoman born in 1303. She married at fourteen, had eight children, went on pilgrimage to Santiago de Compostela with her husband and was widowed by forty. Of her eight children, four were daughters and four were sons. Two of her daughters got married but only one had children, the other two daughters became nuns. Two of her sons died while young, one son became a knight and a politician, but the other son was the 'son of tears'. He was a scoundrel and a playboy!* There's a black sheep in every family …

Normal procedure in medieval times would have been for a widow's family to marry her off to a new husband but St. Birgitta decided to become a nun instead. It probably helped that the family was so rich and powerful that they didn't need her to make another economic, social, or political alliance.

*When she was just ten years old, St. Birgitta started receiving revelations and visions – over six hundred throughout her life. She was incredibly blessed to receive all those visions, and doubly blessed that they were accepted as real and valuable by the church community. Most importantly, she not only re-membered them in great detail but was able to get them all written down.*

Some aspects of medieval religious painting can be traced back to these visions: Jesus as a baby with light emanating from his head, Mary with blond hair, and Mary and Joseph kneeling in adoration before baby Jesus.

*As a result of her revelations, St. Birgitta had three main objectives during her time as a nun - to build a new monastery at Vadstena, to convince the Pope to return to Rome from Avignon, and to put a stop to the Hundred Year's War by negotiating a peace between England and France. To this purpose, she went to Rome in 1350 and never went back to Sweden. One of her daughters, St. Katarina went with her. While in Rome, St. Birgitta kept herself busy doing good works, looking after the sick, the poor, and the destitute and generally making herself very loved. She went on pilgrimage to Jerusalem in 1373 when she was seventy years old and died soon after her return to Rome.*

The Birgittine monastery at Vadstena was built while St. Birgitta was in Rome. She never saw it while she was alive, but her body was taken there in a wooden coffin six months after she died. The coffin is still there, on display in a cell in the monastery. Each year, thousands of pilgrims come to this monastery to pay their respects to this most de-voted nun, one of the six patron saints of Sweden.

Contrast that story of devotion to a higher good to the following story of Cecilia, second daughter of Gustav Wasa, King of Sweden.

*Princess Cecilia was born in Stockholm in 1540. She had four brothers and four sisters. Their mother died when Cecilia was eleven years old and the chil-dren were cared for by a collection of aunts and their new stepmother who happened to be their first cousin as well. By the time she was eighteen, Ce-cilia was quite a beauty and needed a husband. Her older sister was also on* the marriage market. Sweden needed the girls to play their part in helping the country in its political ambitions.

A treaty and a marriage alliance with Ostfriesland was suggested. Ostfriesland was a rival to the Hanseatic League based in Lübeck. King Gustav was quite keen to break the Hanseatic League's domination of trade in the Baltic area, so he was interested in having the Ostfriesians as partners in trade and they had a couple of princes available: Edzard and his younger brother, John.

Prince Edzard of Ostfriesland came to visit Stockholm to choose a wife. He chose Cecilia's older sister, Catherine. Edzard and Catherine were married a year later. On their way home to Ostfriesland after the wedding, Catherine and Edzard stopped at the castle in Vadstena for a while to visit Catherine's brother, Magnus, who lived there at the time. They were accompanied by Cecilia, her oldest brother, Erik and also Prince John of Ostfriesland.

While staying at the castle in Vadstena, a man was seen climbing into the window of Cecilia's bedchamber at night, not just once but **at least three nights in a row**. The guards informed Erik who set a trap. John of Ostfriesland was caught in Cecilia's room with no pants on! Erik was furious but not nearly as furious as King Gustav. Between them, Cecilia, John and Erik had destroyed all Cecilia's value as a bargaining chip, an absolute disaster!

King Gustav had John thrown into prison, he sent Catherine and Edzard into house arrest because they hadn't chaperoned Cecilia properly. Erik and Cecilia were recalled to Stockholm. Erik got into huge trouble for making the affair public. He should have kept it all quiet and they could have somehow swept Cecilia's loss of virginity under the carpet. Cecilia was dragged across the room by her hair by the king. Her suitor, George John I, Count Palatine of Veldenz, decided he didn't want her anymore. He married her younger sister, Anna, instead. Cecilia was left on the shelf, soiled goods.

Six months later, John was released from prison and sent packing. Catherine and Edzard were released from house arrest. King Gustav died soon after, and Erik became king. When Erik discovered Cecilia and a sister having **a party** in their rooms a few years later it must have stirred up bad memories because he banned them from going out in the early mornings or late at night, banned them from receiving visitors at night, and banned them from receiving letters. Cecilia must have stressed him out no end.

Eventually, a husband was found for Cecilia. Christopher II, Margrave of Baden-Rodemachern was a young man with a title but not much money. He can't have been too worried about Cecilia's reputation. They married only three months after they were engaged, when Cecilia was twenty-four years old, way past marriage age. Cecilia had six sons with Christopher, but her dowry was never paid out, so they were always short of money.

The rest of Cecilia's life was equally colourful. She was a friend of Queen Elizabeth I of Great Britain until she and Christopher wore out their welcome there by living in grand style and refusing to pay their debts. She was given a fleet of ships by her brother, King John III, as part payment of her dowry. He also gave her permission to attack British and Dutch ships trading with Russia. That wasn't enough, her men attacked friendly ships from Denmark too and even the odd Swedish vessel. Cecilia travelled the courts of Europe, engaged in diplomacy on behalf of the Swedish crown, met, loved, and lived in sin with a Spanish ambassador and bore him a daughter which caused a great scandal. Cecilia died in Brussels at the ripe old age of eighty-six, having outlived all her bossy brothers and having had far more fun than her respectable and well-behaved sisters.

What a life!

# | 20 |

# Back Amongst the Vikings

## Vadstena to Helsingborg 375 km

I headed to Rök to see the rune stone which has the longest inscription of any rune stone in the world. It was created in the ninth century and was a memorial stone set up by Varin to commemorate his dead son, Vämod. Even though historians can read many runes, they still can't agree on the meaning of all the text on this one. I took a stack of photos like I usually do and cycled on, following the shoreline of Lake Vättern for quite a while, it was a slight downhill gradient the whole way with the lake far below me on my right. The morning rain had stopped, there was only a slight wind and the sun shone weakly, ideal weather for cycling.

Shortly before Gränna, I came to a most interesting building with a standard wooden ground floor topped by a second floor all of glass. It was an eco-house offering coffee and meals, so I pulled in for a coffee stop. I stepped through the front door into a veritable greenhouse; this end of the house was a hot, steamy jungle. A staircase led to the second floor and around the corner was an eclectic collection of easy chairs and coffee tables for visitors. There were two other sitting rooms on the other side of the internal wall and a deck outside which looked over the water. The walls were rough boards painted white/off white. The floors were wooden boards and there was a lovely Arabic/Turkish carpet in each room to brighten it up. The coffee and cake had eco prices, no surprise there. Unfortunately, I couldn't go upstairs because there was a function on.

When I surfaced from my eco-coffee induced daze, I wandered outside and discovered it was raining again so I cycled further down-hill into Gränna which is a centre of the red-and-white striped candy industry. I bought some candy and, keen to stay out of the rain, hired a cabin for the night.

From Gränna, I had a morning of hilly, agricultural countryside to cycle through before a long, steep downhill slide into Huskvarna, town of chainsaws and sewing machines. I noticed the town was spelled slightly differently to the products, Husqvarna, but had no idea why. Was it a wise commercial decision by the founder of the business or was it an accidental error? A typing mistake which couldn't be quickly rectified way back in the olden days?

Further around Lake Vättern, I cycled through Jönköping, a lovely student city with a great pedestrian mall in the centre and any number of cafes to select from for a short lunch stop. As I chewed on my lunch, I gloomily looked at my navigation app. I had cycled down a steep hill in the morning and I knew that this steep downhill was going to be followed by an equivalently steep uphill. If I had studied the maps properly before I set off in the morning, I would have noticed a possible alternative route following the top of the ridge above the lake and avoiding both the steep descent and the steep ascent. However, now that I was at the bottom, at lake level, there was no other option. I had to go up! I was a very hot, sweaty and puffed out cyclist as I entered the Lovsjö campground a few hours later.

Lovsjö was another beautiful campsite on the shores of a small lake. I spent some time in the evening sitting on an old jetty, watching the ducks, the changing light and the reflections in the water. I took quite a few photos then settled down to transfer all the photos from the previous few days to my laptop. When I was finished, I double-checked my work and was astonished to see that most of the photos had completely disappeared from both my phone and my laptop. I searched, looked and despaired but couldn't find them anywhere. My dozens of photos of the eco-house and rune-stone at Rök from the previous day had been accidentally deleted. Only three photos of the ducks on the lake in the evening sun had survived the purge. I was quite unhappy with my stupidity until I got a grip on my emotions and remembered what is important in life and what isn't. Travel photos, while important for me, are actually fairly low on the list of all of life's dramas.

One of the photos which survived the accidental purge is one of my all-time favourites. On the bottom of the photo are the front of my filthy shoes, the middle of the photo is taken up by the lake with clouds from above reflected in the fading light. The upper third of the photo has a solitary duck swimming ahead of trailing ripples in the water. Behind the duck are reflections of trees in the water, with the actual trees and then the sky framing the photo at the top. I love this photo. Even though it was taken with my phone and was just a quick snap with no forethought or planning involved, it encapsulates, for me, the peace and contentment which I felt as I cycled through this part of Sweden.

Nothing special happened on the ride from Losvjö to Värnamo. I just cruised slowly downhill all day and enjoyed the scenery as I went. Of note were the many small artistic displays which the local farmers had placed at the entrance to their driveways. Some people had followed their Viking heritage and placed large boulders surrounded by a few plants or over-shadowed by a large tree. Other folk had built a display stand and had placed a milk can filled with cut branches, a pumpkin or two, or some farming implements on it. Once again, it was the small things which I spotted when cycling which gave my travels so much interest and enjoyment.

There were two Belgian motorbike riders at the camp at Värnamo. They were terribly proud of their shiny, new machines which they had specially bought for their travels to the North Cape and back. When they asked where I had been and was going, they were so amazed that they couldn't stop talking about my journey and asking questions. "Well, f#%k me!" one kept saying. He was just gobsmacked.

The washing machine and the dryer at this camp cost fifty kronor each to use. I was washing too often. The problem was not only the cost but also the amount of time it took to organise the key, the token or the correct coinage; to place the clothes into the washing machine and hang around waiting for it to finish; to transfer the clothes into the dryer and wait for it to finish … I felt that if I organised myself better, I should be able to wash every five days instead of every three days. On the other hand, I could have just given up on washing at all. I figured that if I cycled fast enough, I would be long gone before people started to wonder where that appalling smell came from. Campgrounds, on the other hand, were more problematic. If I wasn't on the move, I would be surrounded by a fug of odour as it radiated from my clothes. Stinky!

From Värnamo to Ljungby was more downhill cruising, past lakes and over rivers. I had just cycled past Toftaholm when I saw a picnic table and seats of stone. Just behind was a wooden stile going over a fence into a paddock full of grass-covered mounds, each over a metre high and a couple of metres across. "What's this?" I asked myself. I turned around, cycled to the information board and discovered there were about a hundred iron-age burial mounds there. There was also a runestone dating to about 1,000 AD and the ruins of a medieval manor house. Of course, I investigated the mounds, cycled to the rune-stone, went to the manor house which was on an island, walked around the island and had a lovely time. The manor house, being just a couple of piles of rock was a real fixer-upper! Walking back off the island, I stopped at the bridge and took photos of the light and the water. They turned out to be quite nice and perfect compensation for the photos which I lost. It helped that I only had forty-five kilometres to ride so I knew I had plenty of time to spare for diversions such as this.

Further on, at Hallsjö, I spotted more mounds which also had some medieval church ruins nearby. There were about fifty mounds there and another fifty in another field further on. Rune-stones and iron-age burial mounds; they were just everywhere.

I had booked the Linnea Hotel at Ljungby because I couldn't find a campground mentioned anywhere in my tourist information. Of course, I cycled past one on the way into town. An internet search for campgrounds always ended up at a particular website which didn't seem to have all the campgrounds on it. I decided to do a search for camp-grounds at a particular location in the future, maybe that way I would come up with better information.

Staying at the hotel in Ljungby turned out to be a great idea, any-way. The hotel was managed by a lovely young man, Johann, who was also a cyclist. He was so interested in my journey and quite in awe of what I had achieved so far. He asked whether I had a blog, so I gave him one of my cards. He offered the use of the family's washing machine even though that wasn't normally hotel procedure and the following morning he gifted me a tube scarf to wear. I still wear that scarf in cold weather.

We had a good chat about runestones, so Johann gave me directions to an excellent one to which he had been unwillingly dragged as a child. It was about eight kilometres out of town but well worth the extra cy-cling. This runestone sat by itself in the centre of a small park with the standard information boards giving information in Swedish, Eng-lish and German. The inscription on the runestone read: "Götrad made this monument in memory of Astrad, his father, best of kinsmen and of land-owners – who in times past lived in Finnveden." There were more burial mounds there too. By this point, I had more than made up for the lost photos and was feeling in travel photo/rune stone heaven.

Leaving Ljungby, I had a choice of cycling either fifty or eighty-one kilometres. I was keen to get the greater distance done because I wanted to get moving! I was suffering again from that eternal dilemma; cycle slow and see the sights or cycle fast and miss almost everything. I had stopped numerous times in the previous few days and had seen so many Viking sites, but autumn was coming with its usual unfriendly weather. It was time to get cracking! I was quite worried about the distance but by lunchtime, I found I had cruised through thirty-eight kilometres and still felt full of energy. I stopped a few times in the afternoon, once for a coffee, a little later for an ice-cream.

I stopped outside a farmhouse and was puzzling over my navigation app. The indicated route didn't seem to exist. A lady came out of her house and told me which way to go; along the old railway line and through the forest. I followed the proposed route. The path began as a wide trail of compacted sand, then the surfacing changed to hard stones and weeds, the path itself narrowed and narrowed further. I found myself pushing my bike over sharp rocks and through overhanging bushes. I prayed that there were no hungry wolves in the area. I was also stressing in case something broke on my bicycle or I got a flat tyre. I was nervous, worried and scared … all at once! Then I got a grip. "This is southern Sweden," I told myself. "No-where is more than a few hundred metres from a house. Just because I can't see any houses doesn't mean I'm lost in the wilderness." I broke free of the thick undergrowth to emerge onto a sandy road with piles of logs waiting for collection by the timber companies. Safe again!

On my last full day in Sweden, I cycled the fifty-seven kilometres from Örkelljunga to Helsingborg. My app took me through the Woodlands Club which was a golf course with fancy accommodation sprinkled throughout and a very nifty clubhouse which I didn't photograph because there were cameras everywhere spying on me. I had the very strong feeling that I shouldn't have been there anyway even though all the men (I only saw men) smiled and said "Hey" when they saw me.

From there, my app took me along a very narrow path through forest (again!) but I figured that I had done this before and survived so it wasn't too bad. I also reminded myself that this part of Sweden was so developed that any patch of forest couldn't be very big therefore if the very worst (flat tyre?) happened, I wouldn't be too far from a house or assistance. I made my way calmly through the forest and only allowed a small moment of hysteria to surface when I could already see broad daylight through the trees ahead of me. So much for all my courage that people were commenting on. I felt that I spent considerable time worrying about wolves or bicycle dramas instead of joyfully rising to each challenge.

I stopped for a coffee in a small village. The owners spoke excellent English and were quite intrigued by my journey. I left there pondering the necessity of creating a simple A4 size map of Europe to show my wanderings as I was so often being asked to explain my route, both completed and proposed. Such a map could help conversations along too. I have found that most people in Scandinavia spoke excellent English, but those people who didn't were just as interested in my cycling trip and would perhaps have appreciated a visual explanation to help them understand. I quite enjoy drawing maps, and I enjoy writing my diary, and reflecting over each day's events. Then it hit me! Maybe I should write a book! Would anyone read it?

# | 21 |

# Denmark – Flat and Very, Very Wet

## Helsingør to Vordingborg, 157 km

Helsingør was my re-introduction to Denmark, but this time it started to rain as soon as I entered the country and never eased off at all for the whole twenty-five kilometres to Hillerod. The campground at Hillerod was exceptionally well set up for travellers. The manager was a very welcoming lady with excellent English and a big smile. The kitchen was large and well equipped, the dining lounge area had everything possibly needed including a library of tattered books and a play area full of toys for the kids. But the rain, for which the manager kept apologising, was impossible!

I cycled to Frederiksborg castle in the late afternoon. It was built for Christian IV in the early seventeenth century but as so often with these old buildings, had been largely burnt down and rebuilt since then. The castle is spread over three islands in a large lake and is quite imposing with high solid brick walls around a series of courtyards. A whopping great fountain in the front was joyfully shooting out water, just in case people worried that the rain and the lake were not enough to keep the air cold and damp.

Inside the castle, there was one room after another, dozens of rooms and passageways, full of paintings and old furniture. Every inch of wall space had paintings hanging on it, even the ceilings had been converted into artworks. There were so many paintings of the various members of the royal family but with all the kings, except for one, since 1448 being named Christian or Frederik, it was a tad confusing, to say the least. I kept getting lost somewhere between Frederik V and Frederik IX.

I found my way to the Great Hall which had been completely destroyed by fire in 1859 and then completely rebuilt according to a series of sketches made only the previous year. Once again, every inch was covered in paintings or tapestries, even the ceiling and window niches were painted with images from industry, agriculture, and trade. The large paintings on the walls were exclusively of the Kings and Queens of Denmark with a few related European royals such as the Czar of Russia thrown in for balance. I was happy to see a large painting of Queen Margrete II, Crown Prince Frederik and Prince Christian as a little boy. At least I knew who they were.

There was a long, wide passage with important pictures along parts of it, leading to an audience chamber with ceiling paintings representing four of the continents: Europe, Asia, Africa and America. Australia was missing. The most impressive item? – a chair elevator! It was a chair in the corner of the room which could be raised from and lowered to the floor below, so the king didn't have to walk up the stairs and along the passageway like other mortals.

The royal chapel had hundreds of plaques on display, each with the name of a member of royalty around the outside edge and their coat of arms inside. I spotted the plaques of the current royals including that of Princess Mary who hails from Australia. There were also other royals from some other families represented such as a Prince Edward Albert of Britain with the motto "Ich dien." (I serve)

There were so many cupboards in so many rooms. How did a servant ever keep track of the king's stockings?

"Get me a fresh pair of stockings!"

"Yes, Sir! From which cupboard?"

What happened when the king called for the document that he had been writing the day before, and fresh quills? Where would he have left his work? Where were the quills? Or did they have quills in every room? Did a servant boy hover forever in the background with a jar of quills at the ready? It would have been easier living in a small house. At least there wouldn't have been too many places to store the quills or the stockings.

It was still bucketing rain when I peeked out of my cabin the following morning and the camp manager apologised yet again for all the rain and the soggy lawns. Not that there was anything which she could do to stop the rain.

I cycled back to the castle to have a look at the gardens and photograph the castle from outside. Afterwards, I pedalled at my top speed, against the wind and in the rain, to Roskilde. I met an American couple on the way who were doing a five-day self-guided tour from Copenhagen to Helsingore, Hillerod, Roskilde and back to Copenhagen. There were on eBikes supplied by the tour company. All their luggage was taken from hotel to hotel for them, the hotels had all been booked and the route was set out. All they had to do was follow the route, enjoy themselves during the day and turn up at the correct hotel every evening.

Roskilde's main drawcard was a museum for five Viking ships which were excavated from their dumping ground in the fjord. They were scuttled there on purpose a thousand years ago as part of Roskilde's defences against possible attack. The fjord was only navigable along a few narrow channels so blocking all but one of these channels ensured that maritime traffic could be supervised, controlled, and taxed by the rulers of Roskilde.

The five ships consisted of two fighting vessels, one large and one small, two merchant vessels and one fishing ship. They were excavated as 100,000 pieces of a massive jigsaw puzzle. Archaeologists worked for twenty-five years to put half of the pieces together to create sections of the five ships. No doubt many years of playing LEGO helped them work out where to put all the bits.

The ships were originally decorated with carvings, banners and shields and painted all over in bright colours, probably to be seen from afar and to strike fear into the hearts of their victims. I wasn't so sure about this rationale for the bright colour schemes. I think the Viking warriors were really repressed artists and actors who were just longing go on stage, singing, dancing and blowing kisses to their audience. Painting their ships in bright colours was the only way they were allowed to get in touch with their creative artistic side.

Next to the main museum complex was a shipyard. Archaeologists and boat-builders work there together to recreate ships from the Viking era using exactly the same wood, tools, and techniques. They have recreated all five of the ships in the museum and take visitors sailing in them in summer. Of course, the season was over, so I wasn't able to go out on the water. It was raining all the time anyway. It was no wonder so many Vikings went to Normandy and forgot to go home again. They were desperate for more sunshine and Vitamin D.

After a Viking lunch of meat and bread, I cycled to Roskilde Cathedral, a UNESCO site and home of the tombs of most of Denmark's kings and queens since the year dot. I wandered around the cathedral, admiring all the massive and ornate tombs, wondering all the while what happens with the deceased's bodily fluids. All the information talked about the kings and queens being buried but they weren't buried; they were stored in perpetuity inside solid stone, marble or wooden tombs.

Like Sweden, Denmark also has some very interesting women of history to be proud of. Margrete I was a powerful woman who takes pride of place both in Danish history and in the cathedral itself. This is her story:

*Margrete was born in 1353, a Danish princess, and was married as a ten-year-old to King Haakon of Norway. Her son became King Olaf of Denmark and Norway while still a child so Margrete ruled in his stead as regent. Unfortunately, he died suddenly as a teenager without leaving an heir. Margrete continued to rule both countries and two years later took over Sweden as well. In 1389, she adopted her sister's grandson, Bugislav of Pommerania, as her heir and renamed him Erik. She then united all three countries in Erik's name as the Kalmar Union with one of its main aims being to counter the dominance of the German-led Hanseatic League. The Kalmar Union lasted about 150 years. It was the first and last time that all of Scandinavia was united under one ruler even though each country was ruled as a separate entity.* Margrete's tomb is directly behind the main altar of the Roskilde Cathedral.

I left Roskilde in the early morning and cycled hard in an effort to get to Køge before the rain started to bucket down again in the afternoon. Following the E6 for most of the way was not the most exhilarating experience. It was time to rethink my cycling strategy if the best I could aim for was to dodge the rain and miss the beautiful countryside. It streamed rain all afternoon.

From Køge, The E151 took me direct to Vordingborg rather than the longer, scenic route along the coast with its UNESCO rated white cliffs. There was no rain but such a strong southerly wind that it made life terribly difficult. Looking on the weather app, I could see there was only rain and strong winds forecast for the next ten days at least. It was mid-September and I couldn't realistically expect an improvement in the weather. In addition, my research showed me that much of the cycling infrastructure, the cycling ferries and bridges, were closed and many of the campgrounds were also about to close for the winter.

I had to go back to Australia sometime soon anyway, so I decided it was an appropriate time to call my ride quits for the season. I hadn't made it to Berlin, but I had made it to the south of Denmark. By this stage, I had ridden over 2,800 kilometres from the North Cape and had about 4,700 kilometres to go. I had also ridden another thousand kilometres extra in my training ride in Denmark, and in the detour with my cousin in Germany and Poland. I was quite happy with what I had achieved and planned to continue on from Køge the following year.

# PART 3

## The Middle Bit

---

*Central Europe*

*Copenhagen, Denmark to Ancona, Italy*

*2,558 kilometres*

Central Europe

2558 KM

2018

DENMARK

Copenhagen

Berlin and Potsdam

Dresden

GERMANY

Prague

CZECHIA

Innsbruck

AUSTRIA

Bolzano

Verona

SAN MARINO

Ancona

ITALY

# | 22 |

# Copenhagen – A Cyclist's Dream

By late June 2018, I found myself in Copenhagen Central Station. I had just travelled across from Sweden, it was 11.30 in the morning and I had generously given myself three days in which to see all the major sights of this much-loved city. I left all my luggage in the storage area under the station, bought a ticket for the Hop-on, Hop-off Bus and set off to explore.

There were thousands of bicycles everywhere! Bikes propped against walls and lamp posts, parked under trees, and sheltering under weather-proof awnings. People in suits rode to work, others, more casually dressed, were busily going about their day. There were bikes laden with shopping and bikes with large boxes on wheels attached to the front of the bike with young children peering over the side. I found a free-flowing wood and steel bridge which went up and down like a wave, twisting and turning to give cyclists more zing for their ride. One diversion ended in a steep slide with an abrupt descent into the water. The locals were keen to explain that the river water was clean enough for swimming.

Later in the day, I decided that I was brave enough to cycle to my accommodation in the outer suburbs. At first, I was daunted by the sheer number of cyclists. 50% of Copenhagen's population commutes daily to work and to school. Everyone was quite civilised. We all obeyed the cyclists' traffic lights which worked in sync with the vehicle lights. It felt amazing to be in a group of fifty people bunched up waiting for the lights to change. We all took off together and everyone was very patient with the children, slower cyclists and tourists like me, laden down with tons of luggage. No swearing, yelling at people or racing past, as I've seen in other cities.

By watching and following others, I learnt how to turn left. We positioned ourselves to the right side of the stream of cyclists, rode through the intersection and indicated we were about to stop. Once through, we waited for the through cyclists to pass, then manoeuvred our bikes to point them to the left. When that light turned green, we cycled through the intersection, followed by more cyclists coming from our right side.

It was necessary to be quite vigilant when riding. There were always slower people ahead, faster people coming up and passing from behind and a smorgasbord of cycling infrastructure to negotiate. Sometimes we were on a raised cycle path next to the footpath, one direction only. Other times we were on the road, separated from vehicles by a white line, a concrete barrier or even a line of parked cars. Our cycle lane often turned into a wide blue painted strip at intersections so there was no confusion about the correct route.

Five kilometres into my ride, the cycling numbers decreased. I chugged along with only about ten other cyclists. By the ten-kilometre mark, I was on my own, but often being overtaken by others. I focused on obeying all the rules, signalling my moves, staying on the right side of my lane and generally being a superb Australian cyclist in Copenhagen. By the time I arrived at my accommodation I felt very pleased with myself and ready to become a bona fide naturalised Dane.

I was once a librarian in a past life, so I was keen to see The Black Diamond, a new extension to the old Royal Library. Facing the river, the library glistened in the sun. People lounged on deck chairs outside while the reading rooms inside were almost empty. The weather was just too beautiful to spend time holed up in a dark, quiet room like a troglodyte in a cave. The new library had two wings of book storage and reading rooms. The centrepiece was a huge atrium with escalators going up the middle. A ginormous clear glass window gave an uninterrupted view onto the water below. Standing on the escalator, I could see crowded tourist boats chugging along the river, their passengers snapping away, taking photos of the library.

Next up was the Amalianborg Palace but there was no-one home. The Crown Princess of Denmark was born and raised in Tasmania so it would have been nice to have knocked on the door and been invited in for a cuppa. I headed into the Palace Museum and swotted up on Danish Royal Family history and culture instead. All those Christians and Fredericks! Denmark's kings have been recycling their names, Christian and Frederick, since the early 1400's. At last count they were up to Frederick IX and Christian X.

Quite a few of Denmark's kings were gallantly riding a horse in a statue somewhere. Unfortunately, many of them were rather difficult to photograph because they were surrounded by machinery, earthworks and general chaos. Copenhagen was busy building three more lines for their metro system. They already had two lines but seemed to want more, or maybe they just wanted to create chaos out of order.

One exception to the rule of chaos was Frederick V riding through Amalienborg Palace Square. I'm sure the Royal Family didn't want a Metro stop in the centre of *their* square. Tourists were snapping selfies and chattering, gathering for the Changing of the Guard but Frederick V just kept riding along, gazing calmly ahead, and quite oblivious to the excitement and hubbub beneath him.

In addition to the equestrian kings, Christian IV, who was not riding a horse, stood and watched his people go about their daily business. Denmark owes much to him for his enthusiasm for building big things like palaces, new cities and islands. Joan of Arc was resting in Ørsteds Park while Bishop Absalom, the founder of Copenhagen, was off to deliver a sermon with an axe in one hand to help the heathens concentrate. I heard a rumour that Moses was also in town, but he must have been quite shy and in hiding somewhere. Ripleys even got in on the act with a life-size model of the tallest man in the world in front of their gallery. At 2.72 metres tall, their model didn't need a horse.

On the third and last day of my sojourn in Copenhagen, I decided I needed to get some more cycling practice in before I set out on my long journey south, so I cycled into town. I toured the Round Tower, a wide and not so high tower built in medieval times for the university and its astronomers. Most of the way up was on a wide, sloping passageway, not the usual steps. Part way up was an old toilet, a hole in a seat and a long way down. The last section went up increasingly narrow steps until I arrived at the top for a 360° view of Copenhagen. I had to step aside on the way down. Lots of young boys were running full pelt down the steep, circular passageway with no way of stopping or avoiding other tourists. Luckily, no-one was injured.

I cycled through the Latin Quarter; the historic university area and its main square, Gråbrøtorv; to Amalianborg Palace for a second go at meeting a Danish prince or princess. There was still no-one at home, but I watched the Changing of the Guard instead. The Queen wasn't home either, so the ceremony had no uplifting military music, just a great deal of marching around and not much else. Watching all that marching made me hungry so I cycled off to Torvehallerne, an upmarket foodie place where I looked in vain for some hot dogs. I had been told that hot dogs were the Danish food of choice. Years ago, it might have been fish, but times are changing. I tasted an egg kebab instead, like a souvlaki but rolled in an egg omelette rather than a flat bread. Over lunch, I pondered a very serious question. What next? Would I rather cycle along Copenhagen's famous green cycle path or would I rather go on a hunt for souvenirs? I figured I would have enough cycling through greenery in the following weeks, so of course, I voted for the souvenirs.

I was looking for a piece of modern, Danish design which would go well in my future house. No snow domes or plastic Guardsmen in fluffy hats for me. My trusted guidebook suggested I check out some different designers; Normann, Designer Zoo, or Stilleben amongst others. I pedalled out to Designer Zoo. It had shut down. I couldn't find Normann; it was hidden somewhere amongst all the Metro excavations in the town square. I did find Stilleben and immediately fell in love with a range of small sipping cups. Never having had a sipping cup before, I didn't quite know what to look for, but I chose two pretty ones anyway. Both were a cream coloured ceramic, one with a blue glaze on the top half, the other with a yellow glaze and both were very modern, even if they weren't quite so elegant. The designer was Anders Arhøj of Studio Arhøj. A tourist shop nearby had a Copenhagen patch with a bicycle on it and a tea-towel, also with a bicycle – both very appropriate, designers unknown.

# | 23 |

# Island Hopping in Denmark

## Copenhagen to Gedser, 276 km

I cycled out of Copenhagen on a beautiful, sunny day and covered the first forty kilometres towards Malta. The route was straightforward and simple to follow; Route 03 to the coast until it morphed into Route 151 then south to Køge. Too easy.

In September of the previous year when I had arrived in Køge, I was sopping wet and shivering. The autumn rains had settled in for the long haul, so I had decided soon after to call it quits for season 2017. This time, I arrived sunburnt and sweating. Spring had been exceptionally warm and dry. It looked like summer could be more of the same with daytime temperatures already reaching the low thirties.

I only rode forty kilometres because I wanted to start off gradually, allowing my ageing body and creaking knees to slowly get fit over time. My knees had been good so far, but I was starting to suffer buttock soreness. I needed to find some stretching exercises to deal with this. I cycled slowly and rested often, even when I didn't feel like I needed it, but I was still tired and very glad to call it a day by the time I arrived in the campground.

Køge was a lovely old town, ideal for an afternoon coffee and a spot of people watching in the main square. Frederick VII was already there but without a horse, keeping an eye on things. I spotted an archway with a quaint looking alley beyond. It was lined with Tudor era shops;

a florist, a hairdresser, a technology repair shop, and around the corner – a coffee shop. A coffee in the peace and quiet of this old alley seemed just the thing. People watching could always wait for another day and another old town square.

From Køge, I wanted to ride along the coast. I had missed that the previous year because of the poor weather. I aimed first for Vallø Slot, just a quick flick of the pedals south of Køge. It was the stuff of fairy tales; a tall, slender castle with two towers surrounded by a garden of lawns, lakes, and forest. A terrace on a buttress jutting out over the moat caught my eye. What a splendid spot for a coffee and a chat! I wondered whether I could get some-one to invite me in.

Until 1976, the castle was reserved for unmarried noble women, supposedly so they could all live together and spend their lives doing good works for the community. If anyone wanted to escape, they could always hang their long and lustrous hair out of the top of one of the two towers and hope for a lost prince to come sauntering by with a beautiful white palfrey in tow. This very pleasant retreat for female wealthy aris-tocrats and royalty has since become the home to the castle trust which manages the thousands of hectares of farmland and forest which belong to it.

I wandered up to the door in the entrance archway. There were the usual apartment style name tags attached to doorbells so visitors could request that the door be opened by a mysterious being from afar. This might be a modern electronic concept, but it seemed quite magical to me, straight out of a fairy tale. All the names next to the bell buttons were pretty standard. None of the them started with Princess or Lady. A pity, they would just have to miss out on meeting me.

Twenty kilometres further on from Vallø Slot was Stevns Klint, a UNESCO site of chalk cliffs with a layer of black stuff through it. This black stuff was once ash blown out of a volcano and has since given sci-entists the world's best information on the demise of the dinosaurs. A flight of sixty-nine very steep metal steps led down to the beach from which I then had to ascend another thirty very rickety wooden steps.

The platform at the top was so unstable that I felt in imminent risk of demise myself.

A short walk and clamber took me to the bay from which I could study the cliff face. I couldn't spot any dinosaur remains and remained cheerfully clueless. I was, however, deeply impressed by the beach. Not a grain of sand was to be seen. Instead, the beach was a mass of dark grey stones, each one shaped and rounded so as to fit snugly into my hand. At water's edge, they glistened black where the waves washed up and over them. The stones murmured and chattered as the waves fell back with a whoosh and a sigh, gently massaging the stones against each other and softening their harsh edges. To think that this dance of the waves and the stones goes on all day, every day without a break for coffee or a chat.

There was a church at the top of the cliff. Originally built in the thirteenth century, it was abandoned in 1910 due to safety concerns. Ten years later, the wall behind the altar fell into the water below leaving a gaping hole and a fine view of the sea from the pews. The hole was still there, a balcony had been built so that tourists could step through the void and admire the spectacular view of sea, beach and white chalk cliffs; a view even God could be proud of.

I hauled myself into camp at Rødvig having cycled a fairly impressive forty kilometres. My knees and my backside were complaining, they just didn't want to do more yet. It was apparent that I would be taking the slow version of this race to the south. Anyway, it was so lovely and sunny in Denmark so what was the point of rushing?

I left camp relatively early the following morning, had a sedate lunch at Faxe Ladeplads where I bought a huge filled baguette and scoffed the lot without hesitation. I then stopped for a break shortly before Praesto when I spotted a picnic table in a rest stop. The road was busy with cyclists; a few other touring couples loaded up with gear breezed past. A young man on his high-tech bike was followed by two more racers chatting as they skimmed by. A group of fifty riders, in pairs, all in matching yellow shirts and black shorts buzzed past. A minute later, another fifty dressed the same. They looked like a swarm of bees and sounded just the same too. Lastly a van with spare bikes on the back followed the group. I was glad that I was resting as they went past. Their slipstream would have knocked me off my bike and that would have caused quite a mess.

Next to arrive was an open truck blasting upbeat pop music with twenty excited teenagers on board. Their flat sailors' caps indicated that they had just passed their secondary school matriculation exams. Reason enough to be singing, dancing, and drinking while being driven around the countryside in the back of a cattle truck. I waved and clapped in congratulation which just enthused them even more. The truck lurched off, teenagers squealed and fell in a heap, and two cans of drink flew overboard spinning a fountain of alcohol in the warm sun.

From Praesto, I took the wrong route out of town and ended up following the main road for about eight kilometres until it crossed the No. 9 Route. From then on, I weaved my way along quiet country lanes, up hill and down dale until Kalvehave. Just before Kalvehave, I cycled over a glass bottle which had been smashed into a thousand bits and left lying on the path. I wondered if that bottle would come back to haunt me.

I met two German ladies on the way who told me about an old ferry which traversed the strait between Kalvehave and Stege so of course, I was into that. The ferry was run by four or five retired gentlemen with nothing better to do than to play around with old boats, a bit like those chaps who like to drive old steam engines. They each wore a bright red shirt as uniform and enjoyed their hobby so much that they just sparkled with pleasure. They loaded our bikes on board for us, motored the boat under the Dronning Alexandrine's Bro (bridge), showed us with great pride that an image of the bridge was on their five hundred kroner note and then turned around and motored slowly and sedately back under the bridge to Stege.

Stege was on the island of Møn and everyone who goes to Møn just has to go to Møns Klint, a set of spectacular chalk cliffs, 128 metres high. Two churches at Keldby and Elmelunde were on the way. These two churches were both decorated by the "Elmelunde Master" at some time in the fifteenth century. The decorations were frescoes which covered the whole ceiling of each church. They depicted scenes from the bible such as the Garden of Eden, complete with snake and apple. Jesus was born, worshipped by the magi, baptised in the River Jordan by John the Baptist and so on. There was a shocking depiction of Herod's soldiers slaughtering the infants while the next panel showed the Holy Family fleeing to Egypt. There were also numerous scenes showing people the perils of being a bad Christian. People were dragged off to hell by the devil while their more virtuous friends queued up at the gates of heaven. Set against the pure white background, the reds, browns, blues and greens of the paintings were still as beautiful as when they were originally painted. The pictures were so simple, that the stories and morals they told could be easily understood and contemplated, even by a modern pagan like me.

As well as their Christian heritage, Møn also had 119 Stone Age burial sites, mounds and tombs. One of them, a large mound was in the yard of the Elmelunga Church. Actually, the church was built next to the mound, another piece of evidence showing that Christian holy places were often placed on top of sites of significance for the pagan population, thus encouraging the pagans to worship at Christian sites and eventually turn to Christianity.

I kept following the suggested route, the cycle path wound up and down and I worked up a sweat as the land got hillier, working its way up to the high point of 128 metres. A Danish couple in Praesto had told me that Møn was flat! The route led past Liselunde Slot, a fine palace set in woodland, so I decided to drop in on the off chance I might find a tall, dark and handsome prince visiting.

No such luck, but I did get a flat tyre on my back wheel. I had brought all my tools with but had forgotten to bring my pump. I up-ended the bike, managed to get the back wheel off, took off the tyre, and pulled out the tube. I found a miniscule hole in the tube and a corresponding sliver of glass in the tyre. That bottle at Kalvehave! I reached down to get my pliers to pull out the glass and lost sight of it. I searched, investigated and studied both tyre and tube but the glass couldn't be found. I replaced both the tube and the tyre but needed to find some way of pumping the tyre up again. I asked some passing cyclists whether they had a pump. Nope. I waited till some more cyclists came by. Still nope. I was about to hide the bike and hitch a lift into town to find a bike shop when two more cyclists came past. I called out to them. They stopped and came back. They had a very small pump for emergencies. Ronald and Josine were Dutch and on holiday on Møn. By the time Ronald had pumped up my tyre and helped me put the back wheel in again, he was drenched in sweat, so I invited them both into the Slot café for a coffee. We had a lovely chat, a bit stilted, but I worked hard at being a good conversationalist. Coffee over, I thanked them yet again and rode off.

More up hill and down dale led me eventually to Møns Klint where I duly admired the chalk cliffs. Five hundred steps led down to the beach from where I got a clear view of the cliffs as they towered above me. It was afternoon, so they were already in shadow, more soft grey than sparkling white but still an artist's dream. The same dark grey stones as at Stevns Klint created the same background music as the waves rushed over them and fell back with a sigh.

The five hundred steps back to the clifftop were not as challenging as I anticipated, I was getting fitter! The ride home, however, was a challenge. Twenty kilometres of winding, scenic but hilly roads with the wind against me when I was already emotionally exhausted from the tyre dramas, pretty well wiped me out. I was so glad to reach Stege and shout myself a Fanta from the local supermarket before I fell in a heap in front of my tent.

Ronald hadn't put quite enough air into my tyre at Liselunde Slot, he had only had a tiny pump for emergencies, so it was quite hard work. I decided to pump up the tyre properly before I set off for the day's adventures. The pump wouldn't fit onto the valve and I lost all of the air out of the tyre. I wheeled the bike to the nearest bike shop and was relieved to discover that it was a valve and pump issue which could be easily solved. The mechanic found an adaptor, screwed it onto the valve, attached the pump, and put some air in. I instantly bought a spare valve adaptor, just in case.

I rode my bike back to camp, packed up, loaded up, rode off, and discovered to my horror that something wasn't right, something was rubbing, and the back wheel was quite off kilter. I turned back into camp, unloaded, tipped the bike over and saw immediately that the back wheel wasn't sitting properly in the forks. I fiddled and discovered that if I unscrewed the central spindle and pulled it out that the wheel slotted in perfectly. I balanced the wheel, poked the spindle through, attached and tightened the nut, tipped over the bike, and went for a trial spin. It worked! I felt very smug.

In hindsight, the most interesting aspect of all this was that I had managed to change the tube, sort out the valve, and solve the issue with the back wheel, with the minimum of fuss or bother. There was a job to do and I just did it without thinking and without fear. Failure wasn't an option, a lesson which I would have done well to remember in the following days.

I cycled into Stege which was having a market. Hundreds of people were milling about but the queues for the food vans were mercifully short. I scoffed a hotdog; the three types of sauce which the cook layered on were quite tasty, but the bread roll was too small for the sausage which hung out at both ends and dripped sauce all down my shirt. I sampled a pancake with honey and almond flakes. It was equally tasty and all in proportion.

Stomach filled, it was time to set off to Klekkende Høj, one of Møn's 119 Viking age burial sites. It was a small detour on my route to Bogø Island, but well worth it. The burial mound had two entrance tunnels running parallel with a burial chamber at the end of each. I crawled along to the burial chamber in one. It was quite earie to think that people had gathered five thousand years ago to build these tombs. Intellectually, I was well aware that every step I took in Europe was on top of the footsteps of thousands of other people through a long period of history, but rarely did I get an emotional connection with our ancestors. Crawling along in the tunnel, seeing the small, flat stones layered between the taller upright rocks, the connection just happened. I could almost feel the people labouring to heave each rock into position, selecting the right stones to place between them, working as they grieved but rising to the challenge of giving their dead an honourable resting place.

Having viewed Fanefjord Church, the third of Møn's churches decorated by the Elmelunde Master with very similar motifs and identical style, I cycled on to view Grønsalen nearby. This was a long barrow surrounded by rows of pinkish rocks. I found the car park easily, a long driveway led to a farmhouse. A sign indicated that cars and trucks were not allowed to enter but it didn't show anything about bikes. I rode in, a farmer came out and observed me suspiciously. Obviously, not many people could be bothered to walk down the long driveway, so the barrow was not often visited. Long grass covered the barrow and the rocks, it all looked rather unkempt and uncared for, so I didn't stay long.

An hour's cycling took me over the dyke to Bogø, which I learnt is pronounced Boh-oooh and a little cottage at the end of a quiet road. The cottage was the holiday home of some distant relatives. I planned to stay only one night but ended up relaxing, working on my journal, catching up with my washing and generally chilling. A longer stay was needed for all this activity so I prolonged my stay to two nights.

Having successfully rested for a day, it was time to move on before I started growing lazy. On leaving my relative's house, I discovered that my phone had completely lost the plot. I wasn't sure what the issue was, it could have been that my SIM card was out of date or that the phone did an update overnight and used up all my credit. Either way, it wanted me to put in my chip pass number which I didn't have and had never needed to put in before. Nothing worked at all on my phone, no camera, no wifi, no What's App or anything else. I had to get this sorted! I hoped I could buy a new SIM card in Rostock, Germany, which was only a few days' ride and a ferry crossing away.

I headed off cross-country to the harbour, detoured to a picturesque windmill and then spotted a piece of white paper on my front tyre. I pulled at the paper, but it was held on by a black drawing pin going through the tyre and possibly into the tube. I would have to keep an eye on the air in the tube. Maybe it was another flat tyre in the making.

Another few kilometres took me through agricultural land, then turned off the road onto a narrow gravel road through the forest. I wasn't happy. Thoughts of flat tyres plagued me, I started hearing weird noises and then worrying about wolves. Images of Little Red Riding Hood flashed through my mind. How would I fight off a wolf pack? Could I throw my bread rolls at them? I also had two eggs, two chocolate biscuits, some carrots and some tomatoes. I started looking about for a tree to climb. Nothing suitable, they all had smooth trunks and skimpy branches. I stopped for lunch and ate the bread rolls. The wolves would have to be content with the eggs. The food calmed my mind, so I peddled on, but I still heaved a great sigh of relief when I came back onto the sealed road and saw a family of Mama, Papa and three children cycling towards me. The wolves could have the children! (For people who don't understand my sense of humour, that was a joke!)

I pulled into camp at Marielyst by 2.30 p.m. It was an early finish but a lack of suitable camp sites closer to Gedser made this an inevitable stop. I wasn't fit enough yet to cycle more than fifty kilometres, then travel two hours on a ferry, and then cycle a further ten kilometres to my accommodation. I needed to factor in time waiting for the ferry, getting myself un-lost and fixing potential punctures as well. Navigation had also been an issue during the day. Normally I used my phone but with it out of order, I had to rely on signposts and my memory of the route. Neither were much good at the task. I asked one cycling couple for directions and was relieved when they said they were going to the same place. My relief turned to astonishment when they just took off and left me. Obviously, they didn't understand that when I asked for help, that it meant that I really didn't know the route. Luckily, the lady was wearing a bright red jacket and I was able to spot it in the distance from time to time.

The manager at the campground looked up the route to Gedser on the computer then printed it out for me to take with. On the negative side, the front tyre on my bike was slowly losing air. I had no doubt that, thanks to the drawing pin at the windmill in Bogø, I now had a punctured tyre which would most likely be completely flat by the next morning.

I was wide awake very early in the morning, so I got up and moving as quickly as I could. I felt quite fragile and unprotected without a working mobile phone and internet connection, so I wanted to get the morning's ride over and done with. I pumped up the very flat front tyre and left camp as quickly as I could, arriving at Gedser by 8 a.m., in good time for the ferry which left an hour later.

I knew this was going to be my last major ferry crossing until the end of the trip when I would take the ferry from mainland Italy to Sicily, and then later the ferry from Sicily to Malta. I had two hours of leisurely cruising across the Baltic in front of me where I would be forced to sit and relax because I couldn't do anything else. What to do? I treated myself to a lavish breakfast, two lovely German bread rolls, two slices of cheese, two slices of salami and a cup of coffee as a reward. My breakfast cost almost as much as the ferry ticket but I savoured every bite as I put my feet up and sank into a soft chair for the duration of the journey.

# | 24 |

## Facing My Fears at Last!

### Rostock to Oranienburg, 299 km

Once in Rostock, I had to rely on my written notes to follow the trail to the hotel. The hardest part was getting out of the harbour area. The vehicle traffic all left by a main gate which led them directly onto a major road without a bicycle path. This was obviously not the correct way to go. Two other cyclists and I circled around for a good twenty minutes before we realised that a small lane off to the left was our exit route. From there, it was a simple matter to follow my notes and the Berlin-Copenhagen bike route signs to my hotel which was directly on the route.

After dumping my belongings at the hotel and locking my bike in their garage, I took the tram into the town centre, headed straight for the first Telekom shop, and bought a SIM card. The salesman was brilliant. He was old and mature enough to understand straight away that I was not a native speaker. He explained everything carefully and set it up but didn't patronise me at all. I was very happy. I walked out of the shop and immediately got a message saying that I didn't have enough money on my account. This sounded problematic so I went straight back into the shop and showed my guy the message. He rang the Telekom people who sorted it out immediately. I was even happier. Then he suggested I sit down and use their wifi to answer all my messages, all thirty-four of them. What a great idea!

The Berlin-Copenhagen Bicycle Route is a very well-known and popular long-distance cycling route. I had followed it for short sections and crossed it a few times in Denmark, but I had been creating my own route according to my interests as I went, so I had not been too concerned about following it. The advantage of following an established cycling route is that they are usually well signposted so that I don't need to focus on navigation or stop and look at my phone so much. There can be more cafes, restaurants and snack options along these routes as well as a greater selection of overnight accommodation. I tried to follow the Berlin-Copenhagen route from Rostock, but it wandered all around the place so in the end, I took a few short cuts to Büstrow.

My tyre needed to be pumped up morning and lunchtime. This didn't bode well. I needed to fix it, but I preferred to wait until I was near a bike shop during opening hours in case something went wrong. In hindsight, I struggle to understand why I was so hesitant to tackle the flat tyre. I had already successfully changed a flat tyre on Møn where my only issue had been the lack of a pump.

Growing up on a farm, my brothers had learnt to use tools confidently, they could fix anything with moveable parts and cobble together a solution to almost any physical issue when needed. Being a girl, I learnt to cook, to clean and to sew (all of them quite badly) but I never had any exposure to tools or mechanics. In my head, I knew that I could solve the flat tyre by simply changing the tube, but I was still terrified and unconfident.

An old fellow in a petrol station suggested I buy a new tube in a supermarket. The town of Bützow had a cluster of small supermarkets, all in a row, Penny, Lidl, Aldi and Edeka. They all had milk and bread, but none had tubes. I asked a couple who had parked their bikes near mine. They suggested that I go to Famila in the industrial estate a few kilometres out of town. I cycled there, bought a new tube and a small fancy gas thing that supposedly inflates and repairs a flat tyre very quickly as a short-term solution. Feeling a little more confident about my ability to sort out my flat tyre, I camped that night in the Bützow Canoe Club for just six euros.

The section from Bützow to Krakow-am-See was a perfect example of the best (almost) of the Berlin-Copenhagen Cycle Trail.

I packed up, pumped up my flat tyre and left the Canoe Camp by 8.30 in the morning. I didn't leave so early to prove a point or to be disciplined, I just woke up very early and was happy to roll out of bed by around 7 a.m. The sun was out but was still relatively shy, there was little wind. I went first to the collection of supermarkets – Penny/ Lidl/Edeka/Aldi on a hunt for some bread rolls for lunch, but all were closed. Many years ago, I had complained that one could die of starvation on a Sunday in Germany. Not much had changed since then. I spotted a man walking along the street with fresh bakery goods, so I knew that all was not lost. I rounded a corner and found a bakery open with all sorts of bread, a variety of cakes, and even fresh coffee.

Panniers filled, I studied my apps to work out the route; over the railway line, over the canal, turn immediately right, and follow the canal for a long, long way. Interestingly, there was not a signpost for the Berlin-Copenhagen Route to be seen, not one! The canal was signposted as the Büstow-Güstrow Canal, so I knew I was right. The path itself was brilliant; two smooth cement strips, each wide enough for a solid tractor tyre and spaced at an appropriate distance apart, ideal for tractors and cyclists.

I followed the canal into Güstrow, walked over the moat, crossed the remains of the old town wall, went through the cobbled streets into the marketplace in the centre, and out the other side to the Duke of Mecklenburg's Palace. The palace had become a museum of religious artefacts, so it didn't really entice me. South of the palace and on a much lower level was a formal garden, all low hedges and geometric shapes except for a huge heart outlined in bricks and filled with bright flowers. The heart was placed in the centre of the garden so that the duke and his guests would have had a perfect view of it from the palace windows. Did the latest duke order the heart to be developed and planted? What sort of man was he? How many dukes would order a symbol like that to be planted front and centre in his formal garden? And why? For whom?

Had I missed a romantic story? Was there a gorgeous prince lounging about, looking for a scruffy elderly cyclist to fall into his arms?

The next dozen kilometres were mainly on quiet country lanes through forest and the occasional village. I loved the forest. There might have been wolves in my imagination but there was little wind and a great deal of shade which made cycling through them just bliss. I emerged into Bellin which the Berlin-Copenhagen website had promised me had a Steintanz (an ancient ring of stones) second only to Stonehenge. I was curious but there was no indication of it in Bellin, no mention of it anywhere. I was gradually discovering that the website was great on flowery statements but rather short on useful detail.

To get the detail, I would have needed to have bought the relevant cycling guidebook. I hadn't because I found the guidebooks had far more detail than I wanted, with a written turn-by-turn description for every part of the route, and large-scale maps which I didn't need. They also had quite detailed explanations of the history of every town, village, church and monument en route as well as explanations of the geography of the area. It was all too much. I only wanted to skim the surface, not become an expert on every small historical or geographical site in the region.

The next village was Groß Breesen (Big Breesen) which had an interesting pillar at one end. It was an artistic work made of numerous panels, each of which explained an element of life in the village. Another informative panel gave a short history of this very old settlement. Groß Breesen was first mentioned in 1303. In 1390 it was granted to the local monastery in Dobberlin. By 1751 Groß Breesen had seventy-six inhabitants of which seventy were serfs, bonded to the monastery. Only six inhabitants were not bonded serfs but there was no explanation as to their position in the village. By 1867, the population had risen to 131 but by 1939 it had sunk again to only eighty-seven so Groß Breesen was a very small village indeed. Was there a place called Klein Breesen (Little Breesen) and if so, what was its population?

Anyway, by 1946, the population had exploded to 346 of which only 120 were locally born. Which means that 226 or about two thirds of the villagers in 1946 had been new arrivals. Were they refugees from the USSR, Poland and other eastern areas? Or were they refugees from Berlin and other German cities which had been bombed to smithereens and couldn't provide adequate accommodation for their citizens at the time? Given the refugee crisis in Europe in 2015 and Germany's role within that crisis, I was curious for an answer, but there was no further explanation.

From Krakow-am-See, most of the day was spent cycling through forest including one section of eleven kilometres on a gravel and stone road. It wasn't good for the bike and I was worried about getting more damage done to my still unrepaired tyre. I was standing at a crossroad in a village, studying my map when a young man pulled up next to me. I spoke to him in German. He looked confused so I asked, "Where are you from?"

"Australia," he answered. Wow! An Aussie, the first such creature I had met on this bike ride. We had a bit of a chat. He was riding a borrowed, old town-bike and had very little equipment with him. He had ridden from Copenhagen in about four days compared to my eleven days and was heading for Berlin too. Chat finished, he zipped off ahead and disappeared in a flash.

Later in the day, I met two Canadian gentlemen who were doing the tour in the opposite direction. They were having trouble locating campgrounds, so I showed them Maps.me. The beauty of Google Maps and Maps.me is that with them, I was never lost. I might not have known where I was, but the navigation apps always did, *and* they always knew how to get me to my destination. I was using Maps.me quite often as I found that it worked well off-line so that was much better than using my precious internet data allowance on Google Maps.

I arrived in Waren (Müritz) very early in the afternoon, set up camp and then cycled into town to have a look around. It was a delightful old town with numerous cafes, a busy town square, and hordes of tourists. I hopped on my bike to return to camp and – oh no! The front tyre was completely flat again. Lacking all my tools and a new tube, I had to walk the bike all the way back to camp.

There was a lesson in this. I first knew about the flat tyre five days previously. Instead of knuckling down and fixing or replacing the tube, I had just pumped it up twice a day and thought, "I'll do it tomorrow." Of course, tomorrow never came and eventually the tube gave out completely. Why didn't I fix the problem? What was I waiting for? The answer was "fear."

*When my son was a small boy, he was exceptionally scared of heights. He couldn't stand on a chair or climb a flight of stairs. He couldn't even stand at the base of Bendigo cathedral and look at the top of the spire. This was a real deep-seated fear. Asking him to walk up two steps turned him into a quivering mess.*

*When he was about nine years old, we had a new garden fence built. It was a real farm fence; posts with wire mesh between and a flat rail along the top to make it look pretty. Three years later, I looked out of the kitchen window and saw my son carefully stepping along the top of the fence. Arms stretched out for balance and face fixed in concentration, he made it right to the end, turned around and walked back again. A little while later, he walked into the house but didn't say anything. I had to ask: "What were you doing on the fence?"*

*"Oh, Mum," he replied. "You have to face your fears." Since then, he has grown to adulthood and faces everybody's fears every day by being a reservist in the army and a constable in our local police force.*

I had my son's message ringing in my ears the whole three kilometre walk back to camp with a sick bicycle. I hadn't made any attempt to fix the issue because I was paralysed by fear of what might happen. I might not have known how to get the front wheel off, I might not have been able to get the new tube properly in place, the tube might have had a dodgy valve, and I might not have been able to pump it up. The worst fear of all was that I might not have been able to get the wheel back on properly. Instead of dealing with a minor problem at my leisure, I was walking back to camp with a major problem which had to be dealt with before I could cycle one centimetre further.

This inability to face our fears paralyses the best of us to some degree. It stops people changing jobs, going on long journeys, facing life alone, committing to deep and sincere relationships, taking a mortgage, enjoying life to the fullest, and so on. The most common question I was asked while travelling was "Are you alone?" The next question was invariably "Aren't you scared?" Yes! I was! But I couldn't let fear stop me because the alternative was to stay at home, growing old and bitter because of opportunities not taken. I just needed to get over my fear and change the flat tyre.

I woke numerous times in the night, each time the thought of the tyre loomed out of the darkness to start me quivering. "Stop being so stupid!" I told myself. "If the worst happens, you can just take the tyre to a bike shop."

When the birds announced that morning had arrived, I rolled out of bed, got myself organised for the day, had breakfast and then, at my leisure, tackled the flat tyre. It all worked without a hitch. The only minor issue was getting the valve to sit correctly so the outer tyre wouldn't pinch the tube. With a bit of thought and wiggling, I solved that issue too.

What on earth had I been I so afraid of? Why had I wasted so much emotional energy being terrified of a small task which I knew quite well that I could successfully complete? At twelve, my son knew more about the importance of facing one's fears than I did, and he was right!

I cycled through glorious countryside, through thousands of acres of forest, past countless lakes and through numerous small villages. Lunch was a picnic on the side of a field. A farmer came along in his big tractor, spreading fertiliser on the field. It was dry manure, crushed to a dust and blowing all over my lunch. To take my mind off the manure dusted bread rolls, I pondered the deep and significant question of the thousand lakes of Mecklenburg. Did someone count them or was that just a wild guess? What was the definition of a lake? Would that puddle a short distance away count as a lake? What if a lake narrowed to a short, wide channel before widening out into a lake again. Did that count as one lake or two?

By mid-afternoon I arrived at the Heinrich Schliemann Museum in Ankersberg. He was an amateur archaeologist in the late 1800s who discovered and excavated Hissarlik, more widely known as the city of Troy, in what is now the country of Turkey. Amazingly, he discovered a cache of treasures which included a magnificent gold necklace and two headpieces which he decided had belonged to Helen of Troy. There's a well-known photograph of Schliemann's wife, Sophie, modelling these treasures. After quite a few adventures, these pieces have ended up in a museum in Moscow, but that's another story.

What is less known about Schliemann was his passion for learning languages – just twenty of them. Schliemann learnt mainly European languages, but also Arabic, Hebrew and Sanskrit which he mastered by inventing his own methods.

- He read passages aloud in the target language, all without translations.
- He spent an hour a day writing in the target language. He sat with a tutor while it was being corrected then took the revised piece away with him to learn. He read the improved copy to his tutor the next day.
- He always carried a book in the target language with him. He spent as much time as he could memorising the book. After a few years, his memory improved to the extent that he could memorise twenty pages after having read them only three times.

Using these methods, Schliemann was able to learn a new language in only six weeks and could learn three new languages in one year. All without Duolingo, Babbel, Skype, or any other modern internet assistants.

Having been made to feel quite useless by the genius of Schliemann, I rode on to my accommodation in Groß Quassow. I had booked two nights at the Storchennest Pension and Gasthof because the weather was forecast to have a big thunderstorm followed by buckets of rain the following day, at least seventy-five millilitres. Instead, the sky, although overcast, only managed about six drops of rain. I spent the day relaxing anyway. I did some stretching exercises and molly-coddled my right ankle which had swollen and was quite uncomfortable. I spent hours updating my journal, calculating distances ridden, and writing emails to friends and family in Australia.

The Pension had advertised that it had wifi but when I asked, I was told that it wasn't working. The manager claimed that the whole village had no internet which I suspected was not quite correct. My phone was picking up the signals of three wifi connections and my own internet was working without a hitch. I had found that this was a quite common issue in Germany which really surprised me. Germany is a world leader in technology yet in 2018, their public connections to the internet were rather poor, being either very slow or non-existent. In other countries which I have visited, every café, restaurant, hotel and pension has had a good wifi connection for their customers. Not so in Germany. In those other countries, the tourist four-week SIM card was always much cheaper and offered a much larger volume of data than in Germany. It was a puzzle, in answer to which I was told that everyone in Germany had such a good connection at home that they didn't need good public connections.

After lunch, I met two Australian cyclists – Toby and Helen. They were cycling the Berlin – Copenhagen route with friends as part of a supported tour. They were organised to cycle a set section each day, their accommodation was pre-booked for them and their luggage was transported from hotel to hotel. It was the same idea as the American couple had been doing in Denmark. The only thing better would be the barge and bike option which friends of mine like to do. They spend a week or ten days based on a barge and their luggage stays for the duration of their tour in their cabin. During the day they have the option of cycling on a set route, but they must be at the pre-arranged meeting point by the correct time every afternoon in order to get back on their barge and have their afternoon drinks. Now that is what I call luxury cycling! But, given my propensity for wandering off a signposted route to investigate something just around the corner, It's probably not such a good idea for me. Maybe when I'm older and not so easily distracted.

Given that there had been so little rain, I went for a stroll around the village to stretch my legs. It was only a small village, so a thorough investigation only took about half an hour. I discovered that Storchennest Pension was named after a stork's nest which sat on top of a neighbouring building. I could see two storks in the nest, fluttering around, bending down to their young and doing whatever storks do. There was a set of information boards nearby from which I learnt that storks usually, but not always, return to the same nest every year. The male arrives first, in April, and occupies the nest with the female following. She lays one egg every two days and the eggs hatch out after thirty-two days. The chicks can fly from about sixty-five days. The nesting pair raises two or three young every season and lives on frogs and other assorted little creatures. The whole family leaves the nest for Africa at the end of August. This particular storks' nest dated back to in 1938. Between 1938 and 2005 there were 160 baby storks reared at this one nest. At the end of all this information, I still had one question - What's the word for a baby stork?

I woke early in the morning feeling really grumpy! All I could hear was the rain drumming on the roof and my brain was going "No! No1 No!! It was supposed to rain yesterday!" Cycling in the rain is never much fun and I almost decided to hide in bed and stay at the pension another night, but my Germanic determination wouldn't let me. It kicked me out of bed and scolded me thoroughly, telling me not to be such a wuss. Lightning was an acceptable excuse to take shelter from the elements, nothing else was.

I did as I was told, climbed into all my wet weather gear and set off - grimly. The rain spattered about a bit, stopped, started, drizzled a few minutes, then stopped altogether. Within another ten minutes I was sweating so much I had to stop and strip off – just the wet weather gear. The route was through fields, forests and past lakes all day. I passed a gentleman who had stripped off completely and was frolicking in a lake. A bit of rain wouldn't have worried him.

The section from Fürstenberg to Himmelpfort reminded me that I was cycling through the old socialist East Germany. I rode past square concrete apartment blocks, along footpaths and cycle paths desperately in need of rejuvenation, past broken houses, and an abandoned farm. Most distressing was cycling past the old buildings of Ravensbrück Camp, a Nazi Concentration Camp for women and children.

On the upside, I ended up at Himmelpfort (Heaven's Gate) and the campsite was indeed heavenly. It was very basic, just a patch of grass dotted with trees, a sprinkling of tents, all with bikes next to them, and a separate campervan section for those lucky people with more luxurious accommodation. Our patch of grass was edged on one side by reeds, beyond was the lake. A short walk took me to a pontoon from which the kids were having great fun swimming in the clear water.

The facilities block was next to our grassy pitch. This is of extreme importance to us cyclists. Spending each day doing so much strenuous exercise, I felt no great desire to have to walk hundreds of metres for every little toilet visit yet in most campgrounds the caravanners were parked next to the facilities block and the tents were placed as far away as possible. This was yet another puzzle, about which I never received a satisfactory explanation. The washbasin section included two tiny washbasins at "little kid" height and a stool for the even shorter ones to stand on.

The manager of the campground was really pleased to have an Australian guest. He had had New Zealanders before, but I was the first Australian. He loved New Zealand because it was small enough to travel in comfortably whereas Australia was just too big and therefore too daunting. I had heard this opinion from a few different people so it must have been a reasonably common concern about Australia; just too big and too far away. Another common reason for avoiding Australia had been our multitude of deadly animals ranging from sharks to spiders to snakes. Whenever I heard this, I used to point out that about twenty-five million people had survived these creatures to that point in time, but this argument never seemed to work for some reason. When people have an irrational fear, like my fear of flat tyres, then a reasoned argument against that fear holds little value.

I had supper at an old mill restaurant in the village. It only had a few tables outside under some grape vines and next to the mill race. The chef/owner served a very refreshing home-made cordial of raspberry with just a hint of fizz. It was served in a crooked beer glass. For the main meal, I chose roast pork with dumplings, beans and something I couldn't identify. It all seemed very German with a twist of hippie organic and I must admit, it all went down *very* well.

Having spent time in the heavenly campground at Himmelpfort, I rolled out of camp feeling very focused and contented, planning to stay in Liebenwalde or somewhere en route to Oranienburg. Knees, legs, backside and bicycle were all humming along nicely together. I spent the morning cycling through the interminable forests, past more of the thousand lakes and through a region which was once the largest brick making area in Europe. The brickworks had made all the bricks for the rebuilding of Berlin since the end of WWII, but then most of them had been closed since the fall of the Eastern Bloc. All that remained were tall, narrow chimneys poking through the treetops and a large museum. The brickworks and their supporting industries would have employed thousands of people but would also have polluted the air immeasurably. Empty buildings, silent car parks and rusting machinery bore witness to the massive changes which this region had seen since the fall of the socialist system. I wasn't surprised that the extreme right-wing party, the AfD had such a strong support base in eastern Germany. When people are under great financial stress and the standard solutions don't seem to be working, they start looking for scapegoats for their problems, and for alternative solutions, even unrealistic ones. Then I cycled past a harbour which was full of large, fancy motorised yachts of the sort which I can only dream about. Maybe not everyone had been left out of the economic miracle.

By lunchtime I was in Liebenwalde where I asked about campsites at the tourist office. Alas, there seemed to be none between Liebenwalde and Berlin. On second thoughts, maybe there was one in Oranienburg.

I cycled on to Bernöwe, mainly following the Havel Kanal. There was an old farmhouse in the village with a café and a tourist office inside. I devoured an ice-cream and asked the lass about campgrounds.

"Oh, yes. There's a campground at the harbour, a very nice one!"

I cycled on, following the Havel Kanal with the occasional barge transporting goods and numerous motorised boats chugging along next to me. Just before Oranienburg was a large lock but I didn't stay to watch. It was getting late and I wanted to get to camp. I didn't feel confident about the campsite, my gut instinct told me that something wasn't quite right. I pedalled into town, past the palace and found the camp site at the harbour. No go! It was only for campervans. No tents allowed. I headed to the tourist office and was pleased to discover that there was a quite basic campground twenty minutes ride down the road. It was easy to find so disaster was avoided. The sky had been rumbling and grumbling for the last few hours and it felt like it would rain so I booked a cabin for two nights. I had no desire to sleep, huddled in the centre of my tent with water dripping all around me. I felt that what I was doing was challenging enough without adding a wet tent and wet clothes to the equation.

# | 25 |

## Two Schrebergarten

### Oranienburg to Potsdam, 77 km

My cousin, Dorothee, collected me at noon and we set off to view her Schrebergarten, or allotment. A Schrebergarten is a simple German solution to the problem of city people living in apartment blocks who would like to have a garden. Blocks of land in less desirable areas such as along railway lines are leased by the local authority and subdivided into garden plots. These are rented out at peppercorn rates to anyone who wants one. The occupants are allowed to build a simple house and a garden shed or two on their plot. They are required to turn the remainder of the block into an orchard, vegie patch and a flower patch and so on.

Dorothee paid €100 per annum for her Schrebergarten. She also had to purchase the block from the previous renters at half of the agreed improved value. The improvements on Dorothee's block consisted of three fruit trees, two patches of lawn, some gardens in a wild state and a small brick cottage of three rooms with electricity connected but no running water. There was a tap outside. There were three small sheds at the back, one of which had a thunderbox toilet in it.

Many people live in their Schrebergarten houses over the summer months when it's warm enough to live (and shower) outside most of the time. Dorothee planned to do the same when her house had been made more habitable. We visited some of her friends who had a similar set-up. Their two smallest rooms were a bedroom, and a bathroom, except for the shower which was outside. The largest room was a kitchen and living room with the smelly, messy cooking also done outside.

What impressed me most about the Schrebergarten idea was the potential for community life and co-operation. The only fences were metre high wire mesh so everyone could look into their neighbour's garden, and indeed, three or four gardens on either side. This meant that the potential for nosy neighbours being a disruptive distraction could be dangerously high, but it also meant that people were under pressure to be good citizens, to care properly for their plots, and to keep their pets under control.

Even in my few hours there, I could see that good neighbourliness also included swapping plants and cuttings, helping each other with more difficult tasks, keeping an eye on others' gardens when people were absent, chatting over the fence, and generally looking out for each other. Dorothee had had some difficulty with removing a screw holding in a lamp. A neighbour came to do it for her. Another neighbour had a trailer and took loads to the rubbish tip for a small fee. A gentleman further down the lane had a collection of electrical tools which he was happy to use, it helped others without those tools, made their purchase more economical, but most importantly, it gave him a feeling of pride and satisfaction in being able to help solve another person's building issues. I could see good economics and positive mental health all round.

To get from Oranienburg to Potsdam, I had to skirt around the edge of Berlin. This section was not nearly as beautiful as the previous week had been. I spent much of the day cycling through suburbs on the outskirts of Berlin with the odd bit of forest thrown in for a change.

Of more serious concern was the German love-story with cobblestones. They were everywhere! And my bike and I did not like them. They shook us around until my teeth rattled and the screws on my bike threatened to fall out from the vibrations. It couldn't possibly be healthy for me or for my bike. Most bike paths in the countryside were bitumen or cement but as soon as we reached any sort of built-up area, the streets became cobblestone. Even when the streets were bitumen, as some were, the intersections were still cobblestone. Maddening! An unusual result of this is that I never saw any teenage boys hooning around on skateboards or young children trying out their new roller skates on wobbly legs.

By this time, I was ready for a few days' break. Potsdam has a collection of royal palaces and I was raring to find that elusive prince. I thought that two or three days would be enough to capture one. I headed off to Sansoucci Palace; meaning "Without Care" in French, which was the language of choice for the rich and powerful in those days. Sansoucci was built by Friedrich der Große (Frederick the Great) from 1745 to 1747. The palace is set in Sanssouci Park which is massive with its hundreds of mature oaks and other splendid trees. Three thousand fruit trees were planted in Friedrich's time as well.

Gracefully reposing on top of a hill, the palace overlooks five or six terraces of vineyards and the park below. Directly in the centre, just below the vineyards, a fountain in the centre of a large circular pool spouted water high in the air. This was set up in Friedrich's era too, but the technology required to power the fountain hadn't developed to the point where it could be used. It took another hundred years before people could stand in awe at the sight of so much water shooting pointlessly through the air; all in the search for beauty. From the fountain, a wide sandy boulevard led through the park to the Neues Palais at the other end. Part way along this path, a circular lawn with classical statues lining the edge sent walkers off into a number of smaller paths radiating out in geometrical fashion. It was all very magnificent.

I toured Sanssouci and discovered it is a very small palace with only twelve bedrooms or living rooms. Friedrich lived here most years from April to October, so I suppose that made Sanssouci Park his Schrebergarten and the palace his summer house. I guessed he didn't need to shower outdoors like modern-day Schrebergarten enthusiasts but then again, people didn't bathe so often in those days.

In the garden on one side of the palace was Friedrich's grave, a simple concrete slab with his name on it. A dozen potatoes had been placed on the grave. Next to Friedrich's grave, I saw some smaller graves with a word or two in flowing cursive script. These graves were too small for adults and I didn't think Friedrich had any children. There was a mystery which needed to be solved! I asked around and discovered the small graves belonged to Friedrich's favourite dogs. He loved his dogs. But the potatoes on his grave? My informant went on to clear up this mystery:

*Friedrich lived in a time of great food insecurity. Wars, undeveloped agricultural practices, the smaller variety of available crops, and unfavourable weather often led to food shortages or even famine. With the discovery of South America, an array of new foods arrived in Europe. Tomatoes, maize, and potatoes had been unknown in the old countries. Friedrich saw these new foods and decided that potatoes could go a long way to solve the issue of food security. He ordered the people to plant, harvest, and use potatoes. Farmers didn't know how to grow and harvest them, cooks didn't know what to do with them, and nobody liked to eat them, so the experiment looked to become a huge failure.*

*Friedrich withdrew to his study and had a long, quiet think. He ordered a crop to be planted nearby and the field to be well guarded by his army. The crop grew and flourished. The people wandering past thought that anything that needed to be guarded so well day and night must be really good, so good, in fact, that they wanted some for themselves. Friedrich quietly ordered the guards to relax their vigilance, to have a bit of a sleep while on duty. The people sneaked past the guards, dug up some potatoes, cooked them somehow, and decided that potatoes were **good**!*

Ever since then, the Germans have loved potatoes whether boiled, fried, mashed, roasted, in dumplings, as chips, or in a soup. And ever since then, the German people have been thankful to Friedrich for bringing them potatoes to eat. To this day, they show their gratitude by putting potatoes on his grave.

I didn't find a prince. I think they were all away on holidays, or something.

# | 26 |

# Two Rebellions

## Potsdam to the Germany-Czechia Border, 319 km

Leaving Potsdam, the route followed the Havel Kanal, through yet more forest, fields and villages. I lunched on bread rolls and cheese in a small village with a miniscule supermarket then proceeded on my way. Having lost sight of the route signs, I checked the route, any route on Maps.me. The app sent me onto a wide dirt track through forest. "OK," I thought, "I'll do this and see what happens. I don't like dirt tracks disappearing into the forest." It only got worse. A sharp bend took me onto a sand path which became a four-wheel drive track with deep loose sand I tried to cycle on the only solid surface, the bit between the wheel ruts. Even this wasn't solid enough and I slipped and slid until I fell off my bike. I ended up pushing my bike and swearing under my breath for the next two hours until I eventually reached bitumen and a proper route sign at the other end of the forest.

A quick cycle early the next day took me to Lutherstadt Wittenberg. Before Luther challenged the established Christian church and became famous, it would have simply been called Wittenberg. Luther had lived in an old monastery. The building is now old and quaint, the interiors are equally old and quaint.

Of most interest to me was Luther's life with his wife, an ex-nun of aristocratic descent, Katharina von Bora. As a priest, he should never have gotten married or had any close physical relationship with anyone at all. They had four sons and four daughters together, money was often tight, they took in students as paying boarders, and often had numerous other visitors as well. Many times, there were up to forty people sitting at the huge dining table for supper. Katharina must have been an amazing woman. While Luther was busy rebelling against the Christian world, she kept the finances ticking over by running a huge garden attached to the house and a couple of acres of extra garden outside the town. She also had poultry, some cows, and some pigs to bring in extra pennies.

After supper, Luther would retire to his study with a group of interested people. There they would spend the evening discussing religion and other matters of importance. No doubt Katharina was busy cleaning up the kitchen and planning the next day's house and farm work while all the rebellious talk was happening next door. The study has been kept as it was five hundred years ago, very simple, bare boards, a few shelves, a bench or two and not much else. Oh, for the simple life; for the men, that is.

At the other end of the town is the church with the famous door upon which Luther is supposed to have nailed his ninety-five theses. Whether he actually did this or not, is a matter of some dispute. Either way, the original wooden door was burnt down when the church was largely destroyed in 1760 during a battle of the Seven Years War. Over a hundred years later, King Friedrich Wilhelm IV ordered new bronze doors to be installed where the old wooden ones had been. The new doors have the text of Luther's theses inscribed on them in their original Latin form. Of course, there was a crowd of selfie-taking tourists in front of them.

By this time, it was late July and the weather began to really heat up. So far, the days had been pleasantly warm, but not too hot. There had been the occasional wind and rain to keep me on my toes but nothing too serious. This was all about to change with a record-breaking heat wave forecast to torture all central and southern Europe. The first signs of the hell to come were already there as I cycled out of Lutherstadt Wittenberg.

Heading to Torgau, I cycled along the bitumen path, caught between the heat of the sun pounding down from above and the heat of the asphalt rising like an oven from below. Foolishly, I had decided to take a short cut from the official shady, riverside route which doglegged around the curve of the river. "Why go around?" I had thought. "Why not just cut straight across?" A great idea, except the first section was on yet another sandy path between the fields until later it became black, unforgiving bitumen. I was caught in the open on a thirty-two-degree day with a hot south-easterly blowing against my cheek. Fields of dried grain stretched into the distance on both sides and there wasn't a scrap of shade anywhere.

I passed a field of sunflowers, their golden-yellow petals shrivelled and fallen to the ground. Their bare, brown heads hung in shame.

"It's not meant to be like this," they rustled as I cycled past.

I stopped and gulped down half a bottle of Fanta and set off doggedly towards the village in the distance. My mind wavered and roamed, no thought stayed long enough to take form or depth. Eventually, "Fuelled by Fanta" stuck as I pondered my need to swig so much sugar. I could become a cycling advertisement for Fanta. Picture this:

*A gorgeous young woman cycles smoothly across a plain, the sun is beating down on her baseball cap perched cheekily on her head. Her long, lustrous hair blows in the breeze. She stops, placing her feet on the ground, and showing well-muscled legs tanned to a soft, golden brown. Cut to her face as she drinks from the Fanta bottle. Some beads of moisture pearl on her smooth skin. Ride a bike, drink Fanta and you too can be this beautiful.*

Sound familiar? How about a reality shot as follows:

*A scruffy old lady in cycling shorts and a fluoro yellow vest is cycling frantically on a dusty path through the fields. She stops, placing her feet on the ground, and showing the abrupt colour changes on her legs, white below the sock line and above the shorts line, freckled brown in-between. Cut to her face as she takes her helmet off and swigs from the Fanta bottle. Wet hair sticks out in all directions, curls grimed by dust and sweat. Her face is red from exertion, her nose is scarlet. A line of sweat trickles down her cheek as her eyes gaze determinedly into the distance. This is a woman who knows the tough stuff. She's a winner!*

I think the Fanta people would rather go for the first advertisement. They'll have to get someone else to do it though, my hair isn't long enough to blow in the breeze. Besides, it wasn't a breeze, it was a hot south-easterly wind.

At camp that night I met two Canadians, Kiersten and Denis, who were doing the whole Elbe route from Prague to Hamburg and then doing some extra cycling in Denmark before heading home from Amsterdam. They were cycling in three-wheeler trikes, leaning back with their legs on the horizontal and Canadian flags flying high above them. They claimed this way was much more comfortable and I suspected that they might even have been much faster than me. This was something else to consider for me to use in the future, although they didn't talk about the difficulties of taking their much wider tricycles on the very narrow cycling paths which we sometimes had.

Cycling from Torgau to Riesa, I seemed to be developing issues. When I left camp, I could feel something rubbing at my front wheel. I flipped the bike over to check it out and in doing so managed to snap a screw out of the front bike stand so it no longer held the weight. I fixed the wheel issue but from then on, I always had to lean the bike against a wall or a tree.

My bank decided to cancel one of my ATM cards due to a security breach and PayPal wouldn't let me log in. They wanted me to verify my account but would only send me the code via a text message to my Australian phone number which I couldn't receive because my Australian SIM was in a secure place in Frankfurt.

Lastly, I couldn't get wifi anywhere. It was the same old issue as further north. It was often advertised but never seemed to work. The Germans all said that this was an issue in Brandenburg, but I suspected that it was an issue across all Germany. I was running out of internet on my phone too.

Then, while setting up camp in Riesa, one of the pieces connecting the ridge pole to the side poles of my tent, snapped and flew past my ear taking my good humour with it. Luckily, I was camping at the Bootshaus, a local boating group which offered basic accommodation to small groups and cyclists. There was a school group of twenty-nine cycling students staying the night, so the manager and his son were cooking a barbeque for them. Next to the barbeque was an open door to a workshop full of shelves, boxes, and drawers of odds and ends. I showed the manager my broken connector. He nudged his son and gestured to the workshop. The son, a young man about twenty years old, took my bits and tried to stick them together with a bit of tape. I knew it wouldn't work but thought he needed to work that out for himself. He thought a bit, scratched around for a few minutes and surfaced with a long section of thin, metal bar, just like a round file. It fitted into the hole, so he cut the correct length off, filed the ends smooth, scratched around a bit more, surfaced again with a few different sized nuts, tried one out, chucked it, tried the next, and gave a happy sigh before handing over a perfect connecting piece with two proper pole extensions and a bit of round file held on with a nut for the third extension. It worked brilliantly. So lucky! What would I have done without this young man and his ingenuity?

Having survived the night quite well in my tent with its newly engineered connecting piece, I paid the manager twenty euros for his son. He didn't want to accept anything, but I insisted on the grounds that the lad had saved me the expense of a night in a hotel and a new tent. First issue solved.

I contacted my daughter in Australia about the PayPal issue. She got on the phone to PayPal and sorted it out. Second issue solved.

I set off for Meissen, found a café en route and was relaxing with my coffee in the shade when a middle-aged couple sat next to me. We started chatting. They were so impressed with my bike ride, my plans, and what I had already achieved that I gave him a kangaroo pin and her a small stuffed koala of the type one gives to young children. They were very keen to pay for my coffee. It was lovely to chat to such supportive people. Unfortunately, I didn't get their names or take a photo which was remiss of me. I have found that I usually only think of these things when it's already too late.

I rode on to Meissen, sorted out my phone with Telekom and put thirty euros onto my Telekom account. That gave me enough data to keep chugging along. Third issue solved.

I went to a bike shop, got the stand screw replaced and got the mechanic to fix me up another replacement piece for the tent connector in case the other one also snapped. Fourth issue solved. What a day!

In amongst all of this, I did a tour of the Meissen factory showrooms to see how Europe's finest porcelain has been made for hundreds of years. They still make the onion pattern porcelain and it's still painted by hand. The museum, with its three thousand pieces of different types of porcelain was enough to make my eyes quite glaze over. I would have like to have purchased something but transporting it by bicycle could become a bit of an issue. I've inherited a Meissen dinner set which has a few broken pieces. It would be nice to replace those. That will go in the "next time" basket. I loved cycling through this area and could envision coming back to it for a deeper, more intense exploration another time.

Cycling to camp, very contented with everything I had achieved during the day, I was overtaken by a young lass flying by on her bike. I overtook her later and we leapfrogged each other into camp. Iris had taken a week off from work and was cycling from Leipzig to Prague. She had cycled about one hundred kilometres on her first day without too much difficulty, but then she was only twenty-eight years old, fit and very active.

I set off for Heidenau, leaving Iris behind. Two hours later, I stopped for a coffee. She found me and we had a good chat about life in general. She left, I followed. I stopped under a bridge to snack on a muesli bar, Iris zipped past and waved. I cycled on and pulled over in a market in Dresden to purchase some supplies for a picnic lunch. Iris tapped me on the shoulder, so we set off again together and enjoyed a picnic in the shade of a tree on the banks of the river. I had bought some juicy cherries. They were delicious! After lunch we accepted fate and cycled on in tandem until we arrived at the Wostra campground where I had planned to spend two nights. I was desperately in need of time to catch up on my diary, to get on-line to do a few posts on my blog, and just to relax for a day. A swim or two were also on the agenda as the weather was still quite uncomfortably hot. Iris cycled on towards Prague.

These were the sorts of short-term meetings which occurred so often on this trail. They were invariably friendly, people helped each other out, talked about possible campsites further on, discussed each other's plans and options. Although I was cycling alone, I was never truly alone.

FKK: Freie Kôrper Kulture, Free Body Culture, Naturism, Nudism. Three short words which encapsulate the German predilection for nude bathing and sunbaking. To be naked may be natural but for some reason society esteems clothing and fashion beyond all measure. "Clothes maketh the man," said Shakespeare in Hamlet, copying the idea from the ancient Greeks.

In more recent times, citizens of the now defunct Democratic Republic of Germany, the old East Germany, became enamoured of the FKK concept. Living under such stark restrictions and such a repressive regime, the ordinary people had had little opportunity to rebel or to voice their displeasure with life and politics. They knew that the authorities disapproved of the rampant freedom implicit in spending a day naked in the sun; what could be more decadent than sunshine, nakedness and just lolling about? The powers-that-be didn't know how to address the problem so the people voted with their bodies and became FKK aficionados. Thirty years after the fall of the Berlin Wall and the DDR, the FKK culture was still going strong in east Germany.

My campground at Heidenau sat between two very different swimming complexes. To the left was a standard, rectangular, chlorinated, child-infested swimming pool. To the right was a lake surrounded by lawn, shady trees and a sandy beach littered with naked bodies. It was thirty-two degrees Celsius and I desperately wanted a swim so in the interest of historical research, I gathered up my towel and my courage with the intention of going FKK swimming.

I had worried about this all morning. What would it be like to undress completely, in the open, in front of everyone? Would anyone look at me? Would they all laugh at all my white skin, rolls of fat and sagging bits? Where did people undress – in the change room? On the beach? Was there shade? Could I wear sunglasses and a hat? Would my white bits get sunburnt? Where should I look when walking towards a gentleman? There were so many questions and so much uncertainty but what's the point of experiencing life if we don't grab our courage by the scruff and push the boundaries?

I planned my attack, went to the shops, bought bread rolls and ham for lunch, rode to the FKK beach, paid my entrance fee, and went in. I found a spot of shade, laid out my sarong, and stripped. No-one watched, no-one cared. I occupied myself for a short while with my lunch, read my novel to its conclusion, and looked around. No-one was looking at me. No-one cared. I sauntered down to the beach, entered the water, swam around a bit. The lake was OK but not brilliant. The water was pretty dark, cool but not cold. It was wet.

I looked around and studied the people. Most were my age group, a few solo women in their twenties or thirties, a few parents with little children, a few older children. Many of the older people were in small social groups, two or three couples chatted together. There were no teenagers. I walked back to my sarong and still no-one looked at me or cared. So much for all my nagging doubts and worries. It was all very civilized, just naked.

The sun was streaming into my tent by 5.30 a.m. Usually I grumbled and mumbled a bit, scratched around for my blindfold and put it on so I could sleep a few hours longer. This time, I got out of bed and got myself sorted to roll out of camp by 7.30. I knew the day was going to be quite warm, over thirty degrees again, so I wanted to make the most of the cool morning. Cycling at that hour was fantastic, compared to later. Not only was the air cool and crisp but the whole environment had been refreshed overnight and didn't seem so weighed down by the heat.

At first, the landscape was similar to the previous few days; the lazy, wide, Elbe River, fields and villages, nothing very exciting. Then, I was heading for some hills, the river wound its way between them and before I knew it, I was cycling in Saxon Switzerland. This is a region well known for its beauty, steep cliffs, and limestone rocks. I lunched in the shade and peered up at a bridge joining two limestone towers. This was part of the Malerweg, (The Painters' Trail) a hiking route starting in Czechia and crossing the Elbstein Mountains before finishing in Pirna. This bridge is featured on the front cover of one of my many travel bucket list books at home and I had long wanted to see it. I had thought that I could cycle over the bridge but hadn't realised how high up it was, that it wasn't possible to cycle up there. Peering up at this bridge and the tiny dots which were the people strolling over it, I immediately put the Malerweg onto my hiking trail bucket list for some unknown date in the distant future.

# | 27 |

# A Quick Lesson in Executing One's Enemies

## Germany-Czechia Border to Prague, 164 km

Nervous with excitement at the prospect of entering yet another foreign country, I crossed the border into Czechia a short time later. This was the most non-descript of borders. A small, white, cement block with a D on the German side and a C on the Czech side, with a small black cross on top to show the exact line ... and that was it! – the border! The saddest side effect of the whole EU concept for us Australians is the lack of borders between EU countries. No passport stamps to collect for bragging rights, no stories of grumpy border officials to embroider, and no great excitement of a new country unless you manufacture it for yourself, which is what I did. I squatted next to the cement block and tried, quite unsuccessfully, to take some selfies with the C and the D. Tragic, really.

The only other cross-border excitement left to me was the search for an ATM followed by the usual confusion as I grappled with a new set of notes, coins and values. The exchange rate was sitting at about fifteen Czech koruny to one $A so one hundred koruny was about $A6.50. Alternatively, one koruna was about 6.6 cents. I could see that my brain was going to get quite a work-out with the mental arithmetic needed for every drink or ice-cream. The ATM very politely asked which combination of notes I wanted, then spat them out with scary efficiency. The notes were all crisp and cleanish with a lady or a gentleman on one side. None of them were looking directly at the user. What were they afraid of? That I'd tell them that they were not important enough to be on a bank note? That they would have to leave and find somewhere else to live?

The coins were a different matter. The one, two, and five Koruna coins were silver and small. The ten and the twenty were dark brown with numbers difficult to read. The fifty Koruna had a shiny copper coloured circle around a brass coloured centre. All these different coins were quite confusing when in the hands of a dumb tourist with poor short-distance eyesight standing at a checkout with an impatient cashier snapping numbers in Czech. I started pouring all the coins into my hand and letting the cashiers choose which ones they wanted, just like I've seen old people do at home!

Supper was a mound of sauerkraut surrounded by eight small potato dumplings filled with minced pork, a real Czech peasant meal designed to fill the bellies of people doing hard physical work every day.

I realised that "Labem" means "Elbe" and "nad Labem" means "on the Elbe." My first full day's ride was fairly uneventful. I was the only one on the path for the first hour or two, then I passed the occasional cyclist. Slowly the trickle of cyclists grew to the usual horde. I passed a few large groups of elderly people cycling in a long row. I stopped at one stage because the path had morphed into a deeply rutted farm track with a surface partly of mud and partly of weeds. A group of about twenty elderly Germans were coming towards me. The big groups were invariably Germans.

One over-sized lady slipped and slid, screeched, then fell off her bike and landed on her side, spread-eagled over the path, ruts and all. I quickly stood my bike on its stand and raced to her side along with two men of her group. Others gathered around. We checked for any injuries, then let her lay still for a few minutes until she was ready to be helped to a sitting position. A few minutes later she was able to be hauled to her feet. The leader of the group thanked me for stopping and then I cycled on, very glad that she hadn't suffered any serious injuries. As I left, the lady was explaining to her friends how she came to fall off her bike, so she was obviously OK.

Later, the sky darkened, the clouds banged together, thunder rumbled, and I raced for a rotunda I could see in a park nearby. Another cyclist had the same idea as well as a young Czech man who had had a bit too much to drink. The young man spent the duration of the storm talking to me in Czech. He could count to five in German, showed me a picture of his two daughters and was quite intense, he was actually a bit scary. The thunder settled, the other cyclist apologised to me for his countryman and we all left, with me racing away as fast as I could.

It was so hot at night that I was quite keen for a swim to help me cool off. I considered jumping into the Labe/Elbe but felt unsure about the safety aspects. There was quite a lot of industry along the river and the question arose as to what chemicals and other rubbish might have been floating downstream, unseen to the naked eye. There was also the other issue of swimming safety. The river looked to be flowing quite fast. I am not a strong swimmer and, being an Australian who often hears reports of drownings in the news at home, I take water safety very seriously. I didn't go swimming but just looked on enviously when five or six young men jumped in the water with a great splash. They had a raucous time throwing a ball around and just generally being young and full of life.

As I left Roudnice, I came across a young German chap, Walter, who was cycling from Dresden to Slovenia. He had so much gear with him that I initially thought he must be en route to the South Pole, but no, it was only a four-week cycling vacation. Rather embarrassingly, I nearly ran him off the path. I misread the sign and turned right; he turned left as we were supposed to do and just avoided me. Whoops! He was very gracious about that too close encounter, but I suspect he was quite pleased when I turned off at my next stop, Melnik.

Melnik is one of those lovely old towns which was established to support a monastery, cathedral or castle. It's high on a bluff overlooking the confluence of the Labe and Vlatave Rivers. I wheeled through the main square, grabbing a local sweet as I went. It was like a donut dough wrapped around a stick, rolled in sugar and cinnamon, then roasted over a grill. Quite delicious.

Hunger and culture satisfied, I headed straight for camp and the huge outdoor pool complex which, fortunately, was just across the road. I was worried that there would be hundreds of people in the pool, but I almost had it to myself. Most adults were sunbaking on the lawn or supervising littlies in the shallow pool section. The teenagers were all at the water slides over in another pool. I swam, then had a chat with two old ladies who had not a word of English between them. I learnt that "dobre" means "good." Our conversation consisted of hand gestures accompanied by "dobre" and many, many smiles. It was all dobre.

Another very early start saw me cycle into Prague by 2 p.m. There were about six or eight campgrounds all in the same two streets near the river. I wanted to stay right at the river itself so was looking for "River Camping." When I asked a local, I was pointed to a narrow blue gate. It was locked. Maps.me insisted that the gate was the only entrance for cyclists and just refused to give me any clues as to where the main entrance was. I went around the block looking for the vehicle entrance and, after much hunting, eventually found it. Even as I was cycling through the main gate, Maps.me tried to tell me to go around the whole block again and enter through the locked blue gate.

The Vlatava looked quite inviting. Steps led down into the water, other people were swimming and splashing about so I figured it would be safe enough for me. By this time, I was so hot and bothered that the thought of a slow and painful death caused by chemical pollution didn't particularly worry me. If I didn't cool down quickly, I was going to drop dead with heat exhaustion anyway!

Following my swim, and feeling much more like a human being, I watched the locals practising their skills on the white-water section of the river. This was an artificial channel set up next to the bank with plastic pipes jutting out into the water from the shore to give the white-water effect. A sign stated that this was the training river for the Olympic team. It was fun watching the young people pit their paddling skills against the raging water. Some zipped through with so much flair and skill while others battled against the rapids, sometimes going forwards, at other times, sideways, backwards and even upside down for a few heart-stopping seconds.

Prague is such a well-known and popular tourist destination that I decided to spend a few days there being a tourist. Unfortunately, it was so hot that a normal day of sightseeing was virtually impossible. The sun beat down on the paving stones, locking in the heat to fry everyone from above and from below. The air shimmered, tree leaves drooped in exhaustion and it all became an energy-sapping endurance test. Some waiters in the main square held hoses and squirted water high in the air for passing tourists to walk underneath. "What a good idea," I thought. Further on, a fire truck was parked, and some firemen were doing the same thing with fire hoses and vastly more force. I walked under one fire hose and delighted in the cool stream as is landed in my hair and slid blissfully down my face and back. I went back for more, and again, until I thought that I'd better stop before I got so wet that I bordered on uncivilised.

It seemed a smart idea to go into a museum, preferably one in an old stone building which tend to stay cooler for longer. I went into the old Town Hall and learnt about Jan Hus and an unusual Czech invention - defenestration, a quick and effective form of execution.

*Jan was born to a poor peasant family in the countryside of Bohemia in 1372. He must have been a very smart lad because he escaped the dung heaps of peasant life and rose to become Dean of Philosophy at the Charles University in Prague. While there, he became known for two completely separate ideas which are still of import in Czech life today.*

1. *Diacritics: Jan invented these little symbols above some letters which aid in pronunciation although they make spelling even more complicated than otherwise. Thus, they have "salátů" (salad), "tuňák" (tuna), "pomerančový" (an orange), and "čokoládový" (chocolate).*

2. *Religious ideals: Jan fought against the financial and corrupt, but very common, practices of the Church which encouraged priests to sell indulgences to sinners and thereby made the Church an extremely wealthy institution. This was at least a hundred years before Luther established the Protestant movement in Wittenberg. Jan also preached in Czech rather than Latin, making the teachings of the Bible available to the ordinary person. Understandably, the Pope was rather unimpressed. Jan was excommunicated in 1410 but that didn't stop him. In 1415 he was invited to Germany to appear before a theological court and recant his views. He was granted safe passage to do so. Jan fronted the court at Constance, but being a stubborn soul, refused to recant. Despite his offer of safe passage to Germany, he ended up being burnt at the stake on the 6$^{th}$ July 1415.*

*Jan's supporters, who called themselves Hussites, were furious! They were so angry that they began to get even more vocal and physical. In 1419, some Hussites entered the Town Hall in Prague and threw seven councillors out of the window where they landed splattered all over the footpath.*

Defenestration, a new and relatively simple method of execution was born. There was no need to pay an executioner, victims were just thrown out of a high window. It was a pity about the people walking underneath.

In 1483, there was another defenestration. The mayor was thrown out of the window to land on the footpath below, alive but with broken legs. No-one took pity on him. He was dragged, broken legs notwithstanding, to the Old Town Square where he was executed.

Prague's third defenestration occurred in 1618 when a group of Protestant noblemen threw two Catholic lords and their secretary out of the window, this time from the Prague Castle. The victims survived by falling onto a dung heap but the act itself sparked the Thirty Years War. Some arguments take a very long time to resolve.

Today more than fifty per cent of Czechs claim to be unconcerned about religion which is probably good for the street cleaners and the pedestrians wandering about below. Jan Hus is commemorated on the 6$^{th}$ July every year when Czechs have one of their many public holidays, twelve at last count. A quick look at the holidays tells all one needs to know about the modern Czech's psyche. Of the twelve public holidays, six are political, five are religious and only one, New Year's Day, is to have a party and celebrate life.

I went back into town on yet another stinking hot day to try to get information about a possible route out of Prague towards the south. I had been receiving messages by concerned friends and family telling me not to cycle through the hills south of Prague; it was too hot, and the hills were not suited for cycling anyway. The National Tourist Office had a small topographical map which indicated that a route west to-wards Regensburg in Germany might be best. An eastern route was a bit flatter but would have taken me to Vienna which was a fair distance out of my way.

When I arrived back at camp in the afternoon, there was a Scottish gentleman with a rickshaw camped next to me. Len was cycling in his rickshaw from Edinburgh to Istanbul, partly to raise funds for cancer research and partly to get into the Guiness Book of Records. He had to document every day of his trip, collect receipts and signatures as ev-idence, record himself talking about his trip for at least ten minutes every day, and he also had to have a GPS tracker monitor his rickshaw's every move for the whole journey. He once lost a whole day because he cycled thirty-five kilometres and then realised that he hadn't switched the GPS tracker on, so he had to return to where he started and do it all over again the next day. This seemed to be an amazing amount of work but as I thought about it, I realised that the Guiness people need to be one hundred per cent certain that the task was actually undertaken and properly completed before they can include it into their record books.

Len was also greatly fuelled by Fanta. Maybe I should include him in my advertisement. His regular routine included a hot chocolate and a huge toasted cheese sandwich on arrival in camp followed soon after by a self-cooked meal, usually of pasta or rice with other ingredients tossed in. He was rather bemused by my concerns about cycling over hilly terrain in the current weather; hot, hotter and even hotter. His theory was that he just cycled slowly and worked through it. "Drink heaps, rest often and eventually you'll get there," was his theory.

So, I decided to stop whingeing and just DO IT!

# | 28 |

## Slowly Roasting in Czechia

### Prague to Babylon, 187 km

How many times have I got lost, physically or psychologically because I was off with the fairies and not observing my surroundings or the people around me? The clues have always been there, but I need to see and evaluate them, join the dots and make decisions accordingly. Leaving Prague, I had a spectacular failure of practical observation and dot-joining.

When I left Prague in the early morning, the sight-seeing boats were all still moored along the riverbanks, the tourist day hadn't started yet. The tourists were all still in bed, except for a few sleeping on the footpath at Charles Bridge and being woken by the police. The sun was low in the sky, gently caressing the river. I knew that in two hours, it would be absolute bedlam all around Charles Bridge with portrait artists, souvenir sellers, ticket touts and con artists all vying for the tourist dollars and euros. I was quite glad to be leaving but just needed a coffee first. A few kilometres of streets lined with old patrician houses led me past a sports centre with big wall advertisements of Fed Tennis and the Davis Cup. Just past that, I spotted a McDonalds – spot on! I knew I'd get a coffee, some carbs and a clean toilet. My requirements were very simple by this time. One coffee, and one egg and bacon muffin later, I set off, having checked my route on Maps.me.

This is where I needed to improve my observation skills. I should have seen that the proposed route was not suitable as it was going on a major road with a great deal of traffic, and a broken footpath which obviously didn't get much use. The footpath disappeared and I found myself riding alongside all the traffic but without a bike lane or any sort of protection. Cars, trucks, and buses were all flying past me with only centimetres to spare, their slipstream causing me to wobble on my bike. An intersection ahead with large overhead signs to regional towns was morphing into a freeway with even crazier traffic. It was terrifying!

What should I do? I certainly couldn't go on in the same direction. I had to turn back, which I did. I walked back on the side of the road with traffic racing past at meteoric speeds and horns blaring at me. It was so dangerous and really stupid! When I was safe again, I headed to the river where a well surfaced bike path promised a much quieter ride. I heard a siren. Was that the police out looking for me?

Having had such a fright, my powers of observation and deduction kicked in at long last. Maps.me wanted to send me off the riverside path into the hills. I noticed the town I was heading for was on the same river and the cycling signs indicated the path would go the whole way to that town but along the river. Why should I take the Maps.me route when it obviously headed into the hills bordering the valley? Why not stick to the river? The river path was a few kilometres longer, but it was cycling heaven compared to unnecessary cycling on the road and up and down all those hills. I followed the river to Cernovise where I met two Dutch people who had cycled all the way from the Netherlands. "Forget the routes, stick to the rivers and you'll be OK," they said. It made sense.

From that day on, I looked at the local labelled cycle paths, at Maps.me, at Google Maps, at local topographic maps on information boards, and at the environment around me. I also asked the people I met, the people running the campgrounds, or the people in the tourist information centres. Only then, did I make an informed decision about my route. Aahhh …. The value of experience.

In Dobřicovice I found a bike shop run by two of the loveliest people on earth. My rear tyre had been a bit soft for a while, but I hadn't been able to get my pump to attach properly, in order to pump it up. The lady gave me a cold water and a coffee, we discussed my Ortlieb bags, and she told me all about her sister who lived in Sydney and whom she had visited a few times. Meanwhile, her husband pumped up my tyres, checked the valves, and checked my pump. It was all working. They suggested I use the pumps at service stations as I had those types of valves. I wanted to pay them, but they just wouldn't accept any money, so I gave them a toy koala to hang amongst their coffee cups instead.

Lunch was a huge toasted cheese, ham and tomato sandwich followed by a chia and fruit yoghurt out of a jar for the princely sum of 130 koruny, from an atmospheric book-lined café. I sat outside in the shade of an elm tree. I loved Czechia! I just wasn't enamoured of their motorways.

I rode on in the heat, following the river and cycling past numerous families cooling off in the water. By mid-afternoon, I had arrived in Karlštejn. The manager of the campground spoke very little English but had a great sense of humour. She beamed over my Australian passport, chortled with glee when I indicated that I was quite hot, and waved me off for a swim before finalising payment. I must have looked just as fried as I felt. Swimming in the river was just magnificent! Waist deep with clear dark water, pebbles on the bottom, and a slow, lazy current; it was exactly what I needed.

Karlštejn has the king of all castles. I was planning to cycle further towards Germany on the following day, but woke up at two in the morning and asked myself: "Why? The campground is pleasant, the river is swimmable, the castle is imposing. Why not stay and be a tourist for the day?" So, I did.

Karlštejn Castle was built from 1348 to 1365 by Charles IV who was the King of Bohemia and the Holy Roman Emperor. He needed a place to store the Imperial Crown, other imperial jewels and some priceless holy relics under lock and key. These items were kept in the

Great Tower until 1421 when they were under threat from the rebellious Hussites, at which point they were evacuated to Nuremburg. The Hussites attacked the castle a year later. Not being able to get inside and throw the enemy out of the windows, they came up with another novel solution to their problems. They catapulted dead bodies and two thousand carriage loads of dung over the walls into the castle grounds, in an effort to spread disease and death amongst the defenders. Is this where the concept of "a sh#t-storm" started?

Back at camp in the mid-afternoon, I had another swim, dried off in thirty-five seconds, jumped into the water again and stayed there for at least an hour. I spent the time pondering how I was going to keep cycling in the record-breaking heat.

The following day was forecast to be yet another hot day, around thirty-eight degrees Celsius, and I wanted to make best use of the cool hours of the morning. That night, I set my alarm for 5 a.m. and lay back listening to the life around me. The campground was full to overflowing, everyone was in a cheerful Friday-night mood. A group of bikers on big, heavy motorbikes rolled up and stood their bikes in a circle; a ring of steel, just like the pioneers of America and South Africa who rolled their wagons in a defensive circle when they stopped at the end of the day. The bar was open. I was not hopeful of a quiet night.

The bikers, a group of hairy, old blokes sat in the roofed shelter, playing country music and blues on half a dozen guitars, some sang in tune, others with enthusiasm, and all were lubricated with very large glasses of beer. Everyone was happy. They packed up and finished at midnight which the whole camp took for a signal to settle down. A few voices murmured in the darkness, then silence drifted over camp. I woke in the morning to find the bikers all asleep on the ground, well protected by their ring of steel.

I rolled out of camp at daybreak, cycled along the river, between cliffs of rock topped by green, red and yellow trees. The summer had been so long, hot and dry that the trees were under great stress. Many had already started to turn colour and shed their leaves, carpeting the ground with crisp crackling detritus instead of the wet, soggy mulch which normally protects the soil from the winter cold. How were the trees going to survive through the rest of summer, autumn, and winter? How many would survive the following year?

Breakfast was a cup of coffee and a filled roll from the railway station at Beroun. The way out of Beroun was up a very long but not too steep hill. I cycled all the way up with a few stops in-between. From then on, it was up, down and around until I reached Horovice soon after 9 a.m. Where were all those dreadful hills which people had been warning me about and which I had been working myself into such a tizz over? I cycled over and around many hills, but none were big enough or steep enough to be considered dreadful.

Horovice. With a name like that, I really had to go there but it wasn't horrible, and I couldn't see any vices happening either. It did have a big hill with the Tourist Information Office sitting on the other side so up and over I went.

I had originally planned to stop for the night at Horovice but couldn't see any point in arriving at my night's accommodation so early in the morning. What was I going to do for the rest of the day? I decided to keep cycling but didn't think I had the required energy to make it all the way to the next campground on my map. The lady at the Tourist Information was fantastic. With very little English, she managed to understand that I wanted to keep cycling but needed to know what other accommodation options were available further down the track. I settled on a hotel in Rokycany which she booked for me. I was quite looking forward to a night in a hotel.

I left Horovice with my panniers packed with three cans of fizzy fruit flavoured mineral waters in addition to my two water bottles, two bananas, a yoghurt, two bread rolls, and a packet of cheese. I had thirty kilometres to ride in thirty-five-degree heat. I paced myself, rested often in the shade, and drank every last drop of fluid as I was going. By the time I reached Rokycany in the early afternoon the sun was a killer, I was sopping with sweat, and I had a lot less weight in my saddlebags.

Hotel Coros was bliss! A room with an en-suite, a real bed, a sitting area, **and** a small refrigerator. By late afternoon, the thunder boomed, the wind howled, and the heavens opened. The outside world was drenched in a matter of seconds, but I was safe, snug, and very happy in my hotel room.

It was only thirty kilometres from Rokycany to Dobrany but that was enough for me. The sixty-five kilometres in the extreme heat the previous day had knocked a lot of the zing out of me, so I was quite content to just tootle along. I cycled along a lane of apple trees and could see that all the leaves had been burnt by the sun along the bottom half. The leaves were not just dry, they were burnt. There were some hills to go over, but they weren't too bad, and I never had the feeling that it was too much. The countryside was just beautiful with long vistas along rolling hills and quiet country roads. I had no idea where the bicycle route was which I had been trying to follow but my various apps seemed to have done an excellent job of selecting a cycling route for me.

After Dobrany, my next target, and my last stop in Czechia, was the Babylon Autokemp. As campgrounds go, it was one of the best with a huge area of green grass, shady trees, and clean facilities. On top of that, the campground manager offered to wash my clothes for me, the German couple in a nearby campervan lent me their clothes rack, and there was a lovely lake just across the road. Clear water, sand and pebbles underfoot, water slides for the kids and a grassy green bank to laze about on; some people know how to live the good life.

I chatted with the German couple in the evening. They were very curious about my trip, as most people I met were. They lived south of Munich and were able to give me some pointers on getting over the Alps which I knew would be a challenge. I didn't think that I could ride up the Alps, that would be just a tad too difficult. Their suggestion was to cycle to Innsbruck and then to keep going to Pfunds, from where I could take a special shuttle bus for cyclists up to the Brenner Pass at the top of the Alps. From the pass, I could slowly meander downhill all the way to Venice. It was great to hear of some possible options from some locals. Apart from the knowledge gained, it also validated my reluctance to try to cycle up such huge mountains. If other people could take a shuttle bus, then so could I.

# | 29 |

## More Tyre Dramas!

### Babylon to Waldkraiburg, 376 km

I left Babylon, with its many languages; German, Dutch, English and Czech, to cycle to the border with Germany at Furth im Wald. (Furth in the Forest) I had no idea where the border was until I came across a gate in a sagging wire fence surrounded by a veritable forest of signs telling me in German, Czech and English that I was crossing an invisible line. The Czechs warned me that I was leaving Czechia, the Germans welcomed me to Germany, and the EU informed me that both countries were members of the EU. A couple of long-distance cycling routes crossed this point as well as even more long-distance hiking trails and short distance saunters. Every route had its pointer on a signpost and every possible destination was noted as well. Having read all of these signs, I knew exactly where I could go in every direction and how long it would take me to get there.

I camped that night in a canoe camp on the banks of the Regen (Rain) River in Cham. The other campers were all canoeists who were doing trips of a few days or a week on the Regen and staying overnight in canoe camps. These camps are run by the various canoeing organisations, are available for any canoeists, cyclists and hikers, and because of this, have a very different ambience to campgrounds aimed at retirees in motorhomes or families on a beach holiday. Being in amongst small groups of like-minded people was very relaxing. There were no screaming toddlers, no dogs and everyone went to bed early!

The ride from Nittenau to Regensburg was one of those days of which we all dream about. The path followed the river, winding here and there through its narrow valley. The trees and hills were reflected in the river, reeds along the bank swayed in the breeze, the plop of fish breaking the surface broke the hum of insects, and an old bridge led to a picturesque church.

Leaving Regensburg, I looked for the Danube River which I was planning to follow until Passau. I easily found a large bridge crossing over a small river but where was the Danube? I was expecting a large, wide flowing river and instead found that it had shrunk to a much smaller proportion of its normal size. The unseasonably hot summer had had quite a dramatic effect to the point that the river cruise ships which are so popular with so many tourists couldn't sail the whole distance on the Danube anymore. In some stretches, the boats were being replaced by buses and hotels.

Mid-morning, I glanced to my right and saw a mooring pier for a river cruising ship. Why would a cruise ship moor there? I cycled to the information board and discovered there was a building called Valhalla nearby. I had never heard of it, although I did have some idea of the concept of Valhalla in Norse mythology. I looked around, checked over my shoulder to my left, and saw a humungous Parthenon in grey sitting atop a large hill, looming over all who passed beneath it. That was Valhalla? To think that I nearly missed it out of sheer ignorance and lack of observation – again!

I parked my bike and walked up the hill to the steps at the base of the building. The view over the Danube and the plains beyond was magnificent and only got better the higher I climbed. Nearly at the top, I was hailed by a middle-aged man, a German speaker with an accent probably as noticeable as mine. Tibor from Hungary lived and worked in northern Germany. He was returning from a visit to Hungary to see his parents.

"You have to get as much out of life as you can. Don't just sit there and let time go by. Get out and do something!" he said. He took photos of me in front of the scenery, I took photos of him in front of the scenery, and then we both went our separate ways to get as much out of life as we could.

I entered Valhalla, not the real one of Viking lore, but this copy on earth. Through the massive door, I gasped as I entered a large open hall with a richly decorated ceiling. Ludwig I, he who commissioned this Hall of Fame, sat in regal splendour at the other end and observed all who entered. The walls on all four sides were lined with a double row of white marble busts representing over two hundred people from the Germanic nations; politicians, kings and queens, philosophers, scientists, musicians, artists, generals, and writers. A few females were there, but not many.

I had a short chat with Martin Luther and explained that I'd recently visited Jan Hus in Prague. Martin was happy to hear that there is now a huge statue of Jan in Prague's Old Town Square and that the Czechs commemorate his sacrifice with a public holiday every year on the 6th July. I admired Catherine the Great of Russia who had a bust in the hall because she was a German princess from the House of Anhalt. I learnt about Konrad Adenauer, West Germany's first Chancellor after WWII. He was instrumental in setting Germany on a path of reconciliation with the rest of Europe and most importantly with the international Jewish community and Israel.

Most impressive of all was the bust of Sophie Scholl. Taking pride of place on a special pedestal opposite Ludwig I, Sophie was chosen to represent all those brave people who resisted the Nazi movement, and a better choice could not have been made.

*Born in 1921, Sophie was a young woman when the Nazis came to power. Through her brother, a university student, she joined a group of resistance fighters named "The White Rose." They were instrumental in printing and distributing anti-Nazi pamphlets. Sophie, her brother and other members of The White Rose were captured, tried and executed by the Nazis on the 22$^{nd}$ February 1943. She was just 21 years old.*

*Her last words:*
**"... What does my death matter, if through it, thousands of people are awakened and stirred to action?"**

Such courage in the face of a brutal and unjust death is unbelievable and deserving of our utmost respect.

On a lighter note, it had started to rain when I went outside and it rained continuously for the remainder of the day, well, sort of. It wasn't so much rain to begin with, as a constant condensation of humidity resulting in a persistent low-level splatter of water from above, a bit like riding through a slow and indolent sprinkler. Even so, my hands, feet and face were soon quite soggy. I decided to stay in roofed accommodation again as I abhor camping in the rain. Straubing seemed like a good place to aim for.

Shortly before Straubing, I was hailed by a local fellow out walking his two dogs. Straubing was having its annual beer-fest, second in size only to Munich's Oktoberfest. 1.4 million people were expected to visit in the next ten days. The beer-fest would open that evening with a grand parade and every accommodation in town and for miles around was bound to be booked out. With that information imparted, he waved a cheery goodbye and walked on in the rain. I was flummoxed. What to do? I looked on booking.com. There was a room available in a hotel in the centre of town for €125. My benchmark figure for a night in a hotel was half that. I hummed and haaad, pondered and debated. Eventually, I decided that the money was irrelevant, I was wet and wanted to sleep in a dry room. The grand parade would be a bonus.

There were more people walking in the parade than had lined up to see it but that's how it often is in small towns. It meant that, with the audience being only one person deep, I didn't have to fight to get a good view. A young lad in a fire-fighter's uniform walked importantly up and down the rope lining the route, keeping the crowd under control. Small children giggled and squealed in anticipation. I was terribly impressed with how many people wore traditional clothing. The men and the boys wore lederhosen with a checked shirt and a matching vest. The shirt sleeves were all elbow length or rolled to the elbow. The women and girls wore frilled white blouses with a deep-cut neckline under a checked dirndl, and a matching half-apron. The feminist in me was pleased to see a few girls and women wearing female versions of the men's leather shorts with checked shirts, and sleeves rolled up to the elbow.

The parade started with a banging of drums, clashing of cymbals, and the shrill notes of various wind instruments. Community groups in traditional uniforms, highly decorated wagons drawn by matching horses, the Beer-fest Queen on horseback, a group of chimney sweeps, and a group of butchers' assistants all walked past, laughing and joking with the spectators. A group of a hundred older men paced seriously and purposefully along the road, tapping knobbly, curved walking sticks on the ground in unison as they went. I had no idea who they were or why they were there, but they were very impressive as they went tapping past to the beat of their drum.

I loved the chimney sweeps; all in black, carrying ladders, cleaning brooms, and brushes. A Roman soldier driving a chariot pulled by four black horses came thundering past but my vote for favourites had to be shared between the two oxen who pulled a wagon of beer barrels and the team of ten black horses who also pulled an enormous wagon of beer barrels. Those wagons were huge!

The children would have voted for all those who threw them lollies. The two kids standing next to me had come prepared, with Grandad holding a big plastic bag. He stood calmly and guarded the treasure while the kids ran about excitedly snatching as many lollies as they could gather from the road. I helped them collect a few but didn't hand all of them over. I'm still just a kid at heart too.

It was a great evening. I could see how proud the locals were of their community and their culture. All the community groups walking in the parade were so pleased to be so honoured. The audience clapped and cheered each group. It was a fantastic public mental health event which originated in the peoples' common love for beer hundreds of years ago. Beer might still be the excuse now but it's really all about community, identity, pride in place and belonging. People came together to celebrate that which binds them and left disunity and dissension for another day. The parade was finished by a few police cars, fire trucks and emergency services; just a gentle reminder to all of us to be sensible and to behave ourselves.

I went back to my hotel and luxuriated in my €125 room. I spread my wet gear over the place to dry, charged my devices, ate most of the fruit and drank all the water, had a coffee or two and a spa. Then I relaxed by binge watching Netflix on their wifi. So good!

I was determined to get my money's worth at breakfast, so I filled my stomach to bursting point then secreted three tiny bread rolls, a muesli bar and a banana in my handlebar bag. The waitress gave me a free bottle of beer to take with. I don't think she realised how much loot I had already stashed away. The bottle had a metal cap and I had no opener, so I left the bottle behind. The waitress then came running after me, bottle in hand. I explained the lack of a bottle-opener, she laughed, went into the kitchen and presented me with a small opener to take with. Problem solved.

The route along the Danube was fairly uneventful. I stopped at the thirty-kilometer point, parked my butt on a seat overlooking the river and drank my bottle of beer. Later, I pulled in at Aldi, a grocery store, in Deggendorff to find three middle-aged French cyclists keen to chat. "Where from, where to, why, how many kilometres per day ...?" As usual, they were quite astonished and a bit disbelieving when they heard that I was from Australia. I had to show them my Australian flag as evidence. They too, were swigging from bottles of beer. It seemed to be the right thing to do.

The route after lunch was a spaghetti mess of detours; miles and miles of gravel, sand, and stony paths zigging, then zagging all over the countryside. I had to be so careful to spot all the signage because, being a detour, there was not much logic to the route. I was sure some of the detour was designed to take cyclists through numerous small villages. I often had to stop at a corner, scratching my head in puzzlement, trying to work out which of the four possibilities was the correct route. At one such stop, I was carefully observed the whole time by granny, sitting in the garden, enjoying the sunshine and a coffee. I'm sure we were better entertainment than TV.

"There was one cyclist, at least sixty, with a bright red nose. She kept turning in circles and glaring at her phone. It was so funny!" would have been her contribution to the conversation at supper:

After an age of zigging and zagging, the path morphed back into the regular Danube Cycle Route with a bitumen surface and regular green signs. The river there was quite low and hardly flowing. Rocks and soil were exposed to the sun, drying in the heat. I could see by the still damp soil where the river level had been until recently. It must have been dropping quite quickly. The rocks looked so sad, just drab and grey, covered in dried weeds and slime.

Further on, there must have been a dam wall somewhere. The river deepened and flowed quite well. The best part of the day was cycling along with a steep drop directly into the river on my right. One false wobble and I could have tumbled through a few trees and splashed into the water. The bank dropped away and widened. The path became a country lane and suddenly there were fishermen everywhere. Behind every tree lounged an old bloke, or sometimes a young fellow, fishing. Three teenage boys told me they had caught four fish. I couldn't understand what else they told me, their German speech was so Bavarian with dialects so thick that it would require a sledgehammer to crack them open and get at the meaning hidden in the centre.

In camp that evening, I sat and chatted with a young German fellow and a middle-aged Frenchman. They both smoked incessantly which is something I saw much more in Europe than in Australia. The German rode about 150 kilometres per day. He averaged twenty kilometres per hour and rode up to eight hours a day. The Frenchman kept getting lost all the time, so he often ended up throwing his bike on a bus and getting to his destination the easy way. Maybe he didn't have a phone or maybe he hadn't heard of Google Maps.

Passau was an easy morning's ride downriver. I set up camp on the banks of the Ilz River, in a campground dedicated to cyclists and hikers, before I wandered into the old town for lunch. I found a Vietnamese restaurant. What else should I eat in Bavaria? All joking aside, I was desperate to eat some vegetables which, although quite plentiful in shops, never seemed to make it into the traditional restaurant kitchens. I found that the Vietnamese and Thai restaurants often solved this issue for me. I couldn't help but hear the Australian accents emanating from the two ladies sitting at the next table. Mary and Julie had just finished a boat and bike tour along the Danube. They were supposed to go as far as Budapest, but the Danube was so low that they couldn't get there so they had finished their tour early.

The afternoon was spent in search of a good viewpoint to photograph the junction of the three rivers for which Passau is known and which made it wealthy. I slogged up the hill to the castle to get a good view of the confluence of the three rivers. No such luck. I could see a park with a children's playground in the distance. Beyond it I could see where the Inn flows into the Danube. The observation tower which might have given a better view was closed for renovations. I walked back down the hill, over the bridge and to the park from where I had a good view of the Danube and the Inn.

The different colours of the two streams were so clear and obvious that you could almost separate them with a knife. The Danube was indeed a blueish colour and the Inn, carrying a great deal of snow melt from the Alps was a murky, cloudy grey. I knew that the Ilz, which originates in the forests along the border of Bohemia and Bavaria, was a clear dark brown. I looked to the left expecting to see its dark brown waters coming down between the hills to join the blue and the grey. Nope! There was a Viking cruise ship in the way.

Now, if I was a producer of a prime TV reality show shooting an episode there, I would have been pretty annoyed at not being able to see all three colours merging at the one spot. I would have stormed aboard and demanded that the ship be moved; or maybe I would have sat around for a day or two until the way was cleared; or maybe I would have sent up a drone. I'm not a producer of a TV reality show so I just shrugged my shoulders and consoled myself with coffee and cake at a nearby café.

Navigating from Passau to Innsbruck was a reasonably simple matter. I just had to follow the Inn River the whole way with a few detours for overnight stops and one break of a few days to visit yet another cousin.

On my first day following the Inn, I cycled from Passau to Bad Füssing. The weather was still unseasonably hot, so I spent the late afternoon wallowing in the local swimming pool. Having set up my tent on a pitch of compacted gravel, I decided not to unpack my other gear until the last minute. I could feel a thunderstorm coming, and while I knew that my pannier bags were waterproof, I wasn't so sure about my tent. It had held off showers quite well in the past, but a summer thunderstorm was a different matter altogether. I was right. Thunder boomed, lightning flashed, and the rain came pelting down, hit the ground and bounced up between the tent fly and the tent inner to wash down into the tent itself. Within seconds, my tent floor was awash in water. Luckily, the campground had very flash facilities including TV screens showing a continuous loop of advertisements on the back of each toilet door. More importantly, two carpeted conference rooms took up most of the first floor. I moved all my gear inside and slept in one of the conference rooms, hoping that a security guard wouldn't throw me out in the middle of the night. In that case, I planned to move into the laundry in the basement.

From Bad Füssing, I followed the Inn to Braunau am Inn, Hitler's birthplace, which they didn't advertise. Then came Marktl am Inn which was Pope Benedikt's birthplace. I'm not a Catholic so felt no great need to go there and find his house. My main aim was to get to Emmerting, a small village near the Inn which is home to a cousin of mine. I wanted to spend a few days there as she was having a family gathering and my brother would be there too.

Having grown up in Australia with all our extended family in Germany, family gatherings can be a bit challenging. Trying to remember who everyone is and how they are connected to us, trying to follow the conversations with their southern dialects, stumbling across cultural differences and nuances of behaviour; I had a lovely time but was quite happy to leave after a few days and keep heading south on my trusty bicycle.

I didn't get very far. I set off from my cousin's house in the morning, bright-eyed and bushy-tailed. Saying goodbye to her and her family was difficult. Who knew when I would see them again? I pedalled to the Inn and turned towards Mühldorf. Five kilometres out of Mühldorf, I could feel the pebbles and the bumps on the path much more than I should – a flat tyre.

I tried pumping the tyre up but then couldn't get the pump off the valve. The valve snapped off, the air whooshed out and I sat stunned with a tyre flat as a pancake. Oh well, I knew what to do. The luggage off, I upended my bike, and took the back wheel off. I took the tube out and searched for the problem. I couldn't find it. I checked the wheel rim thoroughly, but it all looked good. I placed a new tube on the rim, checked for pinches, and pumped the tyre up. It worked, and the tyre held. I inserted the back wheel, tipped the bike up, and I had a trial ride. It was all good so I loaded my bags and set off.

I rode through Mühldorf looking for some lunch and a bike shop. I wanted to get another tube, just in case. I didn't see what I needed so kept going. An hour later, I was getting really hungry so decided to detour to Waldkraiburg. The local service station filled my stomach and fuelled me with Fanta. On returning to my bike, I saw immediately; oh no! The tyre was completely flat again! Why?

I unloaded all my luggage, deflated the tyre thoroughly and attached the gas tyre-fixing cylinder. It was supposed to insert a whole lot of gas and rubber into the tube for a temporary fix, plugging the hole and inflating the tyre at the same time. It didn't. The cylinder exploded and foam went everywhere - over my shoes, hands, bike chain, and cog set. They were all covered in foam. I took out my last spare tube. It had a different valve to my pump but that was OK, I knew I had an adaptor. I fitted the adaptor and attached the pump for a test run before changing the tyre. I couldn't get the pump to fit properly and air was going everywhere except into the tube. I threw the tube and adaptor out in disgust.

I pumped up the existing tube and checked to see if I could find where the air was coming out. I have previously ridden for about five days with a flat tyre by pumping up the tube every morning which then stayed inflated for the whole day. This time, I could hear a hiss of air and spotted a half centimetre tear in the outer tyre. Things were not looking good.

At this point, I had my luggage spread all over the ground, filthy hands, a tyre with a small tear, a tube with a hole, an exasperated soul, a very bad temper and no spare tubes. What to do? It was a Saturday and the local bike shops had both just closed for the weekend. They wouldn't open again until Monday morning. Even if I could find a spare tube or two, I didn't want to risk riding on until I knew the outer tyre was OK. What if it were to split completely when I was an hour's ride from the nearest bike shop and a long walk from the nearest town? I walked to the local hotel and booked in for two nights.

The real life-lesson there, in Waldkraiburg, was all about patience. Having to stay two nights in a hotel when the weather was perfect for cycling and I just wanted to keep moving was frustrating in the extreme. but it could have been so much worse. I could have been stuck in the countryside with no bike shop or accommodation for miles around. Instead, I was in a very clean, almost new and quite lovely hotel with great wifi. I could do a day trip to Munich on the Sunday and see the Residenz which I had always wanted to see. My daughter told me that it was snowing at home. This only happens every thirty years, so it's something no-one is prepared for or knows how to live with. She definitely won in the "Misery" stakes.

By 8.50 on Monday morning, I was at the bike shop and the door was already open. Hallelujah! There was no question about it, the rear tyre needed to be changed. The lady was incredibly kind and helpful, explaining that when the tyre gets so worn down, even a small pebble will cause a puncture of the tube just through pressure. She suggested I replace the old tyre with a Schwalbe Ultra Marathon Plus which is top of the range for touring. These tyres have an extra thickness along the section of tyre which rolls on the ground which makes it much more difficult for a piece of glass or a drawing pin to penetrate and puncture the tube.

An interesting fact: rear tyres need to be replaced four times as often as front tyres. Carrying all the extra weight of a sixty-kilogram body and the larger bike bags at the back puts so much more pressure on the back tyre and wears down the tread so much quicker. An interesting observation: of my five flat tyres so far, four had been on the back wheel.

I watched closely as the young man changed my tyre and tube. I was looking for expert tips to use and he was happy to explain what he was doing. He checked that the outer tyre went on in the correct direction. He also pumped up the tube much more than I did, before placing it on the rim. Otherwise, I had done everything the same, only much slower. I asked him to check the chain and the rear cog set. The chain needed replacing. The cog set was 50/50 so I got it all replaced. The total cost was 150 euros for a new tyre and tube, two spare tubes, a new chain, a new rear cog set and labour. It wasn't cheap but I considered it money well spent if it meant that I could cycle on, secure in the knowledge that I had done all that I could to minimize puncture and chain problems. If I kept having issues, I would seriously consider throwing my bike, the panniers and everything else into the river and walking to Malta!

# | 30 |

## Alps on the Horizon!

### Waldkraiburg to Brennero, 178 km

By lunchtime, I was a much happier cyclist. I sat on a bridge in the forest, listening to the gurgle of the stream as it flowed over the rocks and under the bridge. I had never realised that flowing water has multiple tones at the same time. There was a deep gurgle overlaid by a lighter rush and occasionally an even lighter series of plops which was probably the sound of my brain cells as they melted out of my body and plopped into the water. The heat was crazy! It was only about thirty degree Celsius but even so, that was about ten degrees too hot for comfortable cycling. The only thing to do was to keep plugging on and go for lots of swims.

Afternoon tea was a combination of non-alcoholic Campari, passionfruit juice, mint, lime and ice at a place called "Elend." (misery) How can one feel miserable when drinking a non-alcoholic Campari in the shade of a sun umbrella on a riverbank? On the other hand, it was only a small drink and it did cost €4.90!

I only managed fifty-two kilometres which I found a bit disappointing. I had to remind myself that my daily target was around sixty kilometres, that anything over fifty was quite acceptable when riding through hills in the heat and that I had a good reason why I could only start riding at 10.30 am when it was already so hot.

On the positive side, I had ended up at Erlensee Campground in Schechen, which was pretty close to heaven. There was green grass, shady trees, a restaurant and, most importantly, a lake for swimming. A short while before I pulled in for the night, I had passed a lake with numerous adults sunbaking on the banks and children swimming in the water. It had taken a major effort to keep riding and not ride straight into the water, bike and all. The camp manager of Erlensee reported that the lake was so warm that it wouldn't be terribly refreshing but I wasn't fussed; a swim was a swim, and any water would be cooler than my sweaty body.

My post-swim supper in the restaurant was roast pork with house-made warm potato salad and red cabbage with apple; a good Bavarian meal, to be consumed with a cold beer in a typical Bavarian beer garden. Even the décor was the traditional Bavarian blue and white diamond pattern.

It took me the better part of two days of slow pedalling to cycle the 126 kilometres from Schechen in Germany to Innsbruck, nestled in a valley at the base of the Alps. The weather was still quite hot, up to the low thirties, and exceptionally humid. Dark skies threatened thunderstorms in the evenings, but it was all in vain. All the rumbles and bluster came to nothing, not a drop. I cycled as much as possible in the cool of the morning when the sun was still low. At some stage, I crossed the border into Austria but only noticed I was in a different country when the road signage changed style. Much of the way was through acres and acres of maize being grown for the biofuel industry. Emerging from yet another field of maize, I got very excited when I could see the blue smudge of mountains in the distance - the Alps!

Innsbruck has a plethora of museums, but I was rather over museums unless they were going to show me something unique and exciting. What did I want to see in Innsbruck? What was different about this place which sets it apart from every other town or city in Europe?

I decided to go to the Alpenzoo which focuses on Alpine animals and to Kristallenwelt which is a crystals exhibition and gallery by the world-famous Swarovsky factory. I planned to go to the Alpenzoo on my first day in Innsbruck but fortunately realised beforehand that with the afternoon temperature forecast to be well over thirty degrees that all sensible alpine animals would be panting with heat exhaustion in the shade and fairly unlikely to be bouncing around on show.

The next day was expected to be cooler so I set off in great expectation, along with hordes of other tourists. We all congregated in front of the ticket office, surged inside and then scattered. Almost all went uphill following my theory that one gets the hard work done first and then slowly saunters downhill. The zoo is on a steep site and planning was necessary to avoid slogging up the same slope twice.

Unlike the previous day, when all the animals would have been hiding in the shade, only about ninety-five percent were hiding. Two wolves were stretched out in a bit if scrub, they didn't move all afternoon. The deer, the beavers, the elk and numerous other iconic creatures were also on animal sabbatical, but I did see some lynx kittens tumbling about in their enclosure to a chorus of ooohhs and aaahhs from the admiring audience. The ibex, on full show, stood regally on their rocky platforms, ignoring us all. The chamois were also too busy hopping from rock to rock to take note of us. Two brown bears prowled in their enclosure, one continually brushed against the plate glass which separated us. Magnificent creatures, I wouldn't want to meet one in the wild.

I wandered along the forestry path and discovered a whole lot of interesting, but ultimately useless information. Forty-eight percent of Austria's land is covered in forest, that's four million hectares, 3.4 billion trees. Seventy-two percent of the trees are conifers, the remainder are deciduous trees. There are sixty-five native types of trees of which the three most common are spruce, beech and pine trees.

The Haselfichte, a type of spruce, has very fine growth rings. Anton Stradivari used to wander around in the forest for days on end, whacking trees with the blunt side of an axe to listen to the tones they made. If a tree sounded good enough when whacked, he would harvest it and use the wood to make his world-famous violins.

The wood of the beech tree is hard and heavy. In the olden days, messages were carved into beech wood because the carvings stayed clear for a long time, long enough to be delivered to the recipient. The word for "beech" in German is "Buche" from which the word "Buch" is derived – "book."

Speaking of language; "Schadenfreude" is a German term which has been adopted into English. It means the joy one feels at the distress which another person suffers when something goes wrong for them. Why the German language has a term for this and why English speakers have felt the need to adopt it is a mystery to me.

I was standing next to a family of Mum, Dad and four boys ranging in age from twelve to about six. Youngest boy kept kicking the wires which keep the chamois from escaping their pen, very annoying! His parents and brothers told him many times to stop but he wasn't going to listen. He just kept kicking away until he touched the bottom, electric wire and let out an ear-piercing, blood-curdling scream followed by an instant of dead silence, then a flood of tears accompanied by continuous wailing and roaring. Schadenfreude; the highlight of my day!

Swarovski Kristallenwelt, being all about crystals and bling, promised to be a good counterpoint to the nature on display at the zoo. On arriving at the station, the shuttle bus was already parked at the pick-up spot with a crowd of people waiting for the driver to open the door. I waited patiently then queued to board. In my naivety and general ignorance of the world, I expected the trip to be gratis. I mean, Swarovski is a multi-million-dollar corporation, a world leader in its industry exporting high class products all over the world. The shuttle bus delivers crowds of people to its front door every day, each of whom will pay a small fortune in the entrance fee and many of whom will follow that up by paying a not-so-small ransom in order to purchase a piece of bling for a souvenir. So, I just assumed that Swarovski would perform an invaluable service and fund its victims a free bus ride. Apparently not. A one-way ticket costs five euro, a return was €9.50 hence a saving of ten percent on the return trip. How nice of them! On the plus side, the bus was clean and comfortable, and it had wifi which actually worked.

I knew I was in for a treat as soon as I entered Kristallenwelt. Entry was through a turnstile next to an ivy clad giant spewing a waterfall out of his mouth. The first room had the world's largest and smallest crystals. The largest, with a hundred faces, was the size of a footstool. The smallest crystals, each smaller than the peas stuck forever in my freezer, have seventeen faces on each.

I have often wondered whether crystals are natural, extracted from the earth and then cut and polished like diamonds, or whether they are made from scratch by human hands. I used the local wifi to access Google and Wikipedia (which between them know everything there is to know as well as a whole lot more) and discovered that Swarovski crystals are made of sand and minerals, the exact composition of which is a tightly held industrial secret; a bit like KFC's secret spices. Except that Swarovski crystals look beautiful and presumably wouldn't give me indigestion.

The first room also had a horse dressed in gorgeous trappings dotted with crystals. From its earliest days, Swarovski established partnerships with artists, designers and musicians to create beautiful works of art for display on stage, in designer wear, in movies, and in this museum. This resulted in a magnificent show where every room was even more stunning and fascinating than the last.

The Crystal Dome had me standing inside an igloo of 595 mirrors, each reflecting off the others in an infinite display of colour and light. A single rose in one corner reflected its colours all around the room. I spent an age trying to take a suitable selfie but trying to co-ordinate head position, eyes focused and to the front, no reflections onto my glasses or on my nose and no other visitors in the frame at the same time as a big smile was more of a challenge than I could cope with. The smile was the last straw; I felt more like a robot than a human, so I just grimaced instead.

The Mechanical Room was a delight. A male body segmented into pieces while a set of female legs walked elegantly around them. A wild dance by three sets of trousers heralded a group of business shirts swinging and sashaying across the room, over our heads. Most unusual; I didn't know what any of it meant but I did enjoy it.

The Cabinet of Wonders had a train set! Or at least two trains circling around a mountain covered in snow and dotted with famous landmarks from around the world. The Statue of Liberty, Napoleon on his horse, St. Basils Cathedral and Big Ben, all overlooked by a helicopter. It was only after five minutes that I realised all the posts holding up the front railing had miniature golden human skulls on them.

The last room was much larger than all the rest. This was the "Come hither and spend all your money on pretty but useless bling" room. I found the café instead.

Being an absolute wimp when it comes to cycling uphill, I had decided weeks before that I would take the train up to the Brenner Pass and to cycle from there. I wasn't the only one. There was a whole busload of cyclists heading for the top the easy way, but I did notice that I seemed to be the only cyclist on a long tour. The amount of luggage I was schlepping sort of gave it away. The rest of the cyclists only had one or two of the small panniers; probably a small repair kit and a substantial picnic lunch. The first stage was by bus due to work being done on the railway line. We had to disembark half-way up the mountains and transfer to a lovely, clean and sparkling regional train which took us into Italy.

# | 31 |

# Four Solo Female Cyclists

## Brennero to Niederrasen, 83 km

All went well until I had to leave the station at Brennero. There was no elevator, so I had to unload my bags off the bike, carry my bike and bags separately down a flight of steps, load the bags back on the bike, wheel it all through an underpass, unload, lug it all up two flights of steps, load up again and get out of there! The only thing to do was to keep calm and carry on. Which I did. All that work made me hungry, so I splurged on a last German currywurst as a pre-lunch snack.

Feeling quite contented, I searched for the route down to Bressanone. A number of other cyclists were also reading every sign they could see in an effort to find the correct route. They were all couples, as usual, except for one lady. She called out to me, we started a conversation, and decided to ride on together. Andrea had cycled up from Innsbruck the previous day. The road wasn't too steep, she said, but it was exceptionally busy with cars, trucks, and buses. With no bike path to ride along, she thought that taking the train would have been a better idea.

We cycled the rest of the day together, along the most glorious bike path, downhill almost all the way except for a detour which took us over a humungous hill. The views were magnificent, and the sun was shining. We cycled through the historical centre of Vipiteno Sterzing, oohing and aahing as we went, then past a ruined castle on a hill,

193

through apple orchards, under the freeway, and past a massive fortress at Fortezza.

Afternoon was fading into evening as we pulled into the Vahnersee campground. A young Scottish female cyclist was checking in at reception, so we agreed to pitch our tents together. Our neighbours were a lovely, mature but newly married couple from Cologne, Brigitte and Manni. They were staying in a campervan, pulled out chairs for us, and were fascinated with our various cycling stories and itineraries.

As darkness fell, we three cyclists headed to the restaurant, where yet another solo female cyclist was waiting to order her meal, so we invited her to join us. Four solo female cyclists sitting in a restaurant and eating a meal together. What a coincidence! I thought hard but could only remember coming across one other solo female cyclist, Iris. The others had only met very few, we were a rare breed!

Andrea, a nurse from the Netherlands was on a two-week holiday. She was cycling from Innsbruck over the Alps towards Kitzbühel. It was her first solo cycling trip, so she had bought all her camping equipment quite recently. She was still getting used to putting up her tent, packing her sleeping bag, working out what she needed, and how to pack it.

Connie was the youngest of the group. She hailed from Aberdeen in Scotland. She had left her home at the end of June and cycled through Belgium, Luxembourg, Germany, France, Germany again, Austria and Italy. She was heading towards Slovenia and Croatia, planned to cross over to Bari in Italy and eventually end up in Malta. Connie worked in industrial design but had resigned from her job in order to go on this adventure.

Beth was from Oregon, in the USA. She had been about to buy a house at home but then had decided she would rather go cycling instead. She had flown to Sarajevo and cycled through Serbia, Croatia and Slovenia into Italy. She planned to meet her parents in the French Alps a few weeks later. Beth was an expert medical professional but had also resigned from her job in order to fulfil this dream. She rode a mountain bike with the absolute minimum of luggage. The following morning, when I saw how little Beth was taking with her, my jaw dropped in astonishment. She was one tough cookie!

We all shared our breakfast supplies with Brigitte and Manni. Porridge, coffee and pleasant conversation with like-minded people makes a great start to any day! Beth was heading north to Innsbruck. Connie and Andrea were planning to cycle east and check out the Pragser Wildsee, a well-known beautiful alpine lake. I was pining for a bit more female company, so I agreed to go with them. I was also keen to see a bit of the Dolomites before I headed further downhill onto the hot plains of the Veneto.

Connie, Andrea and I cycled into the Puster Valley, through Brunico and to the campground at Niederrasen. It was a hard slog! Beautiful, but hard. The hills might not have been so big, but I found them really challenging anyway. Connie, with less luggage and with youth and strong legs on her side could just zip up them but Andrea and I found it much more difficult. On the other hand, age brings wisdom and caution. We had to go down a very steep hill with an S bend at the bottom. Connie flew down, missed a curve and landed in a heap in the ditch with her bike on top. We old ladies took a more leisurely pace and were able to pull her out of her ditch, check for broken bones and concussion. All was well, so we kept going.

At Brunico, we stopped for ice-cream and coffee. I stayed back to buy a SIM card for my phone. TIM, the telecommunications company, became my instant best friend. It was love at first sight! Thirteen euros bought me a SIM card and activation. Another ten euros gave me thirty gigabytes of data valid for one month. I was supposed to have phone credit too, but I wasn't really sure whether I actually had it or not. I didn't particularly worry about that. Given that I didn't speak any Italian at all, I saw limited value in phone credit. I was much more concerned about having a massive data allowance.

It was a really cold night, but we were in the Alps. I woke the next morning with a flat battery in my phone and learnt about the effects of cold on phone batteries. I had had no idea. Connie also taught me about a navigation app called Komoot which is specifically for cyclists and hikers. Then she showed me how to block all the spam which kept arriving on my blog. Three useful things learnt from one person in ten minutes. It was powerful stuff.

Phone sorted, our task for the day was to check out the Pragser Wildsee, known as Lago di Braies in Italian. We had to take a bus, a train, and another bus. The first bus and train fares were covered by the tourist fees which in turn were included in our camp fees. We had to pay three euro per trip for the last bus only.

The lake was so crowded. Thousands of visitors jabbered away in dozens of languages. A small lake, emerald green in colour, surrounded by forested and bare mountains, it was a jewel in its environment. Connie and I both went for a swim. The water was really cold but so refreshing! Andrea amused herself by taking hundreds of photos of Connie as she posed, first this way and then that way, in her bathers. We had been laughing at other people doing exactly the same thing while we ate our picnic lunch, but Connie's chestnut hair against the green of the lake proved an irresistible combination. She flicked her hair, pouted on command and looked beautiful. After the hour long, five hundred photo session, we walked on around the lake. We found the jumping off point for the very popular Alta Via trekking route which Beth had recently completed, admired the hundreds of little rock towers which tourists have built over the years, walked up the hill to the scenic lookout point, and then continued back to the car park. It was all irresistibly photogenic so it wasn't our fault that we took dozens more photos en route, as all the other daft tourists were doing. Having worn out our phone batteries and Connie's camera by taking photos, we set off for "home," our trio of tents set amongst the trees.

The restaurant at the campground offered a whole range of meals including that Austrian favourite – schnitzel with chips and salad. The waiter was an incredibly friendly chap who gave Andrea all the information she needed to plan her route further east. The road over the saddle was closed, she should go via Lienz, and so on. We also quizzed him on language and identity in South Tyrol. All the towns, villages, and natural features there have two names - one in Italian and one in

German. So, did he identify as an Italian or as a German? He identified with neither because he was from South Tyrol; he was a South Tyrolean first and foremost. Interestingly, there are still very close ties between South Tyrol in Italy and Tyrol in Austria. The provincial officials from both areas have regular meetings and often co-operate for their mutual benefit.

Furthermore, everyone in South Tyrol speaks both German and Italian. That's the standard there. Children are taught in both languages at school and are equally fluent in both. They also learn at least one foreign language, usually English. People in the northern regions are more likely to speak German at home, those in the south tend to prefer Italian at home. Ladin, a Rheto-Romanisch language directly descended from Latin, is still commonly spoken in some valleys. Those children learn all three local languages equally and none of this is seen as at all remarkable, it's just how it is.

We three shared our breakfast supplies again, then headed to the restaurant for coffee and croissants. I think we were all a trifle sad that we were splitting up to go our separate ways. It was so nice travelling with other like-minded people, but Andrea had to be in Kitzbühel within a week and Connie wanted to go east while I was fixated on going south. I hoped that I would be able to meet them again one day, but I knew that it was quite doubtful. That's the reality of long-distance cyclists and hikers; we meet, we enjoy each other's company, and we swap contact details, but we somehow never manage to keep the contact going. Real life intrudes and those fleeting moments of companionship become nothing more than hundreds of photos, and many pleasant memories.

# | 32 |

# Freewheeling Down the Alps

## Niederrasen to Verona, 216 km

Having waved a cheery goodbye to Connie and Andrea, I rode to the station at Niederrasen. The ticket machine could respond to me in Italian, German, Ladin or English but it couldn't give me change for a fifty euro note. Luckily a gentleman nearby had enough change, so it wasn't a huge drama for me. The train was perfect; clean, modern, and not too fast for me to enjoy the scenery which we had ridden through, two days previously. It took an hour to reverse that whole day's riding into the Pustertal.

At Fortezza, I left the station and set off happily until I noticed I was cycling up-steam. Whoops! Wrong way! This sort of thing happened to me constantly in Europe. My brain didn't seem to be able to adapt to me being in the northern hemisphere so I regularly found myself going the wrong way or else going the correct way and feeling that it must be wrong. Do our brains have some sort of chemical which always points to the north or the south pole? Are the chemicals in my brain so stubborn, that they just won't swing around to point to the north? Is this just a mad, unscientific theory? Maybe, but my inability to find the correct direction when I'm in Europe is not a theory, it's an undeniable fact.

It started to rain but then luckily petered out. The route to Bressanone was a bit topsy turvy, up-hill and down dale, crossing a river here and there, curving all around the place. After Bressanone, it settled down to a steady slight downhill slope following the river until Bolzano.

Ötzi is the world's oldest celebrity, dating back to about 5,300 years ago. He grew up in the mountains and valleys of northern Italy, was possibly a shepherd and was killed in a fight when he was about forty-five years old. Soon after he died, his body was covered in ice and snow, only to be found by some hikers in 1991. He is Europe's oldest known natural human mummy and is to be found in a specially designed museum in the centre of Bolzano. Visiting Ötzi was my main reason for crossing the Alps at Brennero and entering Italy from there. He was the only item on my agenda for the day.

It was pouring with rain, so hundreds of other people also had the brilliant idea of a museum visit. The queue to get inside the museum was long, I waited for an hour, the queue didn't move, so I went to have a coffee. The queue was even longer when I returned but at least it was moving. I walked up the steps, through the entrance, bought my ticket and joined another queue. Eventually, the queue reached the beginning of the exhibition and we patient queuers were able to study each bit of information as we filed past it. And so it went – queue, read, look, queue, read, look, until I got to queue to see Ötzi himself. I stood on a small platform by myself and peered through a tiny window.

Ötzi lay on his back with one arm crossed over his body, just like he has for the last 5,300 years, but now covered in a sheen of icy water instead of a glacier in the Alps. Over one hundred teams of scientists and archaeologists have investigated nearly every aspect of Ötzi's remains so they can tell a great deal about him, his life, the area, and the time he lived in. He was 160 centimetres tall and weighed just fifty kilograms when he died. He ate a meal of ibex meat and bread two hours before he was killed, but he also ate red deer, chamois, bread, herbs, and berries. His clothes were mainly of leather, but his cloak was made of woven grass. Strips of leather were sewn together with sinew to make his coat, belt, leggings, and loincloth. There was much, much more, but some questions will never be answered unless we solve the mystery of time travel.

We call him "Ötzi," but what was his real name? Did he have family? Were they waiting for him to return from the mountains? Did they ever know what happened to him? Why was he in a fight, and who shot the arrow that killed him?

The care taken to preserve Ötzi's body, his dignity as a human being, and all his possessions is remarkable. Ötzi lay in Innsbruck for years after his discovery before he was transferred to Bolzano. On the day of the transfer, both autobahns from Innsbruck to Brennero and from there to Bolzano were closed so that he had an uninterrupted journey, top notch security, a police escort and journalists from twenty newspapers in attendance. Now there's a celebrity!

It was still bucketing rain the next day, so I spent the morning in a laundromat and hoped the rain would clear after my washing was washed, dried and packed away, smelling beautiful. I was impressed that there always seemed to be a coffee shop next to every laundromat. I ordered an Americano with a long dash of milk. The waitress spoke no English or German, so she asked a customer to translate from German to Italian. The coffee was perfect, so I asked how to order a coffee like that in Italian. A long intense discussion ensued. Our translator couldn't cope with a long black coffee with some milk added. For him, coffee was small, black and so strong that one could mortar bricks with it, or it was a cappuccino. In the end, he suggested I ask for a "brown coffee."

I set off in the rain. The main issue with cycling in the rain was that it would only take five minutes for my shoes to get wet through, and a full day of sunshine to dry them out again. I had no spare shoes with me, so once my feet got wet, they stayed wet until my shoes dried out again. Even wearing overshoes didn't help because my feet sweated so much in them that they got soaked and smelly in no time. However, I wasn't going to be beaten. I packed my shoes into a waterproof bag, inside another waterproof bag, just in case. I fished out my flip-flops and pulled the overshoes on over them. My feet were going to get wet anyway and the flip-flops were designed to get dry quite quickly. The overshoes protected my wet feet from the cold wind and also helped keep my feet on the pedals as I was riding. When the rain stopped, I just dried my feet, and put my shoes and socks on again. Another problem solved.

The route followed the Adige River and went slightly downhill all day. The valley was bordered by huge limestone cliffs towering above me to meet the sky. There had been a massive landslide in prehistoric times which left an enormous white cliff-face devoid of any vegetation high above a tiny village. The base of the valley was home to a freeway, a country road, a railway line, the river, a cycle path, and numerous villages. Every spare plot of land was taken up by apple orchards which went right to the base of the cliffs on either side. The apples were a red variety. I picked one to sample, but it wasn't quite ripe so one bite was enough for me.

The rain didn't stop for the next few days, and constantly flicking water out of my eyes was fast losing its charm. I stopped at a bici grill (a café and bicycle repair station on a bicycle path) for a hot drink. On discovering that I was not only wet, but cold as well, I booked a hotel for the night and spent the afternoon researching my route through Italy instead. I needed to decide where to go after Verona – left or right? Left would take me to the Adriatic coast south of Venice. I could then follow the coast road, which seemed very flat, to Bari or even Brindisi, before working out what to do next. There seemed to be some bits and pieces of cycle paths but nothing as organised as a completed long-distance cycle route. On the other hand, turning right would take me, mainly on bike paths, over the Appenines to Rome. From there, I could take a train to Naples and a ferry to Sicily, avoiding the busy southern roads which had no cycleways. Hills scared me. I elected to go left.

Leaving the hotel, the rain had stopped. The sun wasn't exactly shining, but it was all okay. The route kept going slightly downhill most of the way but instead of resolutely following the river, it zig-zagged here and there, sometimes along the river, sometimes through orchards, other times next to the freeway or along a channel high above the valley. It was constant left, then right, short uphill burst, steep downhill with a "STOP" sign and a T intersection at the bottom. All this twisting and turning, crossing roads and waterways really slowed my cycling down so that, despite going downhill all the way, the eighty-one kilometres took just as long as if I were cycling on a straight, flat road.

Gradually the apple orchards gave way to vineyards. The grapes were a small purple variety with the bunches hanging below the vines, so they would have been easy to cut. Harvesting was in full swing. I had to watch out for tractors and trailers as well as everything else. I pedalled through some villages, each seeming less Tirolean and more Italian than the last. Square houses with flat roofs, gardens full of vegetables, a sprinkling of olive trees, church bells ringing and clanging, narrow winding streets. It all spoke of the Italy of epicure and home-decorating magazines.

Thirty kilometres before Verona, I was admiring a castle on top of a big hill when the path took a sharp turn and sent me on an exhausting push and shove, up past the castle to a village right at the top. Sweating, puffing and panting, I stood at the lookout point, observed the busy country road winding past the base of the hill and wondered why the bike route had to go over the top. Did the planners think that cyclists needed to see the castle from above? Did they want to give us a change of pace? Did they own an e-bike shop somewhere close by? Or were they just bored?

A steep drop down took me to the same channel which I had been following back in the valley, but which had disappeared before my excursion up and over the hill. I suspected that the channel cut straight through the middle of the hill in a tunnel. I spent a pleasant ten minutes visualising a raft system whereby cyclists could get a free ride on the channel, through the hill and over the valleys. I mean, why not?

The high point of the day was cycling across three aqueducts with a fast-flowing channel to the right, and the valley floor down below to the left. It was a weird feeling to be cycling along, looking through the fence at the treetops below me.

I soon came into another village which had a row of cafés in the main street. A coffee revived me. A couple nearby were speaking English, so I joined them for a chat. Colin and Sharon kindly invited me to share dinner with them, but I knew that my campground was on top of yet another hill and I feared that once I arrived, I wouldn't go downhill again, even for a meal. We discussed e-bikes. They were both avid cyclists at home and had borrowed e-bikes for the first time, that day. They were quite enamoured of their experience so far. Colin claimed he could probably ride straight up a wall on his – an exaggeration, to be sure, but he was making a point. I liked the idea of an e-bike more and more. If I had one, I probably would have gone out to dinner with them, because the post-prandial ride up to the campground wouldn't have been so daunting.

The campground in Verona was in the remains of a castle, overlooking the town. Section B of the campground was reserved for cyclists We had a walled enclosure roofed with green grapevines. Outside the enclosure was a terrace with a simple camp kitchen, outdoor tables, and a tremendous view of the river and the town below. The cyclists were mostly Dutch, with a few Germans, one Belgian, and me, a lone Australian, there to add a bit of exotic to the mix. The Dutch and Belgian were all cycling a well-known tour from Amsterdam to Rome. They had guidebooks with written directions and maps.

The Belgian chap let me photograph all the pages from Verona to Ferrara, so I decided to go that way instead of on my previously planned route, which was down to the Po River and then east to the coast. The new option was completely flat, considerably shorter, and had a few campgrounds on the way, all of which were significant positives. I had slept so many nights in hotels during the last four weeks due to the inclement weather that I felt it was time to reinvigorate my love affair with my tent.

People were cooking dinner and chatting. Most were having pasta. I had bought a can of vegetable soup from a supermarket, two frankfurts, and a skinny roll speckled with bits of olives, all for five euros. I heated the soup, sliced the frankfurts into it and wondered why people went to so much effort lugging all their cooking equipment around, shopping for fresh ingredients, keeping it all cool, and then cooking it all. The thought of having all those bits and pieces of unused foods – ½ cucumber and ½ jar pesto in my panniers was enough to give me the shudders. Some people just love cooking, of course.

In the morning, I walked down the hill, crossed the bridge, and stepped into another world. Streets lined with old buildings opened onto plazas and courtyards, a turn of a corner revealed an old Roman wall, a fountain, or a tomb of a member of the Scali family high on a pedestal. Cafés bustled with patrons enjoying a coffee or an ice-cream piled high in sparkling glasses. A light tenor sang an aria, its notes drifting through the September sunshine. Shakespeare would have loved it!

The biggest crowd was in Capello Street where the city authorities had decided to place Juliet's balcony. It's all a big con, of course. Romeo and Juliet were a figment of someone's imagination, even if the plot was quite plausible for that era. Even though it's well-known that there is no historical basis for a Juliet balcony in Verona, people still flock there in their thousands. The arched entrance to the courtyard was covered in sticky notes with the names of couples deeply in love. A succession of women, some very young, and some for whom youth is a vague memory, appeared on the balcony to be photographed by their doting partners hanging out of a neighbouring window. Many in the crowd took snapshots too. I later saw a sign to Juliet's tomb, another con.

After all the excitement and drama of doomed love, I headed for the post office. A kind lady there found the correct sized box and coached me through the whole packing and addressing saga. I registered the parcel because Connie had told me a sad story of her contact lenses lost somewhere in the postal system. Registering the parcel cost thirty euros which was more than the contents were worth, but I didn't want my precious items lost – my swimming vest, two pairs of riding shorts, a book on Ötzi, an assortment of maps, and a couple of country specific cloth patches. All were of terrific value to me, but of no real value at all. After this little expense and having previously paid fifteen euros to send three measly postcards to Australia, I figured that I really needed to stay out of Italian post offices.

I thought I would trot off to see the Basilica of Some-one but then realised how far away it was. I would have had to pass so many ice-cream shops on the way. Italy has a wide variety of flavours, and in the interest of unbiased research, I needed to test them all. Hard work, I know, but some-one has to do it! I tested a mint flavour that day and forgot all about the basilica.

On my walk back to camp, I came across a poster for the Orchestra Machiavelli. What were their internal politics like? I saw Romeo and Juliet high on another balcony in a completely different street, so I could only assume that rumours of their demise were unfounded. They had simply run away and were in hiding in another part of town. A café was selling Guilatta Focaccias for €8.50. Romeo didn't get a focaccia, poor lad.

# | 33 |

# Across the Veneto Plain

## Verona to Rimini, 288 km

Following the route set out in the Dutch guidebook worked well. I didn't follow it exactly but made sure that I went through most of the villages they had marked. The land was as flat as a tack, there were quiet country roads in all directions and none of them seemed to have an official bike route set out, so it didn't really matter which way I went.

By this stage, I had Komoot, Maps.me, Google Maps and photos of the guidebook maps to follow. Interestingly, none of them agreed on the best route. I did see a sign for a cycle path at an intersection at a bridge. It pointed to a path along the river which none of my maps had included in their routes. It seemed a reasonably good option except that it was gravel instead of bitumen. I took it anyway because it was direct and uncomplicated whereas the mapped routes were full of "turn left, go one hundred metres, turn right, cross the bridge..." That was the main issue with following a map rather than a signed route. I constantly had to stop to check where I was and where I was going next which slowed progress considerably. I hadn't yet learnt to set a route and let my phone talk to me. That came later.

The day's ride out of Verona was through vineyards, apple orchards and market gardens. Cycling east, the blue smudge of the mountains in the distance reminded me how lucky I was to be riding on the flat Veneto Plain. I cycled past many old abandoned buildings and some magnificent mansions crying out for love and repair. A church with a crumbling vestry had its windows bricked up. Expats from wealthier, colder countries have been keen to buy and salvage older buildings in Tuscany and other more scenic, provinces. Was there anything in this area to draw people to it? Apparently not.

A family of three which had camped next to me in Verona arrived at the agriturismo, a farm which has a small campground on it. "You left so early and have just arrived," they said. "Did you look at things on the way?" No, I didn't. It took me all day to cycle the sixty-six kilometres. They, being father, adult son, and mother on an e-bike could go much faster than I could. After supper, I wandered over and we spent the evening chatting about e-bikes. Annika confessed that she hadn't really wanted a new bicycle, but her husband had convinced her to try one. On the past trips, he and the son had had to give her much more support than they were all happy with. Now she absolutely loved her e-bike and quietly wondered why she hadn't gotten one years earlier. She could carry her fair share of luggage and more. She could zip up hills with no effort and she could very easily keep up with the men in all terrain. Most significantly, she had the time and the energy to enjoy the journey instead of feeling guilty for being such a drag on the group. She arrived at camp each afternoon bursting with enthusiasm, buzzing with energy, and happy to take her share in all the evening chores and rituals.

One of the most exciting aspects of travelling through Europe, for an Australian, is the number of old towns and villages just waiting to be discovered by wide-eyed tourists. Italy has so many towns dating back to pre-Roman times, and often with Roman ruins or medieval walls. In fact, there are so many of these old towns around that I was starting to get rather blasé about them. Yep, there's another old town with really old tombs/churches/town plans/culinary traditions/festivals/monuments/rituals....

The town of Montagnana is surrounded by a complete set of city walls dating back to medieval times. Two kilometres long and from six to eight metres high, they are said to be among the best preserved in all Europe. I didn't stop to look at them, just admired them as I cycled through one of the main gates and into the old town. Inside, there was a market in full swing, and all of the local citizenry were out in force, doing their weekly shopping. As well as all the fruit, vegetables, bread, cheeses and meats were shoes, handbags, tea towels, kitchen wares and a whole host of other items. Having little need for a kitchen sieve or cooking pots, I escaped the marketplace with my wallet unzipped, and headed out again through another gate in the magnificent wall.

Another of the most fascinating aspects of cycling through a new culture is the focus on a new language. First up were always "Hello" and "Good morning" followed quickly by "Please" and "Thank you." The niceties having been learnt, it was then time for a few numbers beginning with zero to ten. Language is everywhere and my learning never stopped. All day long, I read road signs, the front covers of magazines, advertisements in shop windows, restaurant menus, and anything in print that I cycled past. In Europe, it's amazing how much an English/German speaker can pick up just by looking at words and looking for connections with their own language or with words learnt from other languages.

The downside when cycle touring across countries, for me, was that I would get immersed in one language, cross a border, hit another language and get thoroughly confused. All my bits and bobs of different languages would come out like a brightly coloured salad being presented for dessert – right word, wrong language in the right place but at the wrong time. I mixed up "Buenos dias" with "Buongiorno," and replaced "Grazie" with "Gracias" or "Merci" or even "Tak." By the time I got my miniscule vocabulary under control and was able to understand the camp managers' instructions, it was time to cross another border and start the learning all over again. But a smile needed no words and could be understood by all.

Ferrara is a UNESCO city, something to do with renaissance palaces, a nine-kilometre wall, and churches. There was a colonnade with a pasticceria, so I ordered an Americano (I didn't think asking for a brown coffee would work here.) with some milk on the side, and a pastry. I sat at a table in the colonnade to people watch, as one does in Italy.

My language lessons continued unabated. I had already learnt that "senza lattioso" means "without lactose" which was handy to know when buying milk. My neighbour was reading the morning paper. The heading on the front page proclaimed "…senza…" Somebody was missing something but who the poor sod was, and what he/she was missing were beyond my comprehension. I was senza a clue.

The waiter came flouncing up to me with a tray upon which were set two jugs, a cup, my pastry, and three small saucers. With a flamboyant wave of arm, wrist and hand, he grandly deposited each saucer individually on my table. The cup went on one with a theatrical flourish. The pastry on another with the same pompous gesture. The jugs were placed in an artful triangle with the cup and its saucer. Finally, with an even greater flourish, the docket was ceremoniously placed on the remaining saucer. What a production for four euros!

I scrabble in my wallet with the broken zip and handed over a five euro note. It was quickly and smoothly pocketed without any sort of flourish at all. The waiter chatted briefly with a lady passing by and disappeared from view.

Would I get my change? I did. By the time he returned, I had disarranged the artwork, scoffed half the pastry, spread crumbs all over the table, and was busy fishing out the sugar sachet which I had accidentally dropped into the coffee cup, splashing coffee onto the saucer and contributing my very own artwork to the tablecloth.

Coffee drunk, it was time to saddle up my bici and head to the Este castle in the centre of town. It was very imposing, but of greater interest to me was the market in the main street and the drumming that I could hear in the distance. There's nothing like a good bit of drumming to get the heart racing. I fought my way through the market, past the shoes and the handbags, the tomatoes and the cucumbers, past the buckets, colanders and rolling pins and all the other necessities of life in Italy, to the arched entrance of a large piazza.

Tiered rows of benches had been set up around the edge and the centre was squared off with a low barrier. Something was going to happen! Teams of people in coloured shirts milled about. Team Green met in the centre, the drumming began with a dozen drummers marching up and down. Suddenly, the drumming silenced and more Team Green bearing trumpets took over, squealing and wailing their timeless music. The trumpets were the long variety which we see in movies set in medieval times. It was a thrilling, heady racket. I had stumbled on a full-dress rehearsal for a big competition at the weekend.

Practice finished, Team Green left the arena and Team White walked on, the same collection of drummers and trumpeters but with a difference. A dozen people with multi-coloured flags formed up too. The music began with a mighty crash of the drums and blast of the trumpets. The flag bearers began a choreographed dance, marching and weaving around each other, waving their flags, throwing them in the air and catching them again. They tossed the flags to each other, spun around them, danced over them and never missed a beat.

Team White were followed by Team Yellow who were even better. This group integrated their drummers, trumpeters and flag dancers in one large musical dance. Drummers marched through the flag dancers, trumpeters blasted their way from one end of the square to the other, always in step, flags dipped and waved, then flew high into the air to be caught again as they zoomed down. Amazing!

Lastly, Team Red formed up in the square and went through their routine. Drums beat a heady rhythm, trumpets rang out in unison, flags waved, spun through the air towards the sun and were caught at the last second. Other groups were gathering outside the barriers for their rehearsal. It was getting late for me, so I marched my way back to my bici and cycled out of town.

Two days later, I stayed at another agriturismo campground, this time at Anita, next to a region of lake and wetlands. This agriturismo was once a standard farm but changed to hosting bird watching exhibitions as well as running a guesthouse and restaurant. The owner offered me a single room, dinner and breakfast for only ten euros more than camping would have cost, so I slept in a real bed again, which I thoroughly appreciated.

Dinner was a traditional Italian four course feast. The first course was a salty prosciutto, rock melon and quiche accompanied by a roughish red wine and fresh home-made bread. The second course was green ravioli filled with cheese. This was followed by a large tray of grilled vegetables – red and yellow peppers cut into wide strips, zucchini and tomato pieces, from which we could take what we wanted. Each guest was served their own piece of chicken, roasted with yet more tomatoes and some lemon. The dessert was a lemon gelato.

I love flat land and good bitumen roads. Twenty-four kilometres of rapid cycling took me to yet another agriturismo campground on the outskirts of Ravenna. This one was labelled as "bio" but I wasn't sure what that meant. There was no loo paper at all in the toilets. Did that make them bio? They had a big coffee machine and the owner cooked piadina on request. This is a local food which I had seen advertised on a number of café menu boards. It is a flatbread stuffed with a variety of fillings such as olives and tomatoes, and I can highly recommend them to any hungry cyclists.

I rode into Ravenna after a bit of a break to begin the arduous process of touring the eight UNESCO sites, and most importantly, to buy a new camping mattress.

From the outside, the Basilica di San Apollinare Nuovo looked pretty ordinary, a brick building with a few arches in front and a tall conical tower next to it. I walked inside and my jaw hit the ground! Two rows of columns divided the space. Above them were the most glorious mosaics. A row of sedate virgin maidens trailed behind the Three Kings as they walked towards Mary with the Infant Jesus on her lap. On the opposite wall, twenty-five saints walked calmly towards an adult Jesus. Above them all shone various snippets from the Old and the New Testaments. A square at one end showed the Port of Classe, just outside Ravenna, and a fleet of trading ships in the harbour.

I visited all the other well-known mosaic sites and was equally impressed by each of them. The colours were so vibrant, the figures had been created with such delicate detail that words alone are completely inadequate to describe the beauty of these mosaics. One of my favourite images was The Baptism of Jesus in the Battistero degli Ariani. The water rippled across His lower body, stylized yet lifelike as it shimmered and distorted the body behind it.

To think that over 1,500 years ago, artists planned, designed, and drew each of these images from their imaginations. The merger of mathematics and art was of supreme importance. If a designer wanted twenty-four holy men in a picture, he needed to make sure that they all fitted comfortably. A picture of three people nd ten sheep needed to be balanced, if not, the sheep might have ended up sitting on someone's lap. And how did the artists design pictures which had to follow curves or go around corners? Climbing high up on ladders or scaffolding, they spent hours, days, and months gluing tiny pieces of coloured stone, tinted glass, and gold leaf onto a background to form intricate pictures for the Glory of God. And of course, to trumpet the glories of Emperor Justinian, Queen Theodora, and Archbishop Massimiano.

While in Ravenna, I made sure to spread the sight-seeing over three days to avoid sensory overload. In-between, I went mattress hunting. My camping mattress, which consisted of a dozen or so long, narrow air channels, had rebelled. Some of the walls between the air channels had exploded so that whenever I lay down, all the air underneath me got squashed and rushed to any section which didn't have a body part on top of it. The result was that I slept on the ground with a great big balloon of air on either side of my legs or between my knees. It was very uncomfortable. Sadly, none of the camping shops in Ravenna could sell me a decent air-mattress. The only offering was far too long, it wouldn't have fitted into my tent.

On my last morning, I had one more historic site to visit before cycling on towards the east coast of Italy, so I pedalled the short distance to Classe to check out the Basilicata di Apollinare there. Walking past the three tour buses disgorging their loads of elderly German and Dutch tourists, I wheeled my bicycle into the basilica garden and chained it to a tree, fairly confident that none of the walking-stick wielding tourists would steal it to cycle off into the distance.

Inside the basilica, above the apse, God held a book, watched by the four evangelists while twelve lambs walked towards them in heaven. Below them, a large gold cross sparkled inside a circle of glorious blue with ninety-nine gold stars. More sheep ambled across green fields shaded by trees while Moses and Elijah hovered above them in a shimmering golden background. The images are packed with coded meanings, easily read by anyone with the relevant knowledge, but what struck me most was the timeless beauty of this scene. The contrast of the white sheep on the green fields under the golden sky was a glory of colour. Indeed, the overall vision of all those magnificent colours and shades – blues, greens, golds, reds, and white, the golden stars in the deep blue sky … these images will stay with me forever.

The route to the coast led me along the railway line and into a large forest reserve. Interestingly, cycling signs led me into the forest … and then deserted me with no indication of where to go. Without my trusty phone, I would have had to rely on breadcrumbs to get out of there. Emerging on the other side, I came into a marshy plain, divided by a river with numerous trabucchi lining its banks.

Trabucchi are wooden huts standing on stilts and connected to the shore by a gangplank. Long poles jut out from the trabucchi and hang over the river, fishing nets dangling below them. It was a warm day with the sun beating down from above so there was no fishing happening. No doubt that would occur in the early morning or late evening when the light and shade conditions were optimum for catching fish.

A short while later, I turned left and saw and smelt the sea in front of me. The Adriatic! I had reached the sea! The remainder of the day, I cycled due south along a beach road between hotels and restaurants to my right and the beach to my left. "If the next five hundred kilometres are like this, it'll be a breeze," I thought, contentedly.

My accommodation for the night in Rimini was a top bunk in a four-bed female dorm with three young German lasses. Everyone in the hostel was super friendly. Free pasta and sauce were available for supper, but I paid five euros for two mini sausages and a cremated hamburger with white, sliced bread, lettuce and a few bits of tomato. A backyard BBQ with burnt meat – so like home!

Once upon a time, Italy as a country didn't exist. Instead. It was a motley collection of independent city-states such as Venice, Genoa, Florence, and San Marino. Each city competed with all the others in trade, politics, and warfare to gain wealth, power, recognition, and influence. Over time, the city-states all combined to become a new country: Italy. All that is, except for the Vatican and San Marino. Splendidly isolated on its mountain top, San Marino is still an independent entity, living in co-operation with, but also thumbing its nose at its powerful neighbour, Italy. I took the bus from Rimini, curious to know how a tiny independent country, landlocked and surrounded by only one neighbour, can survive in the modern world.

The old city of San Marino consists of three old towers, a few linking walls, a series of piazzas joined by old buildings on romantically twisting cobbled streets, and the most magnificent views over the surrounding countryside. It was nice, but nothing superlatively special. Without its status as a miniscule, independent country, San Marino would not attract nearly as many tourists. Hundreds of tourist shops, restaurants and cafés lined every street and open area, beckoning visitors with their wares and goodies. Remarkably, the shops were quite varied, although definitely aimed at the tourist market. A postcard stall nestled next to a leather-goods store full of shoes and handbags. Ceramics, T-shirts, cushions, and jewellery were all for sale. There was a lively trade in San Marino stamps, tea towels, mugs, and assorted tourist stuff. There was even a shop for yellow plastic ducks – the type that little children play with in the bath. They probably sold more ducks than the neighbouring shop sold of its Swarovski crystals.

I elbowed my way through a crowd to watch the Changing of the Guard. It was picturesque but rather useless in these modern times of cyber-attacks and terrorism. It was quite tempting to see this as a show just for tourists, but it probably wasn't. If so, it should have been held in the broad expanse of the piazza with standing room all around for the curious, and with souvenirs for sale. It wasn't. It was held in the portico of the government offices where only rude people like me could see what was happening, and it was over in minutes. If so few people could see the Changing of the Guard and it didn't serve a rational purpose in protecting the building or its occupants, I was puzzled as to why it is still performed in this manner.

I couldn't see any evidence of normal, everyday commercial business in the old city. When the tourists returned to their hotels, when the shopkeepers locked their doors for the night, when the last cars had left the seven or eight carparks – what life was there in the old city? Maybe just the mangy cats who woke and prowled the streets pouncing on dropped French fries and scavenging for pieces of leftover piadinas.

Further down the mountain, life was as busy and as hectic as along the coast. Cranes were dotted along the roadside, their drivers helping to build yet more apartments and office space for the modern digital economy. San Marino has one of the highest GDPs in the world and all that money has to be invested somewhere.

# | 34 |

# Meltdown in Ancona

## Rimoni to Ancona, 95 km

From Rimini to Marotta was fairly uneventful. I left in the morning, rode south all day, then arrived. I breakfasted on the beach at Marotta thinking that this was going to be my life until I eventually wheeled into Bari, where I planned to store my bicycle somewhere while I returned home for a four-month break. How wrong I was! That calm and sunny day had a big lesson in store for me.

The sea shimmered a pale silver in the early morning light. Not a wave or ripple disturbed its stillness. A few rocks in the distance beckoned in vain, there were no swimmers to disturb the calm, An army of umbrellas, green and white, folded down and hooded for the night were yet to be awakened. They stood in silent rows, waiting, waiting, waiting for the command to establish a territory and guard their users from that daunting feeling of openness which plagues the modern soul. To sit on a beach is to be open and unprotected from the sky, the gods, our prehistoric instincts, our enemies. Put a roof, an umbrella, over our heads, no matter how insubstantial, and the uneasiness fades. All is well, we can enjoy this, our own spot of sand, and focus on protecting our territory. Beware all who dare to walk into my shade or kick sand onto my towel!

A lone walker strolled along the water's edge where the sand was packed hard. Another came lumbering towards the café. Walking over deep sand is difficult for the inexperienced. All the action, for the moment, was there in the café.

"An American coffee, please."

"You are welcome."

The waiter thought I was German and answered my Australian accented "Grazie" with a "Bitte." There, on the beach, languages flowed and fluctuated. German, Dutch, English, and French, but mostly Italian. It didn't really matter, we all needed our morning coffee and struggled to walk on deep sand just the same.

Being such a short cycling day, without any hills and with a room at a cheap hotel in Ancona booked, I felt quite relaxed about the day ahead. I fiddled around at camp, had a nice breakfast on the beach, and allowed my washing to dry properly before I packed up and left. The first fifteen kilometres were along a quiet beach road with a great bike path, hotels to my right and cafés on the beach to my left. It was all good.

I turned into a supermarket and bought the makings of a lunch – bread rolls, some cheese, a tomato, an orange, and a drink. Then, I headed back to the beach to look for a bit of shade and have a picnic. The only shade was at the beginning of a walking path leading from a car park at the end of the beach road. There were rocks and sea in front, a wire fence and derelict buildings behind me, an industrial site of chimneys spurting oily-looking smoke in the distance, and rubbish everywhere. It was a far cry from the elegant hotels of the morning ride.

A tall man walked past me, went to his car and got out a towel. I focused on my lunch. When I looked up, I was amazed to see him sitting stark naked on the rocks directly in front of me. With his legs splayed wide and everything on show, I didn't know whether he was a creepy individual, or just being an Italian macho male. I packed up my lunch and left.

I had initially planned to cycle along the walking path and avoid much of the SS16 but I was a bit concerned about Cassanova. It seemed wiser to go back to the busier road. A few kilometres later, as the road entered the next town, it began to get quite hectic. I studied my Maps.me and saw that if I cut through some long grass and rubbish, I could cross a car park and take a quieter road around much of the chaos. I proceeded in this manner, always checking the route and looking for quieter options.

At one point, my route passed under the SS16. It dipped sharply, evened out under the bridge, and then rose sharply on the other side. Alternatively, I could walk on the pedestrian path which stayed on the same level but was a good deal higher than the deepest section of the road. As usual, when in a tricky cycling situation, I chose to walk. This was fine at first, the path had a secure wire fence separating me from the speeding traffic. Then the path narrowed and narrowed until it was so narrow that my bike bags were scraping the fence on one side and the wall on the other side. I had to manoeuvre first one bike handle, then the other, around each drainpipe which protruded onto the path. I was ten metres from the end when a tall skinny lad approached. He saw that I was taking up the whole width of the path with no room to spare. Did he wait for me to exit and leave the way clear for him? No, he didn't. He walked up to me and stopped. There was no way to pass each other.

I shrugged my shoulders and said: "Bad luck, mate. You need to go back." He didn't understand English. After a few seconds of nervous stalemate, he climbed onto the fence, over the other side, and with a drop of at least four metres below him onto the road, spidered his way along the fence until he had passed me. Brave, athletic, and totally pointless. Two stressful situations in one day. Was there going to be a third?

After this little entertainment, all went well until the last eight kilometres into Ancona. The SS16 narrowed, the verge disappeared and there were no quieter options to be found. I was cycling on a major road with four lanes of traffic and nothing protecting me from the trucks, buses and caravans which were flying past me at breakneck speed only a metre away. I was distinctly unhappy.

Every so often, there was a small lay-by, an entrance to a driveway or just a break in the fence. I started waiting in each lay-by until there was a break in the traffic coming up from behind, then zipping out and riding like a bat out of hell, as fast as I possibly could, until the next lay-by. I rode in this manner until I came to a fork in the road. The right lane went to the harbour, the left lane dipped down a steep incline and into Ancona. I couldn't see whether the steep lane went into a tunnel or just under a bridge. After some considerable hesitation, I waited for a gap in the traffic, gathered all my courage, and rode down at top speed, praying that I wouldn't hit loose gravel or a hole in the bitumen. The road levelled out and I could see that I had just ridden under a bridge. More trucks swept past me as I shot off the road, flew between some parked cars and stopped on the broken footpath. I was shaking, but safe. I decided then and there that this type of cycling was not for me. I needed to seriously think about what I was doing.

I spent the remainder of the afternoon considering all my options and studying the map carefully. There seemed to be some smaller roads on my route south, but they were only in short sections and always ended up merging with the major road, the SS16. Should I keep cycling and risk more dangerous roads? I didn't like this option. In fact, even considering it made me slightly hysterical. It was difficult to feel confident about the day ahead when I didn't even know if, or when, my route would morph from a lovely flowing tarmac bike path to a dangerous dodgem game. Cycle-touring should be enjoyable, maybe even educational, not a life-threatening disaster.

Should I take some trains and avoid the worst bits? It was difficult to identify where the worst bits were, and the trains didn't seem to be too easy either. Should I pull the pin altogether, go somewhere else and come back another year with an e-bike? I could then cycle the quieter hill roads and see more of the countryside rather than just a narrow strip of hotels and beach cafés.

I considered spending two nights in Ancona which would give me time to rest and ponder the various options, but Ancona didn't inspire me. I had no desire to stay there at all. I just wanted to get out. Being exhausted and needing a solution, I decided to go to Padua for three nights, Venice for a week or two and then fly back to Australia from there. I booked accommodation in a hostel in Padua.

One of the questions I get asked the most is whether I enjoy travelling alone. Usually, the answer is "Yes," for a variety of reasons, but sometimes the answer is "No." On that day, I had experienced some of the worst aspects of solo travel. The man on the beach, and the young lad in the road underpass had made me face up to everybody else's fears for my safety. The stresses brought on by cycling amongst so much traffic and the need to navigate my own route were building. The need to do all my own research, make decisions when exhausted, book accommodation, organise food and drinks for myself and maintenance for my bike – it all added up to a great deal.

Having made the decision to go to Padua, the resultant feeling of dissatisfaction at having stopped before the end of my trip kept me awake for most of the night. By early morning, I had decided that what I really wanted to do was to spend a few weeks on Malta and put closure on this particular adventure.

I cancelled my booking in Padua and booked three nights in Bari instead. I breakfasted, packed, and was at the station by 7.40 a.m. to get on the first train to Bari. The ticket seller shook his head in dismay when he saw my bicycle. They can only be taken on regional trains. One had just left less than ten minutes ago. The next wouldn't leave for another four hours. Four hours to wait! I could have stayed in my hotel room and had another few hours' sleep. Additionally, it would take four trains to get to Bari and I would only get there by 10 p.m. at the earliest.

Given that I had four hours to wait for the next train, I decided to go away, calm down, relax, and think about it all. The obvious solution was to take the first two trains, changing at Pescara and finishing at Termoli. I cancelled my Bari accommodation and booked one night at Termoli. This inability to make a solid decision was getting quite expensive, each cancellation cost me a fee because the cancellations were so late.

I arrived in Termoli exhausted and immediately booked a second night in my pension so that I could spend a day reading, resting, and slowly meandering around the streets.

It was in Termoli that I fell in love with Italian town planning. Almost every town in Italy has a square in the centre, a meeting place, a marketplace. The square is the focal point of the passegiata which I saw for the first time in Termoli. All the shops were open into the late evening. The bakery was doing a roaring trade selling slices of pizza, while the queue at the gelateria snaked out their door and into the street. Hundreds of people just walked slowly up and down the pedestrian mall, and into the town square. Old couples wandered along arm in arm, sometimes stopping to chat to friends; families strolled along waiting patiently for their toddlers to stop screaming long enough to catch up; little boys chased around in small groups, laughing and yelling in excitement. Little girls skipped in unison, their older sisters giggling on their phones as they sashayed past. Where were the teenage boys who should have been hanging around in groups admiring the girls from the safety of numbers? I only saw a few young men, so I wondered whether they were mostly at home playing computer games or chilling somewhere else.

Meanwhile, the low wall across the bottom of the mall was sporting a collection of old gentlemen, twenty of them, all in a row like sparrows on a power line. They had a good view of all the action and didn't even have to move about in order to be part of it. They chatted and murmured amongst themselves. What were they discussing? The morning's fishing? Alberto's new motorbike? I gave a quick and terribly fluent "Buona sera" as I went past. Some smiled, perked up and responded with a torrent of conversation. Others were smarter, they just laughed at me, knowing quite well that I had reached the limit of my Italian.

For some unknown reason, I didn't even consider cycling any further south which was really, really daft. There was a vague cycle route from Termoli all the way down to the southernmost cape of the heel of Italy. I took two more trains to Bari instead. Three stations, each one a complete unknown as far as stairs and elevators were concerned. Up and down steps and stairs with my bike and all my panniers. At Bari, a cleaner started to tell me not to dump my panniers at the bottom of the stairs as he was about to wipe the floor. I was so fed up that I yelled at him, but he didn't even blink. Expressing oneself quite forcefully seemed to be quite acceptable.

I had another day of ignoring my travels. I think my funk at Ancona was much worse than I had thought, or maybe it had been building up for a while. I found McDonalds and spent all morning sitting over a cup of coffee and reading a book on my phone. Book finished, I strolled through the newer part of Bari with its well-planned grid of straight streets, over the dividing road, through the old town wall and into the maze of twisting, turning streets and piazzas which are so characteristic of medieval town non-planning.

I passed a young man from Portugal sitting on a blanket with an old bicycle next to him. He had a map of the world and had drawn a proposed tour on it. He was making tiny models of bicycles using coloured wire and was trying to sell them. They were pretty, but quite useless. His money-making method may have been artistic and free, but it wasn't going to improve his finances very quickly. How many little models would he need to make and sell in a day to fund his travels?

Apart from my quiet seat in McDonalds, the high point of Bari, for me, was the Basilica di San Nicolo with the tomb of St. Nicholas, known in the English-speaking world as Santa Claus. I made a point of going there to pay my respects. Poor old St. Nick died in Turkey, but his bones were stolen by Barese fishermen in 1087 and brought to Bari where they were placed in a specially built crypt in a specially built church which is said to be one of the best examples of Puglian Romanesque architecture. I'm afraid my understanding of religious architecture still hadn't developed much further than "Look, there's a church," so the beauty and significance of this particular basilica was rather wasted on me. But I did like St. Nick's tomb, down below in the crypt.

There were two young ladies in my room in the hostel, Sally and Andrea. They were both from Melbourne and seemed incredibly young to me, but that's probably because I'm so old. It was great to be able to speak in my normal broad Australian accents to some compatriots, even with the forty-year age difference. I chatted a fair while with them, mainly listening while they spoke at length about their travels, their lives at home, their hopes and dreams for the future. I looked at their bright, hopeful faces and wondered where the last forty years of my life had gone, never to be relived except in my memories.

It was time to move on and to create more spectacular memories. I left my bicycle in Bari and took a train to Matera, thought to be one of the oldest settlements in Italy. Some claim it to be the third oldest continuous settlement in the world.

Matera is in the province of Basilicata, an area of soft rock riven with streams and steep canyons, pocked by thousands of caves, and noted for the extreme poverty of the local population until recent times. Matera itself, is a jumble of sand-coloured blocks tumbling down the hillside in two areas called "sassi." Sassi Barisano and Sassi Caveoso.

Way back in the "good old days," the town was an urban marvel with a drainage system, cisterns, orchards and hanging gardens. People lived in houses. The caves, with their constant temperature of fifteen degrees Celsius, were mainly used for storing agricultural products such as wine and olives. In 1595 Eustachio Verricelli wrote that Matera was a healthy and well protected city.

The seventeenth century was the beginning of the end of the good times. The development of large modern agricultural estates impacted negatively on the small-scale pastoral and agricultural economy of the region. In 1663. Matera became the provincial capital which brought great development and a massive increase in population. The new arrivals needed houses of their own. Gardens were destroyed and built over, the poorer people were forced out of their homes into the caves and their quality of life went inexorable downhill. By 1952, the Prime Minister of the day called Matera "the Shame of Italy." New houses were built on the flatter lands above the ravine and the locals were forcibly evacuated from their homes.

The sassi were blocked off for many years. Neglected, crumbling and increasingly dangerous, no-one knew what to do with them until they were classified by UNESCO in 1993. Suddenly, the local population woke up to the treasure they had lying at their feet.

House fronts hide the caves which lie behind them. Flights of steps connect levels as they twist and turn in all directions. Long ago, every floor was someone else's roof and every open space was a family's loungeroom. Two steps up and a quick turn around a corner led to a doorway, a rooftop, weeds reaching for life from cracked walls, a hopeful cat cleaning her fur in the sun, or a small triangle of pavement glistened with the last rain.

Matera was a timeless memory of vanished footsteps. I listened for the echoes of life long gone, of people joined together in family, in community and in poverty. Just imagine if the stones could speak! Gone were the stories, the dramas, the joy and the celebrations of the people who lived in each other's lives. Gone too, were the personal memories of squalor, misery and hopelessness. Tourists murmured as they perused photographs, wandered through recreated cave interiors, and planned their evening meal at one of the many modern restaurants on a cave terrace. The clink of coins in the entrance of a cave museum heralded a different time but I wondered what the community had lost in its move to modernisation.

A church, square and solid, rose on the edge of a large piazza. Religious life and churches abounded in the sassi of Matera, at least 150 churches. Although some were merely frescoes painted on a cave wall, they were still considered holy by the local population. The tenth century frescoes inside the Chiesa Madonna de Idris were a reminder of the strength of the people's faith and the very human desire to surround ourselves with beauty, even in the midst of poverty.

When I arrived, Matera had recently been selected to be a European City of Culture for 2019, which had thrown the local authorities into quite a tizz. They had been given enormous buckets of money to spend on upgrading infrastructure and dragging the city into the 21$^{st}$ century. The two sassi were being renovated and revived. It cost up to €4,500 per square metre to bring a cave dwelling up to modern standards of health, safety and beauty. Because these dwellings were so old, every aspect of them had to be respected and treated accordingly. The ceilings had to be covered with either glass fibre or carbon to strengthen and stabilise them. The walls were sprayed with a chemical resin which protects the surface and prevents particles from loosening into the atmosphere. Add to that the modern necessities of electricity, running water and sewerage. Guest houses, restaurants, bakeries, and souvenir shops were the new tenants.

Sassi Barisano had already largely been restored. I walked over to Caveoso which was the poorer of the two areas. There were some caves being renovated but most of the little laneways had been blocked off and safety warnings abounded.

I took a tour bus to the other side of the ravine from where I got a great view of Matera. Unlike Fez, which has sprouted satellite dishes like a plague of mushrooms, Matera still looked positively biblical when viewed from afar. It has been the settings for a few movies set in ancient times, mostly to do with the life of Christ. The harsh rock-strewn landscape of the Murgia Plateau only added to the ancient impression. I could imagine multiple movie producers and directors going hysterical with spasms of delight when they first beheld Matera from a distance.

I stayed at Rock Hostel in the new town above the sassi. It was a lovely hostel: bright, airy, and with just the right level of comfort to soothe a battered soul. It was owned by Francesca, who shone with enthusiasm for her old town. The hostel only had a few people in it, but they were an interesting bunch. A screen writer for British television, a young man who had also cycled all the way from Finland, and another older solo female traveller. Marie, an American with sparkling eyes and a great sense of style, was seventy-one years old but looked to be in her fifties. She had been travelling solo since she was forty-nine and had celebrated her fiftieth birthday with a balloon flight over Ayer's Rock, now known as Uluru, in Central Australia.

Having thoroughly enjoyed the ancient site of Matera, and having relaxed with so many like-minded travellers, I came to a momentous decision. I decided to continue cycling to Malta the following year. It was while I was roaming the steps, terraces and piazzas of Matera that I asked myself what I really wanted to do. From the depths of my heart came the instant response – to pick up again from where I had left off, to start cycling again from Ancona. It felt the right thing to do. I returned to Bari, collected my bicycle and took it back to Matera where Francesca organised for me to be able to store it with a tour company over the winter. They had over a hundred bikes of their own which were hired out to tourists over the summer. Their bikes hibernated in a big warehouse in the off-season,undergoing health checks and repairs in preparation for the following year. I knew that my bicycle would be in good company until I returned for the final leg of Cycling to the Sun.

By this stage, I had ridden over 2,500 kilometres in central Europe in addition to the 2,800 kilometres in Scandinavia, and I had cycled in eight countries. I still had another 1,700 kilometres to go, but only one new country to explore: Malta.

# PART 4:

## La Dolce Vita

*Italy and Malta*
*Ancona, Italy to Malta*
*1,709 kilometres*

*Italy and Malta*

1,709 KM

2019

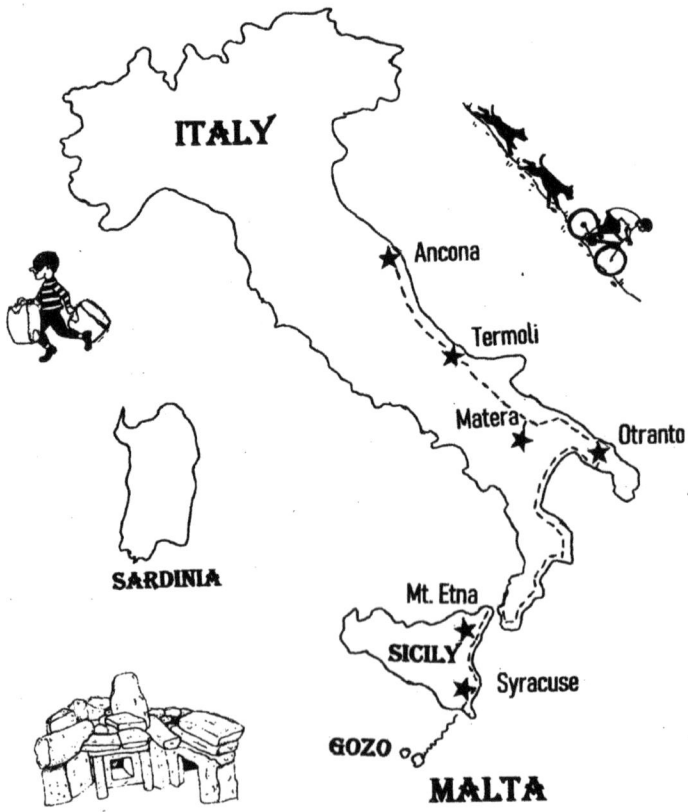

ITALY

Ancona

Termoli

Matera

Otranto

SARDINIA

Mt. Etna

SICILY

Syracuse

GOZO

MALTA

# | 35 |

## Starting Again With a Cycling Buddy

### Ancona to Termoli, 274 km

Anne is one of my many cousins from Germany. She is six years older than me and has an insatiable appetite for life. She is another one of those blessed people who can plough through the bad times and always comes up smiling at the end. An unstoppable, perky optimist, Anne is also a cycling and hiking enthusiast with a bit of a travel bug. She had been very supportive of my ride south from the North Cape and was quite keen to ride the rest of the way to Malta with me.

I was hesitant. On the one hand, it would be a big bonus to have someone to share the navigation, the research and the costs. I knew we have similar travel styles. We both like to take our time, to stop at every point of interest, to take dozens of photos, to be really in the moment. On the other hand, I have developed my own way of doing things, and was aware that I get rather grumpy when things don't go my way. It's not a good trait, one that I have been battling my whole life, and I was nervous.

Anne also had her own fears and stresses to contend with. She seemed blissfully unaware of all that could go wrong with a bicycle - mechanics, tyres and so on. Her main fears were about being caught out in the rain or of being unable to find accommodation for the night. We each carried a tent, but Anne was not so experienced in camping and certainly wasn't keen on stealth camping if required.

The route from Ancona to Loreto was only twenty-five kilometres but that was quite far enough for the first day. We had to slog our way up three steep hills during which I discovered that Anne was much fitter and stronger than me. She rode merrily on ahead and waited patiently for me on every hilltop. So much for me being the more experienced rider leading the way! We had earlier booked an Airbnb apartment in Loreto in the theory that we should start our trip with a bit of luxury and gently ease ourselves into the camping side of things. Our accommodation in Loreto was in "Holy House," an ordinary, not very holy house with an upstairs apartment for paying guests.

After a rest, we set off to see the cathedral which, like most towns and villages in that part of Italy, was on top of another steep hill. Inside, the cathedral's paintings, candles and spiritual ambience muted all sound. Eyes raised high, we peered at a marvellous depiction of the Last Supper painted under the dome but were eventually drawn forwards to look behind the altar. There lay the true treasure of the cathedral and the reason for it being a major pilgrimage site.

A single-roomed house of stone and brick, in all its simple glory, this was apparently the house of Mary and Joseph in Nazareth and in which Jesus also lived as a boy. The house was originally situated in front of, and adjoining a cave in Nazareth, the cave making a second room. In 1291, when the crusaders were expelled from Palestine, the house was transported by angels, first to Croatia and then three years later to Loreto; or so the legend goes.

Either that, or the stones and the bricks were stolen by a noble family from Epirus called the Angeli. There is documentary evidence to support the latter theory. Niceforo Angelo, leader of Epirus, gave the stones and bricks as a dowry when he married his daughter off to Philip of Taranto. In more modern times, the bricks and stones have been scientifically examined and it has been accepted that they did indeed originate from in front of a cave in Nazareth. Whether Mary, Joseph and

Jesus actually lived in this house 1285 years prior to its theft by the crusaders is a different question altogether.

Cycling to Loreto had been a bit of an inland detour. It was time to head back to the beach and the flat coastal roads. The day began bright and sunny; we did too. We set off following our route as planned out for us in Komoot but soon decided that we knew better. For some reason it wanted to take us over a big hill when we couldn't see any hills at all between us and the coast. We followed our noses instead, and went straight to the beach, turned right, and headed south down the coast. We passed numerous hotels and cafés, and even some campgrounds. All was well. The quiet road along the beach soon came to a halt and we had to make a choice – follow the suggested route along the SS16, the major road, or make our own route along minor roads. We opted to make our own route which seemed to work well until we realised that we were heading for the hills again. Any sort of hills were anathema to us. We just didn't have the strength to ride up steep inclines and those hills were all very steep!

We pondered the dilemma over lunch, then decided to brave the SS16, the thought of which quite terrified me. It was a toss-up between hills or traffic. When we reached the SS16, I was quite relieved to see it wasn't nearly so bad as I had anticipated. It was busy and noisy but there was a good verge which we could ride on. I wouldn't call it safe, but it wasn't quite as dangerous as I had feared.

Our accommodation at Porto Sant' Elpidio was a whole apartment again, owned by Valentino and Selena with their six children: three girls and three boys. Child Number Four spoke good English, otherwise we made do with kisses on both cheeks and a lot of good-natured Italian rapid-fire explanations of which I could understand no more than one word in every sentence. It was just as well that there was a recognisably human pattern to our communications. We were tired, they were friendly, we wanted accommodation, they wanted money. The only real questions were: where could we get food? And, what should we do with the keys when we left?

Having handed over the keys the next morning, we continued on our relentless search for The South and soon found a cycle path along the beach. Cycling there was quite pleasant, a wide path with houses and gardens on one side, waves crashing against large rocks on the other side. This idyllic route was short-lived.

We came to a STOP sign. DANGER! Beyond, we could see waves crashing over the rocks onto the path. Undaunted, we decided to risk an instant salt-shower and cycled on. Our bravado was, however, also short-lived. A small stream lay in our path with no way over, except through, depth unknown. We retraced our route, back past the STOP and DANGER! signs and back onto the road. By the time we had cycled through the town, we decided to try the path again. This time there were no warning signs, so we pedalled bravely on, dodging the waves which occasionally came hurtling over the rocks.

Then came a dry stream bed, and no proper path to be seen on the other side. There was just a very rough looking stretch of sand and gravel with the sea held back by big rocks on the left, a fence on the right and a building at the far end. I looked but couldn't see any bicycle tyre marks in the sand, only footprints. I walked along the fence for about a kilometre until it emerged at a road and café. In places, the sand and gravel morphed into a surface of pebbles and small rocks. I decided it was do-able, we could push our bikes through, riding them was impossible. Anne acquiesced, so we set off, pushing and heaving when the wheels got stuck in deep sand or between sharp stones, dodging splashing water as it came over the rocks, weaving between broken glass and assorted rubbish too. We made it through, happily but then agreed that we'd had enough adventures for one day. From then on, we stuck to the Komoot route until we arrived, exhausted, at Porto d'Ascoli where we collapsed in a hotel over-run with school students.

From Loreto to Montesilvano, the route had been quite flat the whole way. Leaving Montesilvano, we could see hills running down to the sea on the cape ahead of us. I hoped there was a path around the base of the hills but didn't feel too confident. At some stage we were going to have to tackle hills again. It actually wasn't too bad. I had to push, but mainly because my gear change didn't work, I lost my rhythm and half fell of my bike. Anne rode almost to the top. A few kilometres along a ridge led us to a steep descent. We could see a lovely bike path at the bottom of the valley. It followed along the beach and went around the base of the next hill. I got really excited because I was pretty sure it would enable us to avoid the steep climb up to Ortona.

We flew down the road and found the track to the bottom of the valley. It ended at a rail line bridge. Then I saw that other people had walked under the bridge. I could see another, smaller bridge on the other side. Was it the bike path? I hauled my bike through and onto the second bridge. There it was – the most glorious bike path leading into the distance, around the base of the hill, as we had anticipated. The path was a wide, bright blue tarmac, with a dotted line down the centre, and … with a big construction fence completely blocking our way!

After ten minutes of abject misery, we hauled our bikes back under the railway bridge and retraced our steps back to the road. We cycled up the long, slow hill into Ortona and collapsed on a bench for our picnic lunch from where we were consoled with a magnificent view of the sea in front of us and of the castle to our right.

The afternoon's cycling was quite different to the previous days. Most of the time we were high above the sea, swooping up and down small rises, but always on the SS16. A sign welcomed us to the Costa de Trabbochi, scattered with a number of the aforementioned trabbochi. These traditional coastal fishing shacks were similar to the ones I had seen along a river further north. Long wooden piers led from land out to the sea. At the end of each pier was a wooden shack with wooden poles hanging out the sides. Fishing nets hung from the poles and could be lowered into the water when the tide and the weather conditions were right.

It seemed appropriate to have a seafood pizza for supper that night. My pizza was not only huge, with lashings of tomato and cheese, but also very tasty with mussels, clams, prawns and some unidentifiable white bits piled high on the top. And carrots! I had no idea how or why carrots got included on a seafood pizza, but they did add a bit of bright colour to this most Italian of dishes.

I had had a quite varied experience of food in Italy by this point. The general perception is that the cuisine there is absolutely wonderful. People rave about it and it has spawned a whole industry of cookbooks, cooking lessons in Tuscany, food tasting tours, cooking utensils and ingredients, and so on.

It made me feel like a heretic, but I hadn't seen much to get so excited about. The areas which we were cycling through did not see many tourists. Most visitors were holiday makers from northern Europe who came to spend a week or two by the sea and were rumoured to bring most of their own food with them. The supermarkets which I had gone to had all been rather small and uninspiring with sad, tired vegetables wrapped in plastic amidst an equally sad and uninspiring collection of the basics of life. The freezers didn't offer any pre-cooked meals at all. Most other countries that I have cycled in have had cafés with simple cheap meals such as a thick pea and ham soup for three euros. As a non-cooking cyclist, I had come to rely on these café meals to keep me energised and pedalling through each long day.

I pondered and worried about this conundrum for days on end. Was I missing out on something? Was I not seeing what was in front of me? Then I had a light-bulb moment. If everyone goes home to a wonderful home-cooked meal every day, they don't need to buy pre-cooked meals from a supermarket or a cheap and filling soup from a café. We didn't have a home and family in Italy to keep us fed, so the only options left to us were to eat in restaurants or to eat pizza. The restaurants were comparatively expensive, and I couldn't face pizza every day. We had already agreed to stay in apartments as much as possible, so we amended that plan slightly to include cooking our own evening meals most days. Neither of us liked to cook much but we were confident that we could bumble along together and create something simple but edible. Every few days we would go to a restaurant and enjoy whatever regional specialities were available.

I had had such a relaxing time at Termoli after my Ancona funk the previous year that I was quite keen to go back and show it to Anne. Komoot showed me a big hill at Vasto, and once again, we looked for any route which would take us around the hill rather than over the top. We followed an alternative mountain biking trail through forest and along a cliff top. It wasn't such a clever idea. I enjoyed the forest and the occasional view over the sea. I did not enjoy the extra kilos of mud clinging to my tyres, blocking the wheel from turning, choking the chain mechanism and making every step hard work. We stopped numerous times to clean the mud off with my extra heavy tyre levers, grumbling and muttering over the mud and getting it smeared all over our clothes. Our alternative trail was beautiful and adventurous but a real time waster.

Termoli was just as relaxing as I remembered it. There was a very civilised cycling path for the last few kilometres into town and hundreds of people were strolling about, enjoying the fresh air blowing in from the sea. We only stayed one night because we had both hit our cycling stride and were keen to keep moving.

# | 36 |

## Through the Olive Groves

### Termoli to Toritto, 236 km

Our route from Termoli turned west, inland. I was sad to be leaving the sea but also excited to be venturing into a different landscape, a hotter, drier countryside of ancient villages amidst the olive groves.

We turned off the main north-south highway onto a narrower country road. The sun was behind our shoulders, but the air still held the early morning chill. We came to a young woman squatting next to a chair, a small fire smouldering at her side. She was putting on make-up to complement her bright red dress and fishnet stockings. Why was she there? Maybe she was waiting for a friend to take her to work? But why the fire? Some ruined buildings stood on the opposite side of the road, an empty chair in front. Puzzling. A few kilometres further, another young woman sat on a chair, then another. The penny dropped. Sex workers. Occasionally a truck parked on the side of the road, or a van parked in a field with an empty chair nearby added more detail. We counted nineteen women in total, mostly from twenty to thirty years old. Some stood around bored, one was picking flowers, another woman was listening to Arabic music. It seemed a dangerous and lonely way to earn a living. We smiled and greeted any who vaguely looked at us, to be rewarded with a return smile and a wave. The last lady was much older with a flash looking car. Was she the madam?

We cycled through sleepy villages and endless olive groves. Thick black clouds threatened to wash us into the gutters but usually passed by to thunder elsewhere. A pack of big, black, mongrel dogs raced to intercept us, slather flying as they tore across the fields, baying for our blood. We fled, to meet up with a super-friendly small brown dog who wanted to adopt us. He accompanied us for kilometres, trotting along beside us, tongue hanging out and panting in the heat, stopping to mark a post or sniff in the roadside weeds before racing to catch up to us. I eventually used my best farmer's language and teacher's voice to sternly send him scuttling back to his home. One cycling buddy was quite sufficient.

The sun bore down on us, the olive groves faded away and we cycled through an area of market gardens and large fields of bare earth being readied for planting. We passed a dozen or so African men working in the fields and a group of twenty more Africans standing around a fire next to a shed. We cycled past a temporary settlement of these field workers and their families. A high cement fence attempted to either give them some privacy, or to hide their appalling living conditions from the world. Children ran through the mud between simple huts of tin and plastic, rags of washing hung over the fence, and a general air of filth and neglect hung over the place. We didn't stop, but we did spend some time comparing the politics and the economics of the immigration issue in Germany and in Italy. The refugee crisis of 2015 had made every German citizen evaluate their own place in the world, their history, their beliefs, and their fears. It was quite confronting to witness how poorly these refugees in rural Italy were being received in comparison to their compatriots in Germany.

We arrived in the old town of Andria, sat at a café for Anne's afternoon coffee and were twice warned by passers-by to keep a watchful eye on our bikes and panniers. Our Airbnb host showed us a large underground garage where we could store our bicycles, but it didn't look very secure. Given the warnings we had just been given, we were not at all confident that we would still have our bikes the following day. Our host was very gracious and made no protest at all when we told him we would like the bikes kept in our apartment. The lift was too short, so he very helpfully took them up himself by standing each bike on its rear wheel and balancing it there while he rode up in the lift. We followed with all our bags and managed to squeeze the bikes into the tiny entrance hall of our apartment.

This courtesy and willingness to help us with our bikes, no matter how wet, muddy or dirty they were, was a common thread throughout Italy. We almost always kept them with us, parked in our bedrooms, in the kitchen, or in the entrance hall. They stood next to us in café gardens and, on one memorable occasion came into McDonalds with us. Only once were we refused accommodation because of our trusty steeds. The hosts were so worried about security that they cancelled our booking and gave us a refund. We found a hotel nearby and the bikes slept next to our beds that night.

Andria was of interest to us because it is near the Castel del Monte, a well-known castle built by Federico II. I had never heard of him, but this is his story:

*Born into the Hohenstaufen family, Federico was a very busy young man. He became king of Sicily in 1198, at the age of three. He was married at fourteen, fathered an heir at fifteen, and by the time he was seventeen he was also king of Germany. Eight years later he added both the kingdom of Italy and the Holy Roman Empire to his lands and titles. Federico topped this off by marrying Isabella of Jerusalem in 1225 and installing himself as king of Jerusalem too. As if all these kingdoms weren't enough to keep Federico occupied, he married four times, fathered at least nine illegitimate children in addition to his ten legitimate offspring, and was excommunicated by the pope four times.*

*Federico had earlier promised to go on crusade to Palestine but kept dragging his feet and not actually getting anywhere so he was excommunicated by Pope Gregory IX. Two years later, he eventually made it to Jerusalem and won it back by negotiation instead of through battle. Pope Gregory was not impressed. Federico had dared to go on crusade while excommunicated, so he was technically not even allowed to go with, let alone lead a Christian expedition.*

*He was promptly excommunicated again – a double excommunication, if such*
*a thing were possible.*

On the positive side, Federico was ahead of his times in his attitudes to the wider world. He invited Greek, Arab, Italian, and Jewish scholars to his court in Palermo. He spoke six languages including Greek, Arabic and German. He established the University of Naples, outlawed trial by jury, and was called "The Wonder of the World" by his contemporaries. Indeed, Federico was one of the first true humanists.

This king and emperor spent most of his life in Sicily and southern Italy with the occasional trip to Germany or on crusade to Palestine. By 1241, the Mongol horde was rampaging through Hungary and pounding on the doors of Europe. The king of Hungary appealed to Federico for aid, but assistance was refused. Instead, Federico focused his energies on improving and extending his own defences. Castel del Monte was built during this time. Why Federico built the castle there is a bit of a mystery though, as it served no useful military purpose. High on a hill, octagonal in shape, with its sheer walls and eight towers, it can be seen for miles around. Looming over their lives like that, it would have scared the local peasantry witless.

Federico was an expert hunter and he had a great love for hunting with falcons. In amongst his many duties as king and builder of castles, he found time to write an extensive and quite authoritative book titled "On the Art of Hunting with Birds." It is possible that he used the castle as a hunting lodge, but no-one knows for sure.

The castle was deserted for many years and its contents plundered. Bandits and shepherds used the cavernous rooms for shelter until the castle was bought by the Italian state in 1876 and restorations were started. It gained World Heritage status in 1996, partly because of the perfection of the building itself, and partly because the building reflects Federico's humanist ideals.

Stripped of marble and bare of all life, Castel del Monte could only hint at all the activity which was once there. The furnishings, carpets, tapestries, and candles which would have added warmth and depth, and livened up the atmosphere have long gone. The frantic servants running hither and thither, the clatter and racket of soldiers practicing their moves, the pacing of sentries, the clink of glasses and the murmuring of the king's companions in quiet corners; all have vanished forever. Now there is the just the chatter of tourists and the constant whirr of cameras as they wander the stairways, gaze out of tiny windows to the olive groves far below, and study the art and science of hunting with falcons.

Castel del Monte can be seen daily by everyone in Italy. It is pictured on the reverse side of Italy's one cent euro coin which in itself raises an interesting question. Is the castle significant enough to be pictured on a national coin, or is it so unimportant that it only gets shown on the smallest and least valuable of all the coins? No doubt there are many Castel del Montes lurking in dusty corners and under the cushions of Italian couches.

It was meant to be an easy day's ride to Toritto, only forty-five kilometres, including thirty-five kilometres of cycleway, but we discovered it was all unpaved. The first section was on farm roads amongst neverending olive groves. After that, we were directed onto twenty kilometres of a disused railway line overgrown with weeds and assorted shrubs. I probably would have attempted this route but, luckily, Anne rebelled. Hunting around for an alternative, I realised that I could set Komoot to "road bike" and found another route, all on quiet country roads. It was brilliant. We zipped along at sixteen kilometres per hour to reach Toritto, another atmospheric old village with twisting streets and a weird numbering system. Our accommodation was in purgatory, Via Cantone Purgatorio. We couldn't find our Airbnb and seemed fated to be stuck in purgatory forever until an old woman hanging out of her window took pity on us and pointed to a quaint front door in the corner of a hidden cul-de-sac.

Antonio, Maria and Alphonso were so very lovely and welcoming. With little English but a great deal of warmth, they showed us through their maze of an apartment. Our bedroom had an arched ceiling, the doorways were arched too, and the floors creaked their own well-worn music. Antonio ordered pizza for us and Alphonso gifted us a flagon of his home-made wine to wash it down.

The next morning, I was admiring some original watercolours in the house when Maria beckoned to me and opened a door into another room. I was absolutely gobsmacked! This room was old, very old. An oil painting of a religious scene hung on one wall. Sixteenth century, Maria indicated to me. Old chairs and furnishings were scattered about. She proudly lifted the lid of a piano but most of the keys didn't work anymore. Above all this splendour hung the ceiling, itself beautifully painted with more religious scenes surrounded by swirls and arabesques of gold. This apartment must have been part of an old palace or maybe a monastery. What other treasures were hidden behind the closed doors? Still pondering, we lugged our bags downstairs, loaded up and peddled off to the railway station where our host found us to give Anne her water bottle which she had accidentally left behind.

# | 37 |

# Dreaming of a Better Future

We took the train to Matera and met a retired Dutch couple who had been staying in Toritto. They had friends there and came for a week's visit twice a year. The husband spoke eight languages of which I can guarantee that he was word perfect in English, far better than me in German, and completely fluent in his native Dutch, of course. He also spoke French, Italian, Spanish, and Russian, and was learning Japanese.

Our Dutch friends explained the phenomenon of all the men standing around in groups in the towns and villages during the day in southern Italy. Traditionally, the women worked and socialised in the home or in the marketplace. The men worked in the fields during the day and very often socialised with their friends in the evenings in the bars or in the piazza. Now the farm work was largely being done by lower paid field hands from Romania and from sub-Saharan Africa. There was very little other work for the local men, so they gathered in groups in the street in an attempt to while away the long hours of boredom. The women still had work to do in the home but there was no way that a southern Italian man could stay home and participate in this. They still had a very traditional mind-set and believed housework to be well beneath their dignity.

With the men unemployed, the women working for no remuneration in the home, and no unemployment benefits, there were whole families living off the pensions of their elderly relatives. As the elderly die out, these families were being left with little or no income and no conceivable pathway out of poverty. Southern Italy has long been much poorer and less developed than northern Italy and we were seeing this discrepancy every day with our own eyes.

I dreamt up a suggestion for the Italian government: borrow swags of money from the EU, employ the local men to build thousands of kilometres of good quality cycling paths all through southern Italy, finance the locals to start up cafés, pensions, B&Bs, lure all those cycling enthusiasts from northern Europe with the promise of ample sunshine and a great cycling infrastructure, and count the euros as they come flying in from all over the continent. Of course dreams don't have to stay small – add in guidebooks, guided tours, English language colleges, mobile bicycle mechanics, bike hire shops …, not just in the main towns but all across southern Italy.

What about a service where a cyclist can travel to any airport or major railway station with their bike in a regulation bicycle box and, for a fee, can have their bike reassembled so they can ride happily off into the distance? Then later, they could ride to another airport or railway station and have their bike dismantled and packed into another regulation bike box for transport back home. If any young entrepreneurs take up this idea and makes their millions from it – remember! – I thought of it first!

We spent the day in Matera which was quite familiar to me as I had already been there three times in the previous six months. There were quite a few new sculptures standing around. A very tall elephant sculpture in the main piazza was a Salvador Dali original, the Space Elephant. It was one of only five pieces which were being exhibited in Matera for about six months because of the town's designation as a European City of Culture for 2019. The Dance of Time II, a massive clock, kept time at one end of the cliff-side promenade while the Rhinoceros Cosmique could be seen standing regally near the top of the Sassi Barisano.

# | 38 |

# Traditional Towns of Southern Italy

## Toritto to Locorotondo, 86 km

We took the earliest sensible train from Matera back to Toritto where we saddled up our bikes again, quickly pedalled past Grumo Appulia, found our route and our stride, and made it to Acquaviva delle Fonti in good order. The only issue was Anne's propensity to race on ahead at times without checking the route so that we over-shot a turn-off and went too far. Normally I was the navigator but that required Anne to check every few minutes where I was. This time, we were lucky. Our detour didn't add much to our total distance, we just had to spend more time on a busier road than Komoot had planned for us, but it wasn't a big deal.

After Acquaviva we found a nice spot under some olive trees for our picnic lunch. We did this nearly every day. A lunch of bread with cheese or salami accompanied by a yoghurt or some fruit, and with water to drink was so easy to organise. Apart from the yoghurt, everything was cheap, fresh, tasty and semi-free of plastic. Olive trees were everywhere, so finding a suitable spot under an olive tree was easy. The hardest part was avoiding all the rubbish, but we soon realised that there was much less garbage further away from the towns and along the quieter roads. It was just a matter of understanding the local situation.

What I really struggled to understand was the locals' love for throwing their rubbish out on the roads to start with. We had seen garbage collection in towns and there were rubbish bins in the public spaces but for some reason, people still liked to throw their refuse out into nature, and not just a few empty drink cans or cigarette packets. Truckloads of garbage were piled high including old mattresses, refrigerators, tables, broken mirrors, and whole bags filled to the brim. There were hundreds of plastic and glass bottles, plastic bags, broken toys and all the other detritus of daily life littering the smaller roads for at least five kilometres on the way in and out of each town. It was quite disturbing. What did the local farmers think of this mass of rubbish spilling into their driveways, rolling onto their lands and piled up under their olive trees? What thought process is established in the minds of someone who throws their weekly rubbish out onto the road? Who do they think will clean it up? Why do they think it is acceptable for some-one else to come along and clean up after them? It was a mystery.

I had informed our hosts that we would be arriving in Putignano at about 5 p.m. At 5.03, I rang the doorbell. Our host opened the door to the longest, steepest flight of stairs I had ever seen in my life! It soared up not one but two flights to a narrow doorway at the top. The stairwell was narrow, with solid stone walls on both sides and a small landing at the halfway point but no other doors opening off it. This stairway only serviced the third floor.

We carted all our panniers up those steps to our newly renovated two-bedroom apartment. After I had stopped puffing and panting, I managed to ask our host about the stairs. She had three children who were all born while she lived in her apartment next to ours. I couldn't imagine how any heavily pregnant woman could climb those stairs. Her belly must have banged against the steps as she went up, and going down must have been terrifying! She laughed at my astonishment.

Going back out on the street, we saw that there were numerous doors opening off the street into each building. So many, that it was quite picturesque. Not only did each building have multiple doors but each door was at a different level too. Some had only one step onto the street, others had five or six steps, up or even down below ground level, before levelling off at a door. Sometimes a set of steps led to a small landing with a door but then the steps kept going to another landing with another two doors exiting off it. The rooms below street level were often storerooms or workspaces. They had no windows, so the doors had to be left open if the occupants wanted any natural light. The first and second floors of our building were interconnected and serviced by their own stairway leading from the next door in the street. I *love* stairs and doors. There is always so much mystery attached to them. We wandered around in the evening and took dozens of photos of steps and doors. Most didn't turn out well because of the poor evening light, but it was fun anyway.

Leaving Putignano, we had to cycle/push up another hill. Anne was not impressed. "Why should we ride these hills when the state road is bound to be much flatter? she wanted to know. Our current route included almost two hundred metres of climbing. The state route had only about 130 metres. We made a short detour to have a look at the state route, but one look at this road with its hectic traffic and without a verge for us to cycle on convinced us to go back to the quieter country road. The hills suddenly didn't seem so bad, after all.

Shortly before Alberobello we came to a T-intersection. Left or right? Both options went downhill. I crossed the road to stand in the shade and look at Komoot on my phone as I couldn't see the screen properly in the bright sunlight. We had to go left. I looked for Anne to tell her but couldn't see her. I called. No response. Where could she have gone? She hadn't gone behind a bush, I would have spotted her bike. I called again and double-looked. Still no Anne. Maybe she had gone ahead of me. I turned left and swooped down the hill and around a sweeping bend but still no Anne. Dang! I pulled over in a driveway and sent her a message.

"Where are you?" A few minutes later – a response.

"I went right. Which way did you go?"

Ten minutes of quietly resting in the shade, then I saw her crest the hill to come swooping down my side to join me in the driveway.

"I thought you had gone ahead," she explained.

We cycled on and began to see some of the "trulli" which the area is known for. Trulli are traditional small round buildings with conical roofs. The walls are made of squarish blocks of stone, the roofs of thinner slabs of limestone. In the countryside, the trulli are nowadays often used for storage and the walls are usually left in their original stone colour but in the villages, when used as houses, they are plastered over and painted white. One explanation for the development of this unique building style is that the locals were so fed up with paying enormous taxes based on the sizes of their dwellings that they invented a house style which could be quickly dismantled when tax inspectors were seen moving through the district. The two trulli districts of Alberobello have been inscribed on the World Heritage list by UNESCO, and draw thousands of tourists every year to view these cute little homes.

We arrived in time to wheel our bikes through the local market on the way to the central, shaded piazza. The fresh fruit and vegetables looked so good that we just had to buy some mandarins and a punnet of strawberries to snack on as we cycled. Arriving at the piazza, there was an older gentleman sitting alone on a park bench in the shade. He wasn't doing anything, just sitting and watching the world go by. Was he waiting for someone? Was he waiting for something to happen to liven up his day? We took it in turns to eat our lunch, watch our bikes and go into a neighbouring ice-cream shop for a coffee or an ice-cream, and a toilet stop. The old gentleman moved to a different bench and began to read a magazine.

After lunch, we wheeled our bikes to the smaller of the two trulli districts to have a look around. I had been there the previous year as part of my "Ancona funk rehabilitation program" but was keen to see it again. We wandered past a group of Dutch tourists sitting at their easels and painting the trulli street scene. We waited patiently for other tourists to move out of the way so we could take some tourist-free photos, and we waited patiently again for others to take their photos before we walked down the street. All those tourists! Eventually, we came across a young lady who had entertained me so much previously.

She was still sitting outside her family's trulli, playing her guitar and singing. Her father brought out some cookies, a glass of red wine, and offered us some coffee which we refused. Anne went off to have a good look around while I made myself comfortable on a chair and listened to the music. The lass sang with such gusto that her good cheer and enthusiasm were quite catching, bringing big smiles on all those who wandered past. When Anne returned, we placed some euros into her busking basket, wished the young lady well, and left to go back to the main piazza.

Anne went off to investigate the other trulli district with its hundreds of trulli while I made a valiant attempt to not fall asleep on my bench. She reappeared quite soon, having discovered that the larger district was over-touristed and overflowing with restaurants, pensions and souvenirs. It was good for busloads of tourists who have an hour or two as part of their Puglia tour, but it wasn't so exciting for cyclists like us who saw hundreds of trulli as we travelled through the countryside. The old gentleman was still reading his magazine in the shade in the piazza when we left, but on a different bench.

Cycling the ten kilometres to Locorotondo was quick and uneventful. We found our accommodation without any great difficulty even though we only had the names of the very long street and the accommodation itself, no street number. Our Airbnb was a trulli in a group of trullis, all owned by a series of cousins, all descended from the same grandparents. Our trulli had two tiny bedrooms with the bathroom leading off one of the bedrooms. The people who originally lived there were obviously rather shorter than us, maybe a bit over 1.5 metres. The doorways were quite short. It was a case of duck the head down when entering or risk being scalped. The kitchen and lounge area were likewise tiny, but spotlessly clean and well set-up. We were quite contented there for two nights.

The son of one of the cousins was there to assist us on arrival. He had recently spent three years in Melbourne and was currently living in Scandinavia. His English was perfect, and he was so pleased that he could translate for us and our hosts. A number of our hosts in Italy had roped in their teenagers to translate which worked brilliantly. The young ones got the opportunity to practise their English language skills and to help the older generation. We got the benefit of clear communication which was great for asking about hot water and determining where to leave the keys in the morning. I made a point of complimenting the young people and their parents on their English skills which brought smiles all around and hopefully encouraged the youngsters to continue on with their studies. I did reflect one day that, even though I was retired, it was impossible to beat the teacher out of me.

We spent the morning in the lovely old town of Locorotondo. Like most old towns in the area, it was on top of a hill, all painted in white and with a confusing mass of steps and stairs, tight corners and narrow alleyways. Apart from pizzas and olive groves, southern Italy is all about nooks and crannies.

Our curiosity was piqued by the number of puppets hanging high above the streets. They ranged in size from doll size to almost human size but each one was a puppet of an old woman hanging by the neck. They were Quarantana, representations of skinny old farming women dressed in traditional labouring clothes including a black dress and large shawl across the shoulders. The Quarantana is said to be Carnival's widow. She dies on Shrove Tuesday and hangs high above the crossroads for the forty days of Lent until Easter Saturday. She is a symbol of abstinence and hangs there to remind people to avoid consuming fats such as cheese or butter. She also reminds people to behave themselves properly in the lead-up to Easter. The Quarantana usually carries other symbols as further reminders. The grater symbolises the avoidance of cheese while a spindle and a pile of sticks remind women of their duties in the home and on the farm. Most frightening of all is if she carries a pair of scissors. Children used to be warned to follow the rules or she would descend from the heights and cut out their tongues! The Quarantana used to be shot down and set on fire on Easter Saturday, thereby symbolizing the change from the deprivations of Lent to the rebirth and the renewal of life on Easter Sunday.

This was all fascinating, but I couldn't help wondering why the Quarantana was always an old woman. Why is it only women who are reminded to look after their homes and do their farm work? Why is it only old women who are strung up by the neck and held responsible for holding the people to account? Why were the old women so feared that they needed to be shot down and set on fire? Feminists would have a field day in Locorotondo.

A much calmer sight to behold was the old Greek church on the edge of town. It was the oldest church in Locorotondo, built in the fifteenth century. We left the confusion of the local market and entered the simple and quiet ambience of this historic building. All was quiet except for the stifled coughs and murmurs of those at their prayers. The interior, of a creamy white stone, glowed with reflected light. Pale pine benches devoid of prayer books or hymn books invited us to sit and ponder for a while. At the front was a very simple altar, a mantlepiece hanging below statues of Mary and Her Child, flanked by four figures: St. Luke, St. Peter, St. Paul, and St. Oronzo. On the floor below the altar were placed vases of red and white flowers, interspersed with bowls of sprouted grains, a vivid green against the other colours and shades. A dozen candles flickered in red glasses. To the left of the altar, in a niche of his own, St. George was fighting his dragon, an image which seems to have spread right through the Christian world. And that was it. No gold framed oil paintings of Jesus on the Cross, no confessional booths, none of all the other symbols and busyness which so typifies so many other places of prayer. A small but steady stream of people came inside, genuflected, sat quietly for a minute or two to pray, and then rose, and left, just as quietly. It was a real communion between a soul and his/her God.

# | 39 |

## Easter in Ostuni

### Locorotondo to Ostuni, 25 km

The route to Ostuni was a real fitness tester with countless small hills to fly down and pedal up. Anne was much stronger in the legs than I was, she could often ride slowly up a steep hill while I would just fall off near the start and have to push all the way to the top. We were still riding through a sea of olive groves, but the hills gave us good vantage points from which we could spy people and machinery working in amongst the trees.

Cycling with a buddy was panning out to be so much easier than cycling by myself. Sharing accommodation costs meant we could stay in apartments and hotels. Planning the trip, navigating our route, researching accommodation, shopping for food, chatting with the locals – all these tasks could be shared between us. Over time, we worked out what our different strengths and weaknesses were. I tended to navigate using my apps. Anne was much more observant of the road signs and much quicker at spotting the cycling paths which would appear and disappear again without warning. When cycling, we took it in turns to lead. Being faster, she usually led when we were on country roads. Using Google Maps, I led in the larger towns with her following close behind and reminding me of the road rules.

We arrived in Ostuni an hour before our agreed time to enter our apartment. Anne was all for going on until we landed on the correct doorstep and seeing whether we could get in early. I was in favour of an ice-cream or a coffee shop. I have never seen much point in racing along without a break, simply to get somewhere earlier. We rattled and bumped along a cobbled street for about a kilometre and reached the main piazza. By the time we got there, Anne had come to see my point of view and was very much in favour of a coffee.

Rested and partially caffeinated, we had wits enough to form a battle plan for locating our street from amongst the maze on the steep hillside behind the piazza. I set off on foot while Anne guarded the bikes. Google Maps was clear that I had to go north from where I was standing but there were three very narrow streets to choose from. I set off up one street, the buildings loomed overhead, the internet signal got lost, Google Maps got confused and so did I. Many false starts later, I ducked down a tiny alley off another narrow streetlet and found a street name and number which seemed to be a shortened version of our address. Bingo!

Our hosts, Marco and his mother, helped us carry all our gear, including the bikes, up fifteen steep steps of this old and atmospheric apartment building. We had deliberately booked a larger apartment than we normally took because it was the Easter weekend. We wanted to relax, spread out and enjoy a few days of rest. We had three bedrooms plus a communal area with a kitchen and a loungeroom. There was a fireplace in the lounge, enough room for our bikes and everything we could possibly need, or not, in the kitchen. There was even a washing machine in the bathroom.

We visited the archaeological museum. I wanted to see the corpse of a young woman and her unborn child from 25,000 years ago. All that was left of her were her bones, and those of the child, neatly laid out in position in a glass cabinet. I always find it astonishing to think that these bones once belonged to a living, breathing, loving person with language, physical skills, and a social life way beyond my imagination.

Another artefact to catch my eye was a blue ceramic jar, about fifteen centimetres high. Once again, it was the idea that someone long ago had held a lump of clay in his or her hands, and had decided to make a jar, give it a handle, paint it sea-blue, and fire it to use at a later time. Someone **made** this. Someone-else used it, someone lost it or hid it from view, or maybe just forgot where they put it. Was this jar precious to them? Did they spend time searching for it? Did they mourn its loss?

During our wanderings in the old town, we came across a shop selling locally produced groceries – mainly pasta and everything which can be served with pasta. After some discussion, we purchased a bag of tri-coloured pasta shells, a jar of tomato-based pasta sauce and a round of cheese for ten euros. I thought it was rather expensive, but I was still keen to try more of the local produce. Anne afterwards fell in love with a small bottle of olive oil from a farm nearby for another 2.50 euros. I cooked the pasta for dinner, it was rather bland and boring. The tomato sauce was also lacking in flavour. The cheese was very salty so that spiced things up a bit, as did the tiny pork sausages which I had bought in a deli. I fried them, sliced them thinly and tossed them quickly in the frying pan again before placing them on top of the pasta, sauce and cheese. It was good!

All this shopping and cooking brought forth yet another mystery. The pasta shelves in the average supermarket usually displayed dozens of different shapes and sizes of pasta. If pasta is made of the same ingredients: flour, water, salt and eggs, do all the different shapes taste the same?

And then – so many of the pasta sauces included either tomatoes or tomato paste. Tomatoes, along with a whole range of other vegetables, originated in South America and were brought to Europe by the Conquistadors. What did the Italians use before they were introduced to the many glories of tomatoes?

Being Easter Sunday, we had an enforced rest day. I spent the morning washing our clothes which was quite an adventure. I loaded the machine full, switched it on, and turned the dial to forty degrees cotton. The light at three hours flashed on. What? Three hours? I double checked, the only other options were six, nine or twelve hours. Three hours for one load! I pushed the start button, nothing. Hmmm. I looked for instructions, couldn't find any. I tossed around the idea of ringing our host but decided to leave him be, it was Easter Sunday morning, after all. I pushed a few more buttons. Nothing. I turned the water tap, still nothing, but I could feel the drainage hose vibrating. Anne suggested I turn off the machine and start again. I pulled the electric plug out of the socket, plugged it in again, pushed the start and BINGO! The machine started to mutter to itself, water started to seep in ever so slowly and we both got really excited.

Then the power went off and the machine stopped. What now? Was the power off everywhere? Just in our building? Just in our apartment? We flicked the light switch in our kitchen. Nothing. I checked the fuse box. All the fuses were lined up the same. I flicked the light switch in our stairwell. Still nothing. I spotted another fuse box at the bottom of the stairs. There were two racks of fuses and one was in a different position to the other. One showed a label with On/Off, the other had the label hidden by the switches. I figured I had a fifty percent chance of getting it right, so I grabbed the rack with the label showing and flicked it up. Lights pinged on again and Anne called out that we had power again.

"I know," I thought smugly to myself. "I did it."

After supper, we walked into the old town again and looked for a wine bar. We found so many open that it could have been a real dilemma, but we came across a wine bar under street level which had a glass floor above the rocky bottom of the cellar. It was fun to sit there, sipping our red wines and watching people gingerly stepping onto the glass floor as though they fully expected it to collapse underneath them.

# | 40 |

# The Salento Plain

## Ostuni to Nardò, 173 km

We left the white town of Ostuni behind us and headed further south onto the Salento Plain in Italy's heel where the land is flat, hot and dry; perfect for the olives which stretch in all directions as far as the eye can see. Many of the trees were heavily pruned until there was almost nothing left of them. Do the trees feel the cuts? We cycled past some truly ancient groves, the broad gnarled trunks twisting this way and that, before sagging, exhausted to the ground, weary with the constant battle against the sun and the wind, and maybe even of life itself. I knew how they felt.

Around the edges of the olive groves, though, and all along the roadsides, butted up against the interminable dry stone walls were literally millions of wildflowers; a profusion of colour, of reds, yellows, and blues, in glorious contrast to the dull green and brown of the olive trees. Bees and other insects, out in full force, hummed, buzzed and zinged as they raced and zipped from one flower to the next.

"Look!" I wanted to say to the olives. "Look at all this *life*, and smile! For the world is a great place to be in!"

A masseria is a huge old farmhouse which was fortified against attack from enemies in the bad old days. There are numerous such old buildings scattered on the Salento Plain, some of which have been given a new lease of life, and offer boutique accommodation, restaurant class meals, or cooking classes for tourists at eye-watering prices.

We booked a night in a masseria, but ours wasn't quite in the same league as most, neither for its offerings, nor for its pricing. The farmhouse itself was an eccentric, rather run-down but still comfortable old lady, a bit like its owner. Francesca was somewhere in her seventies. She had sparkling eyes, and spoke wonderful English, having been an English teacher for many years. She had a lovely warm and welcoming personality to go with her comfortable and solid physical appearance.

Our whole stay there was rather slapdash and casual, some other visitors who spend a great deal of time there suggested we should be flexible and accepting in our approach to life in this masseria. That was okay, I'm rather good at flexible and accepting, but the total lack of hot water in our shower and bathroom did put a slight dint in my equanimity. Anne had a cold shower, but I wasn't having that. Cold showers should be an optional extra, not a standard feature of an overnight stay. I had a hot shower downstairs in a newly renovated bathroom which didn't seem to have a water outlet at all. My shower water just pooled on the floor, higher and higher until everything was sopping wet.

The yard area of this masseria was a delight for the farming part of my soul. Chickens roamed about scratching between piles of wood, the fruit trees and the vegetable garden. A family of goats bleated from their pen, getting steadily louder as one of their young ones pranced and danced over the stone walls. The walls themselves mainly dated back to medieval times, except for one section which dated back to the pre-Roman era. I just happened to mention an interest in history to Francesca and got an immediate and detailed lesson in the ancient history of the Salento area. She showed us some ancient sarcophagi which were well hidden in amongst a patch of brambles, deliberately kept overgrown to hide the great stone coffins from thieves.

The further south we rode, the more we discovered the force of Italian wind. When cycling almost every day, I became much more aware of daily weather and climate. A wind speed of ten kilometres per hour was fine. Twenty kilometres was a nuisance, a fifty-kilometre wind was really bad. A strong headwind slowed us down considerably, a side-wind was acceptable if it wasn't too gusty. A sudden gust could send one of us flying across the road into the path of oncoming traffic. A rear wind was fantastic but, unfortunately, too rare. I dreamt of a fifty-kilometre rear wind – what bliss that would have been!

From the masseria until we arrived in Otranto, the wind came whipping across the sea and the hot plain, a headwind. My weather app reported gusts of up to fifty-one kilometres one day. It was so strong that pedalling furiously, we were almost standing still at times. We knew we were slow, but being overtaken by a young male jogger was the last straw!

"What's with the wind? I asked our host in Otranto.

"It's Lo Scirocco. It comes from the Sahara and brings tonnes of sand with it," he replied. "See all the dust on our cars? That's African dust!"

I had never before come across a wind so consistent and so strong that it needs a name. At home it's just a "f*%^ing wind." Here, if it's a southerly, it's Lo Scirocco or Il Libeccio, Lo Scirocco's best mate. Also coming from Africa, Il Libeccio brings heavy rain and can be quite destructive just before farmers are ready to harvest their crops. La Tramontana is a cold and dry wind from the north, not to be confused with La Bora which is a cold wind from the north-east. La Bora is called Il Grecale down in southern Italy. Then there's also Il Levante, at which point my eyes rolled back in my head and I couldn't take in another word!

Otranto is the easternmost town in Italy. Its other claim to fame is the Basilica Cattedrale di Santa Maria Annunziata, dedicated to the Annunciation of the Virgin Mary. Consecrated in 1088, it probably would have joined the long list of stunning, but largely ignored, cathedrals in Italy if not for two worthy sights. A Tree of Life in the form of a mosaic stretches the whole length of the cathedral. I spotted mythical beasts, demons in hell, and biblical figures such as King Solomon. The story of Cain and Abel was portrayed right up to Cain murdering his brother. Alexander the Great was conquering the world and King Arthur, of British legend, was galloping across the countryside. An inscription at the base of the Tree of Life included the letters INST which the auto-complete setting in my brain read as "Instagram." It just goes to show how modern technology has spoilt our sense of history. The mosaic was impressive, the other sight was rather more chilling.

On July 28. 1480, eighteen thousand Turks sailed from across the sea to attack Otranto. They captured the town after a two-week siege. All the adult males were murdered, their women and children were sold into slavery. Eight hundred survivors fled into the cathedral praying for God to save them. The cathedral was captured in no time, its occupants were offered their lives in exchange for conversion to Islam. Not one person took up the offer so all eight hundred were executed, beheaded. Their skulls and bones were later stacked up behind glass in a chapel next to the main altar.

It was a sobering sight, especially as the whole world was still reeling from the attack and murder of fifty Muslims at prayer in New Zealand, and the following murders of over two hundred people in Sri Lanka. History repeating itself in an endless cycle of religious extremism and violence. Can it ever end?

Leaving Otranto, we turned west and headed across Italy's heel to Martano and from there to Galatina. Navigation was easy, it was a matter of straight roads between towns and circling around the old town centre within the towns. After Galatina, we detoured off the main road and cycled the last section to Nardò through the countryside, mainly slightly downhill and very relaxing. We were heading north again, and for once, didn't have a headwind.

# | 41 |

## Around Italy's Instep

### Nardò to Reggio di Calabria, 656 km

Somewhere north of Nardò we stopped at a café at a beach for a drink and a snack. The owner waved us into his front yard and indicated that the bikes would be safe there. We chained them to the fence as we usually did and sat on the deck overlooking the sea. When we finished, we collected our bikes and saw immediately that Anne's two front panniers were missing.

The owner rang the police, they would come in twenty minutes. We waited twenty minutes, thirty minutes, forty minutes, no police. The owner rang the police again. A long conversation ensued but still no police appeared. They obviously had more important matters to attend to. A young girl came up from the beach and offered to translate for us.

"OK," we said. "Can you ask the owner what he has discussed with the police?"

The girl conversed with the owner and turned to us. "He is asking why you don't ring the hotel where you stayed last night."

"Why?"

"You should ask them to bring your bags if you forgot them, and not the police. He has four security cameras around his café, so the bags were not stolen. You must have left them at your last hotel."

We gave up and left.

If Italy's heel was all about olive groves, wildflowers and wind, cycling around the country's instep was very different. Navigation was the main issue. There was usually only a narrow strip of flat land between the beach on our left, and the hills on our right. A major road, the E90 ran along this strip, parallel to the beaches. Small villages and resorts were scattered along the beaches, connected to the E90 by narrow country roads but there were usually no other routes between the villages. We would have been quite content to cycle on the E90, ducking over to the coast for supplies or accommodation whenever required. There was only one problem – the E90 was a freeway, bicycles were not allowed.

We had previously had a few navigation issues – the cycling routes which ended at insurmountable barriers: a stream, a barricade, or a fence. Each time we had simply waded through the stream, hauled our bikes over the barricades or detoured around the fence. This time was different.

Leaving Marina di Ginosa, we cycled along a lovely country road, under the freeway and along a tree-lined river to start with. Komoot promised to take us a short distance up the river to a point where we should be able to cross over. Following instructions, we veered onto a dirt path and came to an abrupt halt on the muddy banks of the very sloppy, weed infested, insect buzzing piece of water. Komoot wanted us to cross over to the other side, where I could only see more mud and long grass. It didn't look very promising. I scouted around for a crossing point but to no avail. Our choices were to go back to the road and follow the river a long way upstream and into the hills where there was a bridge, or to backtrack and take the freeway.

We cycled up the freeway ramp, under the huge sign which stated emphatically – no bicycles, motor scooters, tractors or pedestrians, and onto the freeway shoulder. Trucks, buses and cars roared by at top speed. Anne was in front, I followed in my fluoro yellow vest. Hers had been stolen with her two pannier bags. I was absolutely terrified, but we pedalled as fast as we could. A police car passed us but didn't stop. Two kilometres later, having crossed the river, we took the first off-ramp and hit a gravel road at top speed, legs trembling and hearts thumping. We did the same four times over the next two days.

At one town we were hailed by an old gentleman with time to kill. He had worked many years in Germany and was pleased to show off his German language skills to his friends. "It's no problem," he explained. "You are not allowed on the freeway, but you have no alternative, so don't worry about it. No-one will stop you." Okay, so no-one was going to stop us, but what about the danger aspect? Obviously, that was fairly unimportant.

Even in the sections where the E90 wasn't a freeway, we were still concerned about the safety aspect of riding such a dangerous road. The traffic didn't slow down simply because the road wasn't a freeway. Everyone still drove as if they were being chased by the devil himself. We took country road alternatives wherever possible, but they weren't always much better. One road took us on a sharp angle away from our preferred route before turning back, a detour of about fifteen kilometres. We thought that that was a small price to pay for the opportunity to ride on a quieter country road. We were wrong. The quiet country road had no verge at all, it hosted non-stop traffic, all the drivers were in a desperate rush to get somewhere and they didn't feel the need to slow down when passing us. Driving in a slight arc around us to give us more room wasn't feasible either. It was even scarier than riding on the freeway.

That night, Anne stated that she didn't want to go on if the roads were always going to be so dangerous. I was inclined to agree but didn't want to give up just yet. We found a great little holiday apartment on the beach at Marina di Mandatoriccio and stayed there for three nights. The weather was predicted to be rather horrible for a few days, so we took the opportunity to rest, relax and recuperate. By the end of our stay, we were more blasé about the dangers and raring to go. It also could have been that we were getting hungry. Our apartment was one of about six hundred holiday units, but we were the only guests in the whole complex. The holiday season still hadn't started so not only were there no other guests, there were no larger stores open and there was little food to be had, except pizza. How often can a cyclist in Italy eat pizza before getting pizza overload?

Travelling through the countryside at such slow speed with our eyes focused on the road in front of us, we got a fairly good insight into the small animals common in the area – tame family pets, rogue pets gone feral, and native wild animals. All were represented in the road-kill which we pedalled past every day. Unlike other countries where roadkill is cleaned up by roadworkers, in southern Italy, these animals were left to nature to deal with as she wished. Every day we saw dogs, cats, birds, hedgehogs, or snakes squished completely flat and left to dry out and wither in the sun and the wind. A scrap of fur, a leathery dark brown carcass, teeth protruding in a frozen grin. They were never a pleasant sight. The eyes were long gone.

From Marina di Strongoli to Le Castella our route went up a long hill to a plateau on top. The gradient was signed to be ten percent, steep enough for the many trucks to find it a struggle. They had to slow down considerably as they went down through the gears, which meant we felt quite safe as we cycled on the verge. Strangely, we were both able to cycle to the top rather than having to dismount and push. I was never able to work out why I struggled so much with some hills but could sail up others with no problems. It wasn't just the gradient, my bike hadn't developed wings, and I didn't feel that I had become so much fitter.

Just before we reached the top of the rise, at a point where no-one could see over the crest, a sports car came racing up at top speed, pulled out and overtook a slower car. My heart stopped as I visualised an on-coming truck pelting over the hill, car parts and bodies flying in all directions. Luckily, all that hit us as we came over the crest was yet another gale-force wind belting us about the ears.

We turned off the main road onto a smaller country road. It was bitumen, but narrower, with a collection of potholes to navigate around, but they weren't the main issue. The wind was appalling! Yet again!

One hundred and fifty wind turbines were scattered over the plateau, their blades spinning rapidly, shadows creating a disco of light and shade for us to ride through. After eight kilometres of struggle and sweat we turned a sharp left. Suddenly the wind was hitting my right shoulder. I angled my body so more of my back was exposed to the wind, turning my torso into a pudgy sail. Cycling became sailing as I scooted along with wind power.

The countryside was very wild, the plateau fell away into a range of rugged hills and valleys covered in eucalypts and assorted scrubby vegetation. The few farm buildings were all deserted, it was far too windy up there amongst the turbines and their hyperactive blades.

We had a spirited descent into Le Castella where a stone causeway led to a rather romantic looking castle surrounded on three sides by violent wind-blown seas. The next morning, the wind had dropped, the waves subsided, and the golden yellow stone of the castle sparkled in the sun. I imagine the blades of the turbines on the plateau high above us also slowed to a standstill as they waited desultorily for the wind to blow its fury again.

Our target for the next day was Hotel Conca D'Oro just past the town of Catanzaro Lido. Anne's husband in Germany had purchased new panniers to replace the stolen ones. He had sent them to the hotel, and we hoped they would get there in time for Anne to collect them. As we mounted our bicycles, we were rather unsure about whether we would ride to the hotel or take a train as far as we could. It depended on the road, the traffic and the weather conditions. It all seemed to be in our favour. So, we pedalled on until I saw a McDonalds sign in the distance. I had a sudden urge to eat some French fries. We pulled in. Anne wanted a snack too. Neither of us wanted to wait outside with the bikes so we just wheeled them into the restaurant. No-one batted an eyelid. A party of little girls was singing happily, maybe it was someone's birthday. Two mothers came over to us. They asked the usual questions and were terribly impressed with our achievements. They turned to the little girls and gestured excitedly. Fifteen sets of eyes swivelled to turn to us, and fifteen little mouths dropped open in awe, before they went back to the serious business of singing party songs. Maybe in twenty years' time, one of those little girls will set off on a long adventure and think of us as she wheels her bicycle into a McDonalds restaurant in some faraway country.

We knew there was a tunnel that we had to go through just before our hotel. I had studied this tunnel on Google Maps, zoomed in as close as I could on the satellite image and worried myself silly over it. I have a serious aversion to cycling through tunnels at the best of times, and the speed of the traffic in Italy wasn't terribly reassuring. We stopped for a coffee at a roadside café. The owners spoke excellent English and assured me that the tunnel was very short and quite safe to ride through. Full of optimism, we rode on until we arrived at the tunnel. Our hearts sank. It was going slightly uphill so that we couldn't cycle fast, it was narrow, there was no verge for us, the traffic flew through at speed, and it definitely didn't feel safe. There was a narrow path on the right. I walked along it but quickly saw that it was too narrow for our bicycles and panniers.

On the other side, the tunnel was open to the outside world for the first fifty metres. I crossed over to have a look and was cheered to see a dirt path running along the outside of the tunnel. The path widened into a lane, then widened further into a road. It was our escape route. The only problem was the roadside barrier which prevented us from accessing the path. Not to be deterred, we waited for a break in the traffic, wheeled Anne's bike across the road to the barrier, took off her panniers and heaved her bike over. Anne climbed over the barrier and I tossed her panniers after her. She gathered all her possessions, reassembled them and wheeled her bike a short distance away. We then repeated the whole exercise with my bike and panniers. Meanwhile a road cyclist came zipping up, hopped off his bike, lifted it over the barrier with consummate ease, hopped aboard again, and rode off into the distance. It was all too easy for him, and such a pain for us. The lesson of the day? Don't be afraid to tackle the unknown. It's often not as bad as you think. Or, maybe the lesson should be: get rid of the panniers and ride a road bike.

We arrived in good spirits at our hotel but there was no parcel with the replacement panniers waiting for Anne. Two mornings later, there was still no parcel, and no indication on the website of when it would arrive. Anne decided to leave without it. Using a translator app, we managed to explain to the hotel owner that the parcel should be returned to the sender if, or when, it eventually arrived.

Twenty minutes later, cycling down to the beach, we were passed by a car tooting its horn. I looked over and saw the hotel owner's face beaming through the window. He had Anne's parcel! It was so lucky that I had been chatting to him over breakfast, using my huge vocabulary of about fifteen words. I had shown him my map of our travels and had told him that we were heading towards Sicily, so he had a good idea which road we would be cycling on. Anne was so happy to receive her new panniers, but the hotel owner was even happier that he could help us. What a gentleman!

Anne sorted out her panniers and we cycled on to Caulonia Marina full of good cheer. We were expecting our route to be quite relaxing because most of the southbound traffic from the previous days would have turned west and taken the direct route across Italy's toe to the west coast from where they could turn south for Sicily, or north for Naples and Rome. We cycled most of the day on quiet country roads with a few short stints on the major state route which was also rather quiet. Two unexpected river crossings with no bridges for us caused a bit of consternation. Both rivers were shallow, only up to our calves, with cool clear water and a pebbly base. There was no mud and only a scattering of insects. My Australian feet loved those crossings. Anne was doubtful but braved them anyway. The road rose higher, looping around headlands and giving marvellous views to the sea. Eucalyptus trees scattered about scented the air and reminded me once again of home.

# | 42 |

# Sicily – The Key to Everything

## Messina to Syracuse, 188 km

A few days later, we took a short ferry trip across the water to Sicily where we rode along the coast, always aware of Mt. Etna silently towering over the land, waiting for its next eruption. The first twenty kilometres we rode through village after village, always at sea level. Villages full of life, with narrow streets, noisy little scooters zipping around ferrying the young folk on missions of some importance, and fruit and vegetable stalls selling big red onions, cucumbers, and tomatoes. We rode past old houses slowly falling apart with washing hanging from their upper windows, bars full of locals downing a quick coffee, and village squares where the older folk settled to pass the time.

We rode up and over a headland to Ali Terme where four old gentlemen were sitting under an awning in a village square. They spoke some English and a smattering of German too. One of them had worked for many years in Germany. He was very keen for us to understand that Sicily had the "good life." There was high unemployment, but life was easy and relaxed anyway. There were lots of fish in the sea, lovely beaches, good weather, and great food. What else could a man want in life? His friends concurred enthusiastically, life was indeed very good for them. Nearby was a van selling bread, cheese, and olives to passers-by. When no new customers walked up, the driver closed his doors and drove off to his next selling stop.

Up and over another headland, we saw a long beach with villages strewn all along it, until it ended with another headland with our route switch-backing to the top. This headland was hard work. We partly rode, and partly pushed our bikes to the top but were rewarded with a view of Taormina on top of the next headland in the distance. Flying down the other side, we passed a lone female cyclist with a Polish flag pushing her way up the hill. She was the first solo female cyclist I had seen since northern Italy. She smiled and waved. I would have loved to stop and chat for a while, but Anne was a long way ahead of me and keen to get to Taormina.

Our road wound its way slowly up and around the Taormina headland. An extraordinary view of a lovely bay with scattered islands in the clear blue sea captured my attention as we cruised to the top. A group of racing cyclists having a break at the crest of the hill waved and smiled. Their flags proclaimed Denmark and Britain. I heard "… rode all the way up … impressive …" before we headed down the other side to our accommodation.

"To have seen Italy without having seen Sicily is not to have seen Italy at all, for Sicily is the key to everything." So wrote Germany's most revered poet and playwright, Goethe, when he visited the island in 1787. He spent some time in Taormina, so Anne was very keen to spend some time there as well. It rained all day, but that didn't dampen the enthusiasm of all the German tourists who were happily quoting chunks of Goethe as they wandered the streets in the old town centre.

I was equally enthusiastic about the cannoli, cannelloni shaped sweet pastry filled with ricotta cheese and crushed pistachio nuts. It's a necessary task of all wanderers to taste the local specialities. In Sicily, that included arancini cones too, rice balls shaped in a pyramid shape and stuffed with cheese and other goodies. I was beginning to enjoy Sicily very much!

We spent some time wandering through the Villa Communale – a public garden established by a wealthy British lady in the nineteenth century. The garden was green, luscious, dripping with rain and quite glorious. People who were tired of admiring green plants could focus on the rocks scattered artfully about, or the many follies which had been built to resemble ancient classical ruins. What must the Sicilian workers have thought of their employer's propensity to spend so much money on lugging rocks around and building inhabitable ruins, not to mention gardens which didn't produce anything edible? At least the gardens were open to the public so the descendants of those workers could wander through them and admire it all too.

We left Taormina on an overcast and humid morning. We hesitated to leave but cycled off anyway because my experience so far had been that an overcast sky only rarely translated into actual solid rain. The weather in Sicily so far had proven to be like an Italian croissant – all show and promise, but with not much real substance to it.

Having cycled almost to the top of a huge hill and careened joyfully down the other side, we pulled up at Aci Trezza with its scenic harbour of fishing boats guarded by three pointed islets, the Cyclops. Each Cyclop was so round and came to such a sharp point that I had to ask whether they were real or not. They were. This was such an impressive sight that the harbour was lined with restaurants to cater for the masses of tourists who hadn't yet arrived because it was still the off-season. We collapsed into seats at an outdoor café and had our usual drinks, cappuccino for Anne and iced tea with lemon for me. I had developed the habit of purchasing a small snack at each stop so that I got to taste the local specialities. This time it was a fish cake, deep fried and very, very tasty.

The last few kilometres into Catania, we had a bright blue bicycle lane to cycle along. We were both rather impressed. There was even a young couple cycling with the full touring outfit, Ortlieb panniers included, but going the other way. They called out "hello," and I suspect they might have been Australians. Once in Catania, the traffic went quickly from extremely busy to certifiably insane. We had our own bike lane, theoretically shared by buses and taxis but also "stolen" by a couple of rogue cars. The road was unusual in that there were three car lanes going east and our bike/bus lane going west so we were going against the car traffic the whole time with nothing but convention separating us from them.

Anne nearly got wiped out by a speeding motorcyclist who decided to veer off and turn right in front of her. This was at the end of the day which had already seen her side-swiped by a car in a very narrow lane in one of the old towns en route. I had also had my own drama when a driver decided to pull off the road into a parking spot in front of me, so I had to slam on my brakes to avoid kissing his side mirror. It was such a narrow escape that the driver behind us tooted at the first driver in remonstration, to no avail. The offending driver was quite elderly and possibly almost deaf as well as nearly blind.

Entering the beach suburbs of Catania, we passed numerous old and often deserted mansions, each one impressive and just calling out to be lovingly restored. However, this was only a prelude to what we saw when riding up the main street of Catania itself. Mansion after mansion lined the side of the street, all needed a good scrub and coat of paint, but each one was even more grand than the ones before. A Sicilian billionaire with a passion for house renovations could have a ball in Catania. I've since read that this town was once a hotbed of Mafia activity, so maybe not.

Our accommodation was not nearly so grand as those big old mansions, but it suited us much better. A small outdoor courtyard with a big steel gate to keep out bicycle thieves led to a ground floor apartment with two bedrooms, both with en-suites, and a kitchen/dining area as well. The kitchen had everything a traveller needs except for a corkscrew, so we bought one and relaxed with a nice white wine over dinner.

# | 43 |

# Sightseeing in Luxury, by Car

## Syracuse – Piazza Armerina - Mt. Etna – Leonforte - Syracuse

By the time we arrived in Syracuse, we decided that we wanted to see much more of Sicily than just the east coast. It was time to hire a car and venture further afield. Anne, being a European, was well able to cope with driving on the right side of the road. We drive on the left in Australia, so I was quite happy for her to do all the driving while I navigated and booked our accommodation.

Hiring a car was relatively cheap but the insurance wasn't. We paid 240 euros for five days, all costs included, and an extra twenty euros for our bicycles to be stored somewhere under lock and key. It was good to know that our bikes were safe and secure as we drove away.

Our first stop was a small hill town with an ancient Greek theatre, a stage, and a semi-circle of seating rising above it on the hillside. This area of Sicily had been a Greek colony in ancient times. There was some sort of drama competition being staged as we wandered around. Hundreds of teenagers from all Italy were swarming about, practising their lines. A group on the stage was performing a classical play with old style costumes and props but with a modern twist to the dialogue. One character turned his speech into a bouncy rap, to great applause from the spectators.

We left the Greeks and drove on to Piazza Armerina, the remains of a Roman villa with fantastic mosaic floors. The largest room had a fascinating depiction of how wild animals were captured in northern Africa and in India, caged on a ship, sent to Rome and released into the arena to do battle with the gladiators or with other wild beasts. A goat was hung in a cage to lure a panther, slaves and soldiers ran hither and thither, ostriches and antelope were carried on board a ship, an elephant was being led onto a gangplank and a rhinoceros awaited its turn in some marshes. It was all action!

In other rooms some gorgeous young women in bikinis practised discus, long jump and relay races. Children raced chariots pulled by large birds – a goose, a pheasant, a flamingo, and some type of chicken. Other children hunted farmyard animals, a boy was harassed by a rooster and another child was being bitten by a rat. Revenge of the beasts, even if they were only very small and insignificant.

We both really wanted to see Mt. Etna as it had been such a presence as we cycled all the way down the east coast. We drove as far as we could, up to the refugio, from which we took a cable car to the next station. I hired some warm hiking boots and we took a 4WD bus up to the top of the crater where there was snow lying everywhere.

Here was a world of colour at its most elemental. Red stones, black rocks, white snow and grey sky. The air was thick with the smell of sulphur. We peered at the highest point of the mountain and walked down into the crater, formed in 2002 when there had been three hours of earthquakes followed by three months of eruptions. We could see a hole into the volcano, which terrified me, although our guide assured us that the vents through which the volcano erupts always fills up with cooled magma, so we couldn't fall in. We walked around the crater rim and peered over the edge into another crater. The ground under our feet was warm. At one metre underground it was eighty degrees Celsius. Steam rose out of this crater as it was still cooling. As we stood there, pondering the forces of nature, a thick mist curled over the ridge, enveloping everything in its path and cutting visibility to a few metres.

Our group turned into a line of vague shapes, shuffling and disappearing into the distance. It was all very "Game of Thrones."

Our route around the base of Mt. Etna and over to Leonforte took us through the sort of scenery we had only spied from a distance on our bikes. Hills were layered upon hills, rugged hills with lumps, bumps and odd bits sticking out. The roads were good, but they wound around curve after curve, up and over the hills to the valleys on the other side. Magnificent vistas from the tops of the mountains showed sweeping valleys and massive agricultural estates with a scattering of buildings. In the distance, hilltop villages poured down the upper slopes like red-gold lava, sparkling in the sun.

Driving down into the valleys, we passed by cattle, sheep, donkeys, fields of grain, long grass for hay. Some hay had been cut, some was already bailed and even being loaded on trucks for transport out. Sicily was known as the breadbasket of Ancient Rome, it was easy to see why. Occasionally, a ruined castle or a solitary tower punctured the sky, memories of medieval power and taxes.

We swept past six road cyclists as they slowly churned their way up a mountain. I smiled.

# | 44 |

## Locked Out!

### Syracuse to Pozzallo 71 km

At Noto, having exhausted all our patience with both driving and sight-seeing, we unanimously voted to spend some time at the beach. This is what the locals do too, after all. As an Australian with a lifetime of summer beach holidays behind me, I was curious to see what the beaches of Sicily had to offer. Fifteen euros got us the use of one beach umbrella and two lounges for the day. I have never in my life paid to use a beach, so that was definitely a new experience for me. I must admit, to lay back on a lounge, in the shade of an umbrella rather than on a towel covered in sand, was rather nice. We lazed about, read, swam, and enjoyed doing nothing for a change.

Noto is known for its beauty, it is a baroque planned town with many stunning buildings, but before we had time to look at anything, disaster threatened to overwhelm us. It had been a constant nightmare of mine that we would one day be locked out of our accommodation, with next to no Italian, no way to contact our hosts and no way of getting back inside our apartment. Anne, on the other hand, was worried that someone would get inside our apartment and rob us blind, or worse. She always wanted all the doors and windows locked, even when we were inside. Fear again.

Our apartment at Noto was half of a house. The apartment opened onto a flight of stairs at the back, the stairs took us to a small landing which was shared with the other half of the house. From the landing, another flight of stairs led up to a shared terrace which overlooked the street below. A table, some chairs, a collection of pot-plants and the view over the street made it a pleasant spot to eat lunch and while away the heat of the day.

We were having our lunch when Anne started to fret that the door to our accommodation was unlocked. Someone might be able to enter from the other half of the house and create some mischief. I sighed, rolled my eyes, and went downstairs to check. There was no-one. Without thinking, I pulled the door closed behind me, and instantly felt the chill of a long-held fear realised. The keys were inside, the door was locked, and we were stuck on the terrace with no way down or out. I confessed the appalling news to Anne. She took the news bravely and we wondered what to do. Neither of us had our phones with us. On hearing some teenage girls chatting below, I hung over the railing and called down to them.

"Do you speak English?"

"Yes."

"Great! Can you look on the painted sign next to the door? Does it have the owner's phone number on it?"

"Yes." Phew!

"Can you please ring them and tell them that we have locked ourselves onto the terrace and cannot get down?"

Twenty minutes later, I heard a voice call me from the street. The owner's cousin had arrived to rescue us. She entered the other half of the house, which was empty, and came on to the terrace. We were safe, but all was still not well. We still had no access to our own apartment. I had left the keys in the door so we couldn't open it from the outside. We tried pushing the key out, but it was stuck firm. We tried prising the laundry window open, it was locked shut. We tried opening the front door, same problem. The cousin was on her phone speaking to a locksmith. This was going to be a very expensive exercise. But then, I had a brainwave! I had previously tried and failed to lock my bedroom window from the inside. It was an old window, warped and ill-fitting.

It also faced onto the street. I hadn't told Anne about my unlockable window which was most definitely not burglar proof. If we could pry the shutters open, we should be able to open the window. I fumbled with the shutters but couldn't work out how to open them. The cousin called to me:

"The window is locked."

"No, it's not. If we can open the shutters, we can get inside."

She was at my side in a flash, reached up and unhooked the shutters. They swung ajar and I pushed the window open. The cousin quickly cancelled the locksmith, brought a chair for me to stand on, and I tumbled into my bedroom. Door unlocked, we all laughed in great relief. What a circus!

"Remember this," I said to Anne. "Whenever things get difficult, remember that we can do anything!" Fear conquered!

That evening we walked along Noto's main street. My guidebook claims it is the most beautiful street in all Italy, and on this evening, as the cathedral glowed a butter-gold in the setting sun, it certainly fulfilled that promise. Crowds of people strolled about, chatting with their friends or just enjoying the balmy evening air. A little girl and her grandfather walked in front of me. He strolled along in his impeccable black suit, holding the little girl's hand, smiling down at her as she skipped and chatted by his side. Her long curly black hair tied with a white ribbon bounced in rhythm as they promenaded, while her frilly white dress, white socks, and shiny black shoes spoke of the love of her family – a gorgeous sight.

Our last day of cycling in Italy was planned to be sunny, with a last picnic somewhere en route. Instead, dark clouds blew in and the air sagged with humidity. Anne was really nervous, she had never come to grips with getting wet, so we cycled on until we found a café/dance bar at the beach shortly before our end-stop. The rain poured down, but we sat cosily inside, drank a few coffees and cleaned out the complementary snack offerings. I had to admit that that was a better option than getting drenched in the rain.

# | 45 |

# Malta at Last!

The ferry from Pozallo to Malta normally only went at night, but over summer there were daytime sailings three times a week as well. I was keen to take a morning ferry as I have a strong dislike of arriving in a strange place at night. There is a strong element of fear in this reluctance, but also because everything is just so much more complicated when it is dark, and services have shut down for the night. It's harder to read street signs, there are less people walking around who I can ask for directions, reception desks at pensions have closed, and so on.

We took a morning ferry and luxuriated in the journey across the waves. It was only two hours, just enough time to enjoy a leisurely coffee before stationing ourselves at the window to take a hundred photos of the island as it slowly grew larger in front of us. We motored past the old fortress of Valletta and entered the historic Grand Harbour. I thought of the Knights of Malta who first arrived there in 1530. They had been thrown out of their base on the island of Rhodes by the Ottoman Turks and were desperate for a new home. The Holy Roman Emperor, Charles V, granted them the islands of Malta and Gozo in exchange for an annual payment of one falcon and a solemn Mass to be celebrated every year on All Saints Day.

What would these homeless knights have thought when they first sailed into the harbour and saw the steep hills on each side with just a few towers sprinkled about as the only fortifications? From then on, Malta took on immense strategic importance in the never-ending battle between the Christian dominions in the west, and the Ottoman Empire to the east. There was a massive siege in 1565. Five hundred Knights Hospitaller led a force of just over six thousand men in defending the island against an invading force of about forty thousand Ottoman soldiers. The knights eventually prevailed, and the city of Valletta was built to defend the island against further invasions. There was so much history in this tiny piece of land.

We disembarked to add our own footsteps to those which had gone before us. I was so overwhelmed by all this history that I completely forgot that Malta had been my end target for all the seven thousand kilometres cycled since the North Cape way back in freezing Norway. It was only as we relaxed in a café and I could order a drink in English that I remembered.

"Wow! I made it!"

# | 46 |

# Luxuriating in Leisure

During the following days, we left our bikes resting gratefully in our apartment's dining area while we set about discovering Malta via her ubiquitous bus system. We went for walks, rode buses, discovered old temples, poked around in markets, swam in the clear blue sea, and generally revelled in walking out the door every morning, leaving the bikes behind. The sun was hot, ice-creams were plentiful, and life was good.

At some stage, I snapped out of my post-ride stupor and began to notice the surroundings. Most of the eastern end of Malta was covered by an uninterrupted spread of buildings. Villages merged into each other, towns spread their tentacles along the major roads, and there was so much traffic, it took forever to get anywhere. I much preferred the countryside where we could see the importance of the landscape in the island's history and defence.

The sea can be a barrier to those who fear to cross its vast depths, but it's a highway for those with no fear – pirates, invaders, Turks on the prowl hunting for slaves, crops or shiny silverware. The Maltese, being surrounded by the sea and with too few people for adequate defence, came to rely on watch towers for early warning, massive walls to hide behind, and huge churches to pray in. They developed into expert wall-builders and stone masons with a serious belief in the power of their religion.

It all began during the Bronze Age with small settlements in defensive positions. The remains of one such settlement lie on top of a narrow promontory with sheer cliffs on three sides forming a natural barrier. A wall built on the fourth side completed the protective circle. Some parts of the wall were still standing to knee height with other rectangular blocks scattered about. Large round holes had been carved into the rock, probably as storage bins for food or water.

Were these the same people who built the oldest free-standing monuments on earth, pre-dating even the Egyptian pyramids by seven hundred years? Just over the hill from the promontory settlement were two of these ancient monuments, Hagar Qim Temple and Mnajdra Temple, just two of the many temples scattered over the countryside of Malta. Most impressive was Ggantija Temple on the neighbouring island, Gozo. Its name was easy to remember, the stones were so big that the temple was obviously built by giants.

The temples were generally circular, consisting of two or more circular rooms. They were originally roofed, and maybe even plastered inside with red ochre. The doorways were built of two standing stones, some still had a third stone laid flat across the top. There were circular holes carved into some of the doorways. The larger rooms often had altars, niches or a small opening carved into the centre of a rock, the opening leading into another room.

The most astounding aspect of these temples for me was the size of some of the rocks. One of these rocks, at Hagar Qim has been estimated to weigh twenty tonnes. Another is over five metres tall. How did the Bronze Age villagers move these massive slabs of rock? Some of them had stone spheres lying nearby, so maybe the large rocks were rolled into place before being heaved into their current position. Even so, moving a twenty-ton rock over such rough ground would have been a feat requiring enormous resources and organisational skills.

Then there is the question of "why?" Mnajdra Temple was placed so that the sun shines directly through one entrance door, and out the opposite side on certain days of the year. Ggantija Temple has round silo holes carved out of the rock on the floor along the central passageway. It's all a mystery.

Moving along through history to medieval times, the Knights of St. John built massive fortifications at Valletta to keep out the Turks. They followed this up with a series of watchtowers around the coastline. When a Turkish fleet was sighted from a watchtower, the alarm was sounded so that the people could leave their fields and seek shelter in one of the inland towns. Mdina is still encircled by sheer unclimbable walls, as is the citadel in the centre of Victoria, capital of the island of Gozo. The resources and organisation required to build these huge defensive structures is just mind-boggling.

Looking out from the safety of the main towns perched high on their hill-tops, we could see how stony the ground was and how that had shaped the landscape over the millennia. When the fields are full of rocks, they have to be put somewhere so the farmers can plant more crops. Pile the rocks up around the edges of the fields, and soon there is a wall, effectively delineating each farmer's land as well. This work is still going on today, forming an interconnected network of stone walls as far as the eye can see.

All this wall-building has an ecological benefit for the local wildlife and plant life. The cracks and crevices in the walls fill with soil blown by the wind, seeds lodge there and grow, the resulting plants give shelter to all manner of lizards, bugs and beetles so that each wall is a self-supporting eco-system. Worlds within worlds.

Having gained so much expertise in building walls, watchtowers and citadels, the people of Malta then devoted enormous resources to building the most magnificent churches in every little village and town. They can be seen from afar, each church crowned by a dome high above the landscape and itself topped by a small spire. Chugging through village after village in our public buses, we would round a corner and see a piazza spread out before us, people sitting on benches having a gossip, and their church standing front and centre, usually on top of a long flight of steps, obviously the most important building in town.

Anne flew back to Germany with her bike while I went over the water to the next island, Gozo, to continue my extensive program of rest and recuperation with a spot of historical investigation thrown in. Gozo was much quieter and less developed than Malta. I wandered the twisting streets of Victoria, the main town, and ventured out into the countryside. I visited Ggantija Temple, swam at a nearby beach and slowly got used to a different way of travel, a much more common way of travel, where the traveller stays in one place, sleeps in a proper bed, leaves their personal belongings spread all through their accommodation, and gets to know all the grocery stores and restaurants within easy walking distance.

# PART 5:

## The Big Picture

---

*Musings*

# | 47 |

# Looking Back, and Forward

|  | Scandinavia, 2017 | Central Europe, 2018 | Italy and Malta, 2019 |
|---|---|---|---|
|  | North Cape to Vordingborg | Vordingborg to Ancona | Ancona to Malta |
| *Total number of days in the area* | 59 days | 79 days | 56 days |
| *Number of cycling days* | 50 days | 56 days | 38 days |
| *Number of days resting and/or seeing sights* | 9 days | 23 days | 18 days |
| *Total distance* | 2847 km | 2558 km | 1709 km |
| *Average daily distance* | 57 km | 46 km | 45 km |
| *Longest distance in one day* | 97 km | 84 km | 65 km |

Sitting in the shade at a café in a tiny square in Victoria, capital of Gozo, enjoying a refreshing orange drink, I pondered over my long journey from the North Cape and all that I had seen, experienced and learnt on the way.

Looking back - The statistics: I travelled 195 days to cycle 7,114 kilometres, as shown in the table on the previous page. Generally, the further south I rode, the more crowded and complex the route became which resulted in slower cycling speeds and shorter days.

The other way of looking at this is that it took me two summers and a spring, spread over three years, to achieve my goal. I was very slow but enjoyed myself immensely as I stopped to poke and to ponder, and to investigate every point of interest along the route.

Next - The highpoints of each country or region which I cycled through, and also the fears which I faced and overcame - or not:

Norway and Finland had constant daylight but were freezing cold. My main fear was that I was not adequately prepared for the climate, my camping gear just wasn't good enough for the cold conditions. Luckily the weather wasn't too bad, and I was able to stay in cabins on the colder nights. There was ice and snow at the North Cape, reindeer and interminable forest further south. I thoroughly enjoyed the landscapes; the rivers, the forests, the lakes, and the long ribbons of road which stretched out before me. Discovering the different languages and the methods which are used to integrate the different cultural groups into the broader society were fascinating. I found the Finns are not nearly as quiet and reserved as I had been told. Hopping from island to island across the Åland Islands was great fun and I will always remember taking a selfie at the recycling centre at Snäckö.

I had thought that Sweden would be quite boring with all those blue-eyed blond folk and their blue and yellow flag. The country started off being quite challenging because "The Season Was Over" but once I got through Stockholm, most of the issues I had been experiencing fell away and I was able to appreciate this region of Scandinavia much more than I had expected. I was pleasantly surprised by the beauty of the countryside with its fields of grain rippling in the breeze and quiet roads winding around the low hills. The Göta Canal was a joy to cycle along as I tried to visualise thousands of soldiers digging away with their wooden shovels and being rewarded with their daily rations of schnapps to keep them happy. History would be quite dry and dull if it wasn't for the exploits of characters like Princess Cecilia and St. Birgitta of Vadstena, and also those Viking heroes of long ago who carved rune-stones for all eternity to be able to bear witness to their successes, their joys, and also their very personal griefs and tragedies.

Denmark was wet, very, very wet, until I came back a second time to a hot and dry spring which promised a blistering hot summer. Copenhagen was a real eye-opener with its strong cycling culture. I was worried about cycling amongst vehicle traffic and thousands of other, more experienced city cyclists. I learnt to take my time, to study the road conditions, and to have confidence that I could do this. I still don't enjoy city traffic, but Copenhagen taught me that I can do it. The fresco decorated churches on the island of Møn were a complete astonishment. I had never heard of them, but they were truly magnificent, both in their colours and their style. More Viking remains, barrows this time, lured me all over the island. I was faced with my second and third punctures while on Møn and neighbouring Bogø Island. I managed quite well with the Møn puncture which should have given me a great deal of confidence. Instead, the Bogø puncture threw me into a deep well of fear and indecision, completely irrational and inexplicable. I got through it, somehow, but vowed to become much more adept at bicycle mechanics before I ventured on another journey. I also worried about wolves, another irrational fear given than I'm too old and stringy for a wolf to be bothered with. On the plus side, a lady gave me a handful of peas to eat out of my cross-bar pouch. I learnt to shell peas with one hand while steering my bicycle with the other, it's not easy!

My fear of changing a tyre came with me into Germany. I was eventually forced to face up to this fear, only to find it was completely baseless, like so many other fears, I imagine. Germany was significant for its lakes in the north, its post WWII history, its brilliant cycling paths and the 500th anniversary of Martin Luther's rebellion against the Church. I visited a Schrebergarten community near Berlin and visited Friedrich the Great's Schrebergarten, otherwise known as Sansoucci, at Potsdam where I found a dozen potatoes sprinkled on his grave. Cycling through Saxon Germany, the weather was warming up to a record-breaking heatwave. The heat didn't worry me, but I did go a bit loopy as I fantasized about filming an advertisement for Fanta. Then I arrived at a nudist swimming pond to be faced with yet another fear, the fear of baring my naked body to the world. I survived, and so did everyone-else.

Czechia was the land of extreme heat, natural campgrounds and swimming in any river, lake, or pool nearby. Prague was so hot that the fire brigade squirted water in the air in an informal attempt to keep temperatures down to a survivable level. Having forgotten everything that I had ever learnt about navigation through urban areas, I found myself in an extremely dangerous position on a multi-lane highway heading out of town. It was too dangerous to be frightening, the fear only kicked in afterwards, and has since morphed into extreme caution in any sort of urban environment, which is probably a positive development. The rest of Czechia was calm, but hot. I cycled along rivers, camped in lovely natural campgrounds and swam every day. Having vaguely conquered my fear of changing tyres, Czechia was where I developed an irrational fear of hills, spurred on by messages from concerned family and friends. They were convinced I would expire in the hills on a blistering hot day, and that they would later find my rotting body lying in a ditch, swarming with maggots and flies. I cycled the hills, sweated, drank, and wondered what all the fuss was about.

By the time I got to Austria, I wasn't really afraid of anything anymore, except urban traffic. I wasn't afraid of the Alps. I simply took a bus and a train to the top. Sometimes a fear doesn't need to be faced if we can just find a way around it instead.

Northern Italy was about amazing medieval cities and I was able to wallow in my love for history to my heart's content. I realised a long-held dream to visit Ötzi, frozen in his chamber in Bolzano and I enjoyed the cities of Verona, Montagnana, Ferrara, and San Marino. I was completely blown away by the Byzantine magnificence of Ravenna. The cycle paths of northern Italy were excellent so I probably shouldn't have been surprised when I met three other solo female cyclists, but I was.

This region of Italy was also fascinating for its complexity of language and culture. One town's signboard had all the street names in Italian, as to be expected. A note at the bottom explained that those very street names had been changed from German without the permission, and against the will of the locals. That said it all. My fear of urban traffic reached a crescendo in Ancona. I had a complete meltdown and fled, determined to never cycle in Italy again. The following year, thanks to my cousin, Anne, I was able to get back on my bike and keep going. The fear wasn't conquered, just kept bubbling away below the surface, but maybe it's better that way. A good bit of fear can lead to a healthy dose of caution, which is not such a bad thing.

Southern Italy was all about long coastlines with the occasional foray into the inner countryside. We stopped at least twice a day at a bar where Anne drank coffee after coffee while I discovered the joys of iced tea with lemon, and the little regional snacks which were on offer. We bought fresh fruit and vegetables every day, and cooked ratatouille most nights, except when we went to a restaurant to sample a better quality meal. I investigated arancinis and cannoli in Sicily, they gave me strength to cycle up and over the interminable headlands at the end of every beach. We chatted with every person who wanted to ask who we were, where we came from, where we were going, how many kilometres per day, and so on. I was still very nervous about urban traffic but found that having a cycling buddy alleviated much of that. Navigation proved to be our main issue. There were few cycling paths, and even those were not reliable. We often turned a corner to find our path blocked by a road barrier, a river without a bridge, a pile of rocks, a fence or even once a huge gate with the path on the other side disappearing into the distance. It was a challenge, but the joy of cycling through such an interesting country with so much history, and the friendliness of the people more than made up for the difficulties of navigation.

Malta was magnificent. A history written in stone, traffic which drives on the left, a far-reaching bus system, surrounded by a very swimmable sea. We no longer rode our bikes, and this led to yet another problem. How was I going to stop eating so much so that I didn't put on all the weight which I had lost?

So, after all this, what did I learn? In short, I learnt that fear is nature's way of telling us to stop, look around, think, and make a rational decision. Having made a sensible decision, get over the fear and move on. With the exception of a pannier-thief in southern Italy, people everywhere are nice. They are curious, keen to chat, friendly and helpful. The world is a truly wondrous place and there is very little to fear in it.

And what's next? I think a world tour might be next on the agenda, but I might need to learn a bit more bicycle mechanics first.

Terri Jockerst is a graduate of Monash University, Australia.

She spent many years as a teacher in her local secondary school and has recently retired from full-time formal employment. She now travels the world, mainly on foot, or by bicycle, keeps a detailed diary, and occasionally self-publishes a book. She doesn't have a home anymore but lives out of two suitcases when roaming around Australia.

www.ingramcontent.com/pod-product-compliance
Ingram Content Group UK Ltd.
Pitfield, Milton Keynes, MK11 3LW, UK
UKHW021336200625
6509UKWH00037B/430